A SAILOR'S STORY

28 April 2004

To Norman Wu...

With great esteem and warm regard

Allan P. Slaff.
Captain U.S. Navy.

A Sailor's Story

Captain Allan P. Slaff

HOBBLEBUSH BOOKS

ISBN: 0-9636413-9-5
Library of Congress Control Number: 2004100372

Designed and composed in Warnock Pro at Hobblebush Books

Printed in the United States of America

Published by
HOBBLEBUSH BOOKS
17-A Old Milford Road · Brookline, New Hampshire 03033
www.hobblebush.com

Contents

I dedicate this book to Mary Lee—my wife, my sweetheart and my best friend—who has been indispensable in keeping me on course and in safe waters during more than half a century.

Preface

OVER TWO HUNDRED years ago, John Paul Jones, our first and great naval hero set forth his views on what a naval officer should be and how he should conduct himself. His views are as valid today as they were in our Colonial Navy.

The Code of a Naval Officer

It is by no mean enough that an officer of the Navy should be a capable mariner. He must be that, of course, but also a great deal more. He should be as well a gentleman of liberal education, refined manners, punctilious courtesy, and the nicest sense of personal honor.

He should be the sole of tact, patience, firmness, kindness, and charity. No meritorious act of a subordinate should escape his attention or be left to pass without its reward, even if the reward is only a word of approval. Conversely, he should not be blind to a single fault in any subordinate, though at the same time, he should be quick and unfailing to distinguish error from malice, thoughtlessness from incompetence, and well meant shortcomings from heedless or stupid blunder.

To that vital set of attributes I have added my own personal underlying philosophy: *The pursuit of excellence is man's noblest endeavor, and its attainment is man's noblest achievement.*

Looking back over my long life, both in and out of the service, I must humbly confess that I have fallen off the trolley more times than I would have liked. I can truthfully say, however, I did my level best.

But judge for yourself, as you read my account of an incredibly exciting and rewarding life, which I have endeavored in the ensuing chapters to chronicle with both sensitivity and accuracy.

Allan P. Slaff
Captain, U.S. Navy, Retired

A SAILOR'S STORY

Chapter 1

My Early Years

T HE DEFINING EXPERIENCE of my early life—as with most of us who belong to the "greatest generation"—was the grinding Depression of the thirties. In 1932 I was nine years old. My dad had experienced enormous reverses in the stockmarket and in real estate. He was able to salvage a small newspaper and magazine distribution company in Wilkes Barre, Pennsylvania.

At least my dad had a job. He wasn't earning very much, but we got by pretty well. He not only struggled to support us but he was also determined to pay off all of his debts, since he refused to consider bankruptcy. I firmly believe that our experience of the Great Depression, combined with our later experience in World War II, shaped the character of our generation. The former taught us the importance of the work ethic, and the importance of fiscal responsibility and living within our means. The latter imbued us with patriotism, the will to sacrifice, and the importance of discipline and teamwork.

I was introduced at an early age to the hard world of coal and coal miners. I went to school with their sons and daughters and learned about poverty and despair. In those tough days, the miner's efforts to improve their lot through unions and strikes were met with belligerency, not only by the operators but also by the Pennsylvania Mounted Police. These troupers were impressive looking indeed. In order to serve, each man had to be at least six feet tall. They were made even more forbidding looking by their high riot helmets. Any attempt at picketing, or any other demonstration, was met by the mounted troopers carrying long riot sticks. Those tactics were not very conducive to labor activity. In those days, however, unions were important. They were the only bargaining tool that the miners had. In later years, the unions were to lose much of their raison d'être.

It wasn't all grim in those Depression years. I had good friends, plenty to eat and great folks. If I were energetic enough to find a sufficient number of soda bottles to return for their deposits, I could go to the Saturday movie, which was 11 cents, and have enough left over to buy a gigantic Babe Ruth candy bar for a nickel.

Even in those days, I was a law and order man. In school—where I did well enough to skip a grade—I was, if not the teachers pet, certainly among the favored few. As a result, important political appointments came my way. In fifth grade, for instance, I was appointed the Boys' Room Monitor. My job included ensuring that no one spoke a word in the boys' room. Taking my responsibilities seriously, I was alert to any malfeasance. One day, Red Shimilbush, one of the toughest miner's kids, talked in the boys' room, more than a little too. I lost little time in posting his name on the classroom blackboard. After school that afternoon I learned a great deal about the limitations of power. He beat the tar out of me. From then on, I tempered my zeal for law and order with considerable realism.

I never liked old Red very much anyway. Actually I was jealous of him. He wore corduroy knickers that squeaked when he walked and had high top boots with a small penknife in a carefully stitched pocket on the side of the right boot. I had neither, nor could I ever talk my folks into buying an outfit like that for me.

During the early thirties, an event occurred that was to have a decisive impact on my life. The United States Fleet was ordered into New York Harbor to conduct a full dress fleet review. My dad, a Navy veteran of World War I, loved the Navy with all his heart. He packed all of us into the family car and drove to New York to see the fleet, and there it was in all of its magnificence. I had never seen anything more exciting or wonderful. The battleships, cruisers and destroyers were moored in the Hudson River with great precision. The white canvas awnings, which each ship had rigged, shone in the bright sunshine. Although the ships allowed visiting, my dad was disappointed to learn that I was not old enough to go on board. It didn't matter to me. We stayed at the fleet landing and watched with awe as the liberty launches carrying the bluejackets, the motorboats carrying the officers, the gigs carrying the commanding officers and the barge carrying the admirals made their respective landings. It was a day that I never forgot and it was on that day that I became determined to one day be part of that great Navy. At the time it made no difference to me whether I was a bluejacket or an admiral. The important thing to me was to be in the United States Navy.

As the years passed, my dad began to prosper a bit, enough so that he was able to send my brother and me to Wyoming Seminary, a private school in Kingston, Pennsylvania, where we lived. My years at Wyoming Seminary were marked by delightful friendships, a budding social life and, finally, as my time there approached an end, the realization of the importance of learning and the importance of excelling in life. I believe that the latter vital lesson—which stood me in such great stead throughout my life—was taught to me by Dean James Adams, a down-Easter from Maine. It is often said that there must be at least one person that teaches a youngster the importance of good living habits, true academic effort and high standards of excellence. In my case that person was Dean Adams. He was not only a great teacher and administrator, but also a fine disciplinarian.

I was never much of an athlete, although I tried my best. I did rise to the important position of varsity football manager in my junior year and I made the first string on the junior varsity team in my senior year. I was also a cheerleader, and an editor of the yearbook, but I was far from being a big man on campus. They were happy and productive years at Wyoming Seminary, and years that readied me academically for what was to come. I graduated in the spring of 1940, as the world went to war.

I had no problem deciding where I wanted to go to college. It was the United States Naval Academy for me. In those Depression years, there was no small number of young men who aspired to attend a service academy. The academies had enormous prestige in a country that loved and revered its military. They offered a superb education, a commission in the regular service upon graduation and, of great importance, especially during the Depression, a free education. It was about the only free education offered in the United States at the time. There were no ROTC scholarships, and no federal student loan programs. For every space at a service academy there were over a hundred young Pennsylvanian men competing. To generate some political cover for themselves, many congressmen and senators gave competitive examinations developed by the Civil Service Commission. My congressman was no exception. I took the examination and failed to score high enough to win an appointment. It was Dean Adams who took me in hand. He recognized my disappointment, but suggested that if I were serious about the Naval Academy, I should go to college for a year and then try again. I accepted his counsel and applied at his suggestion to the University of Virginia, where the president was a close friend of Adams, and through the dean's good offices I was accepted very late in the spring term.

Virginia was and still is a beautiful school. In 1940 it had only 2,700 students, all male. Thomas Jefferson himself designed the heart of the school. It was a great place for me to "regroup" and to try again. And try I did. In the meantime I joined the first class of a new NROTC formed at the university and, because of my enormous interest in the Navy, stood at the top of my class for the entire year. The skipper of the unit was a Commander Kelley, a splendid officer and a Naval Academy graduate. He was a fine first example of what a commanding officer should be.

I also had a small job while at Virginia. It was the delivery of the *New York Times* on Sundays. I made only a few dollars a month but it was enough to support me and a beautiful used Packard convertible my dad bought me to use in my job.

In early spring of 1941, I received a letter from Congressman Harold Flannery asking me to come to Washington to discuss my request for an appointment to the Naval Academy. The time from the receipt of his letter to the day of my meeting with him seemed like three centuries, but the big day finally arrived and I presented myself at his office on Capital Hill.

I didn't know what to expect, but I prayed it would be favorable. He opened the conversation by saying that he knew how very much I wanted to go to the Naval Academy and that he was happy that I was being persistent in my efforts. He then told me that he had decided to offer me a third alternate appointment. That was better than nothing, but not much. The principle and the first two alternates would have to be disqualified or drop dead for me to have a chance. He then said that he had given my case some thought and he was now prepared to offer me the second alternate. Better, but still not great! He then said that he had talked it over with Mrs. Flannery that very morning and she had suggested the first alternate for me. Now I was in business. Commander Kelley had told me that if we entered the war, the academy would surely expand, and the first alternates would probably be qualified to try for admission. The trouble was we had not entered the war. Finally Congressman Flannery laid it on me. He stood up, shook my hand and informed me that on that very morning on the way to his office he had decided to offer me the principal appointment. Damn, I had my appointment.

The rest was comparatively easy, except my final physical exam, which was not given until after I reported to the academy the fact that doctors had discovered I had a sclerosis of the spine. I never knew that I had anything the matter with me. I appeared before a naval board of medical review, which found that my defect was not sufficient to bar my admission. And so—on a hot afternoon in July of 1941—I was sworn in as a midshipman in the class of 1945. Thus began an incredible adventure.

⚓

Chapter 2

The Naval Academy Years

M OVING FROM AN easygoing life at the University of Virginia to plebe year at the Naval Academy was a painful transition. The prewar Naval Academy was a tough place, ruled by a regulation book that had changed little since World War I. Discipline was strict, enforced to the letter, and the plebe experience could be brutal. The result, however, was a magnificently disciplined regiment. Great emphasis was placed on professional training and naval indoctrination. The curriculum was narrow. The midshipmen were free to pursue any major they wished as long as it was electrical engineering. If successful, all midshipmen graduated with a bachelor of science degree in this subject. The only academic choice was in the study of a foreign language. I chose French, because I had already studied it a little at Wyoming Seminary. It proved to be my toughest subject. I could never get the hang of "dago" as the midshipmen for some reason called it. And I resided in the bucket section.

Plebe summer was really an intensified boot camp. While the rest of the regiment was either on summer cruise or on leave, a second class detail was kept at the academy to shape up the new class. During plebe summer the entire class was billeted in one wing of Bancroft Hall. Bancroft Hall was, and still is, the largest resident hall in the United States. It housed the entire regiment of 4,500 midshipmen.

I got off to less than a great start when I reported for my first drill with my leggings on backwards. I know the second-classman in charge of our company must have thought that they really got a live one in me.

Endless infantry drills, sailing and rowing, long, hot days on the rifle range—where I got a fat lip from the recoil of the Springfield 07s—professional education and a great deal of naval and Naval Academy indoctrination in the traditions of the academy and the service—these filled our days to overflowing. This very tough and demanding period changed us from 1200 or so total strangers to a unified class. We were beginning to feel a sense of bonding that was to grow more intense during our Naval Academy years and to continue to intensify in the many years of our life in the Navy, and beyond.

By the time the much-anticipated and universally-feared return of the upper class finally arrived, we had been whipped, and in many cases beaten, into shape, both physically and mentally. Towards the end of Plebe Summer the Plebe Battalion could march as well as anyone in the country. We were sharp indeed. The return of the upper class meant that we were integrated into one of the twenty companies that made up the regiment. It also meant the start of the fall term of the academic year and, of great excitement, the start of the 1941 football season.

Navy had a world-class team, very much in the running for national championship honors. We beat everyone except, of course, Notre Dame. The most important game of the year was against Army. It was traditionally played in Philadelphia on the last Saturday in November. The regiment embarked from the Naval Academy in a special train and arrived to a packed stadium of well over 100,000 very partisan fans. In those days the only way you could get a ticket to that game was to know someone at one of the Academies or someone in politics in Washington.

I shall never forget the regimental march on. We marched with great precision. It was a beautiful sunny autumn day as the regiment marched through the portals of Municipal Stadium to the tune of "Anchors Aweigh." Sustained cheers from the huge crowd greeted us. I was a plebe in the fourth platoon, tenth company, fourth battalion, but as we marched on the field, I was certain that all 100,000 plus people were looking at me. Well I know for sure that at least two were. My mother and father were there. Nothing could have kept them away.

We beat the hell out of Army again that year, which meant that the plebes were permitted to carry on until Christmas leave. It meant that the incessant and tough discipline applied to the plebes was greatly relaxed. We didn't have to march everywhere when we were outside our rooms, or be endlessly hazed by the upper class or suffer all sorts of indignities and discomforts at our meals. The reader will have little idea of the absolute bliss which we felt.

Our great victory over Army and the following celebrations were to be short-lived, because eight days later, on the 7th of December, the Japanese attacked Pearl Harbor. The effect of that incredible news was immediate and far-reaching. The Academy immediately moved to a wartime footing. The civilian guards at the gates, which were fondly called "Jimmy Legs," were replaced by Marines. All sorts of midshipmen security watches were established. On the 8th of December it was announced that the class of '42 would graduate immediately. The date was set for the 19th of December. In addition, the class of '43 was to graduate in June of '42, '44 was to graduate in June of '43 and the great class of '45 was to graduate in June of '44. It was further announced that we were to cover the entire four-year curriculum in three. It was to be done by curtailing the summer practice cruises and by eliminating most of summer leave. In effect we went from a three-term year to a four-term year.

For the remainder of my time at the Academy, I had two principal concerns. The first was that the war was going to be over before I had a chance to do my thing in the fleet, and the second, which was more or less constantly with me, was how I would behave when the shells and bombs were coming my way. I suspect all hands worried about that, but, of course, we never admitted it to each other.

Our professional education was intensified. Ordnance and gunnery included in-depth studies of our latest weaponry, and fire-control systems were heavily stressed, as were lessons learned about damage control and personal survivability. Our life, while greatly intensified, continued in an orderly way. Plebes were not permitted to date and were only permitted to visit the town of Annapolis on Saturday afternoons. My roommate's family, the Peytons, lived in Annapolis while Captain Peyton commanded the new battleship, *Indiana,* in the Pacific. Mrs. Peyton was truly wonderful to me. I was invited to delicious lunches at least twice a month and I had a place to relax a little during my precious free time.

It was the policy of the Academy that all midshipmen had to participate in a sport during each term. Regrettably, I was not a very good athlete. I did participate in battalion boxing and such non-skill sports as pushball. The later was played with a ball about six feet in diameter. The object of the game was to push the ball over a goal line, no holds barred. It was muddy, but a lot of fun.

I did, however go out for, and make, the editorial staff of the regimental publication, the *Log*. This was to be the vehicle for my major contribution to the life of the regiment and the Navy in future midshipman years.

Christmas leave of 1941 was enormously exciting. I attended the formal dinner dance at the Westmoreland Club in Wilkes Barre. I proudly wore my full-dress uniform, which had only recently been issued. My friends who were still in college had not yet been called up, but the conversation centered on that immediate and strong possibility. I enjoyed great prestige, not only because I was at Annapolis, but also because I was already in uniform. Truth to tell however, I was no closer to combat than my civilian friends. I only looked that way.

Plebe year mercifully ended in June, with the graduation of the class of '43. The shortened summer practice cruise was in the old battleship *Arkansas*. The Youngsters, as the third class was called, were billeted with, and worked like, enlisted personnel. We slept in hammocks which we thriced up and stowed every morning to clear the decks for our meals, which we ate on folding Navy tables and chairs.

All the teak decks of the *Arkansas* had been painted deck-gray. One of our many jobs was to holystone them to their original pure white state. This was accomplished by the vigorous back and forth movement of a boiler brick which had been slightly indented on one side to hold the point of a stick. A line of ten or so midshipmen could make some progress if we worked hard enough and did it in unison.

We manned the five-inch batteries and had numerous firing exercises, which we all enjoyed. Far from seeing the world as prior classes had on their practice cruises, we were obliged to stay in the Chesapeake Bay so that we would not be exposed to German submarines that patrolled our coast more or less with immunity at that time, sinking shipping almost at will.

Youngster and First Class year passed rapidly. I had become very used to the Academy discipline and was doing quite well but certainly not great academically. One of the drags on my academic performance was the enormous time I devoted to the *Log*. I had started to accrue considerable responsibilities during my Youngster year and was elected editor in chief in May of '43. This was considered a great honor in the regiment and my prestige increased enormously. I was also a senior editor of the *Lucky Bag*, the Academy yearbook, and editor of other publications such as *The Drags Handbook*. I declined the editorship of the literary magazine *Trident* as I just didn't have the time. As it was, most of the time I edited the 30,000 words of copy that made up an edition under my blanket after "lights out."

Although being editor in chief was a tough and time-consuming job, it had its many rewards and happy moments. We had a superb cartoon staff, many of professional quality and enormously prolific. One of the principal targets of the cartoonists—as well as some of the writers, such as the very popular columnist known by the pseudonym "Salty Sam"—was the officers in the executive department. These officers, either lieutenant commanders or commanders, were assigned to oversee the discipline of the regiment. It was they who did the incessant inspections as well as enforcing the tough discipline of the Regulation Book. The midshipmen assigned nicknames to all of them. Some of my favorites were "Bird Dog Miller," "Cement-Head Ed" and "Fearless Fosdick." Our cartoonists and writers took aim at them in every issue, and I, of course took the heat. What saved me was a coincidence. My faculty advisor was a Commander Edwin B. Dexter who happened to be the DO's boss. He loved our humor, especially when we zinged the DOs, so I had his blessing, as long as it was done in good fun and good taste.

Boy did I need him! I recall one day after an issue of the *Log* appeared there came the unmistakable sound of the DO's class ring rapping against the window of my door. Everyone knew that rap. The door burst open and there stood "Fearless Fosdick" whom we had really zinged in the new issue. He said, "You think you're pretty funny, Mr. Slaff. Messenger, take that man's name." That was always the signal that you were being put on the report. I asked him why I was being put on the report. He replied, "I don't know but I'll think of something!" He never did put me on report because he well knew that I would go right down to see my friend Commander Dexter and tattle on him. Ed Dexter, by the way, rose to the rank or rear admiral and was a close friend of mine until he died.

The *Log* also gave me considerable social advantages. In every issue we chose and published a picture of what we called "The Drag of the Week" i.e. the girl that we considered the most beautiful among those who visited the Naval Academy during the previous week. To be the "Drag of the Week" was an enormous honor both for the girl and her midshipman date. Everyone in the regiment thought that I was the one to choose her each week, so my prestige at a hop was considerable, as everyone invited me to be on their drag's hop card. I truly never had anything to do with the selection but I never let on. It was actually done by Gunner Fussilier, who was our "Salty Sam."

Since all transportation was being used for war shipments and necessary military and civilian travel, it was not possible for the Army-Navy game to be played in Philadelphia. Instead in '42, the Army team came to the Naval Academy. Two battalions of midshipmen were assigned to root for Army. They learned all of the Army cheers and songs and did very well, in a non-spontaneous way. It wasn't too difficult to be good sports, however, because we beat the hell out of Army for the third consecutive year.

As we moved into First Class Year, the fortunes of our war efforts were beginning to change. Hitler had been stopped at Stalingrad. The North African Campaign was going very well and we were starting our thrusts into Sicily and Italy. In the Pacific, we had started our counter offensive after our great victory at Midway. Guadalcanal was in our hands and the Japanese had been stopped in their incredible efforts to take Port Morsby. Australia now seemed more secure. Our Navy was doing quite well, but we were losing a great number of ships and men.

First Class Year was largely spent getting our academics mastered and getting ready to join the fleet. The routine was punctuated in late November by our football team journeying to West Point to play the cadets there, as Army had come to Annapolis the previous year. Ten midshipmen were selected to represent the regiment and I was one of the lucky ten. It was a thrill to travel on the train with the team. I had never been to West Point and going there under these circumstances was exciting.

My host at West Point was a cadet by the name of Fritz Rowe. He was a regimental commander and the editor of *The Pinter*, my opposite number. He was, by the way, one of the handsomest men that I had ever seen. We had beaten Army four years in a row. Army was starting to develop a great team and they were sure that '43 was their year. Blanchard and Davis, however, had thankfully not yet appeared. They were to dominate college football commencing in '44. The Corps was worked to a feverish pitch. I never saw so much emotion and determination. Rowe shared their emotion and their optimism and proposed that, instead of betting the traditional bathrobe and sweater, that we bet my locker against his! Disaster was close at hand. I couldn't decline, because it would have meant a shameless lack of Navy spirit and confidence in our team. On the other hand, if we lost I would be bankrupt. I didn't have enough money to even start replacing all of those uniforms. But I sucked it up and took the bet. We were the heavy underdog but mercifully we beat them 12 to 2. Thank heavens! I took with me all that I could carry in my suitcase and told Rowe that be could keep the rest until graduation. He told me that if he had won he planned to do the same thing. I wonder. I never did receive the remainder of his gear, because a few months after the game I had a letter from his managing editor informing me that he had dropped dead running the cadet commando course. I knew how he felt just before he died because I had gotten to that point myself on our commando course.

I must, in passing, say just a little about the effect of my experience as a publication editor on my future life, both in and out of the Navy. The requirement to get out a magazine or whatever else I was working on taught me more about responsibility and about human motivation than I learned in any academic effort. My ability to get people who were not paid in any way to work toward a common goal in what little spare time they had, and my ability to write effectively, have stood me in good stead during my entire life.

The last months at the Academy were given over to readying ourselves for graduation and for service in the fleet. Officers' uniforms had to be purchased, ship's preferences had to be decided and plans for graduation had to be finalized. Finally, on the 7th of June 1944 as our troops were landing in Normandy, the Class of '45, 914 strong, graduated. What an exciting and proud day! I had reached my life goal. I was an officer in the United States Navy.

I was ordered to the battleship *Massachusetts,* steaming in the Fast Carrier Task Force in the Pacific Fleet. Just what I had hoped for! Before going to the Pacific, the entire class was ordered to Florida for flight indoctrination in all types of naval aircraft. A.B. Shepard, our first astronaut and my classmate, was in my PBY flight crew. As I recall, we were equally bored with those long patrol boat flights. He, however, went to the heights in aviation and eventually to the moon.

From Pensacola we traveled by train to San Francisco. Thus began our long-awaited participation in the Great War.

Chapter 3

World War II

S AN FRANCISCO IN the summer of '44 was a city devoted to the support of the military. It was the principal port of embarkation for troops moving to the Pacific theater. Its Hunter Point Navy Yard worked around the clock repairing and refitting damaged warships. Navy crews found it a dream come true after months and years of fighting in the far Pacific. I found it exciting but frustrating. While there were lots of things to do and plenty of girls, I had my mind on the *Massachusetts* and was anxious as the devil to get to her. George O'Shea, Haskel Hall and I had a great room at the Mark Hopkins and our only duty was to check each day to determine if we were to report to the port of embarkation for transportation to the war zone. After a week of that we were more than ready to go.

At the end of the second week I had my port call. I was to go on board the Army troop transport *Willard E. Holbrook*, the former *President Taft*. When I arrived at the pier, an army band was playing and the last of a brigade of 3000 Army combat troops were going on board. Fifty Naval Academy ensigns and 100 casual Army nurses were next to board. There isn't much to do when you board a crowded troop transport but to go the rail and watch the others come up the steep gangway.

Just as all hands had completed the long trip up the accommodation ladder, a huge black limousine drove onto the pier. Out stepped the movie stars Greer Garson and Richard Ney, who had played her son in the wartime movie classic *Mrs. Miniver,* and had since married. There was a Hollywood goodbye scene and then it was time for Lieutenant Junior Grade Ney to come on board. There, of course, were no porters. Everyone was expected to carry his own gear up that ladder. It was tough for me, and I had the regulation val-pack that had been issued to all of us. Ney had a lot more, and there was no way he was going to struggle up that ladder with any degree of grace. His predictable failure was a source of great merriment to the embarked troops. There were loud and ribald suggestions as to the reason for his obvious weakness.

Soon after boarding was completed, we were underway for the Western Pacific and to unknown battles yet to be fought. The *Willard E. Holbrook* was for us quite comfortable. We were fairly well billeted in four-man rooms and we ate twice a day in the passenger dining room, which was reasonably attractive, especially since the nurses ate with us.

But it was one fouled-up ship. The captain was a naval reserve officer. The navigator, who was also the first mate, was a Coast Guard commander. The crew belonged to the merchant marine, the stewards were in the civil service and the gun crew was, of course, made up of naval personnel. We spent six weeks on that tub. It wasn't all that bad though, since the nurses had left their inhibitions back in the U.S. I believe they coined the expression "half the fun is getting there" on that voyage.

Interspersed with socializing with the nurses we spent our time criticizing the ship and especially the captain. Someone wrote a poem. I don't remember much of it but I do remember a small snatch that commemorated our collision with another merchantman.

> *Why that son of a bitch*
> *Should be digging a ditch,*
> *He ran us smack in the side of a freighter.*

Once in a while we would get the duty to inspect the crew compartment. That was something else! They had the Army troops packed into the holds. Their bunks were stacked five high. There wasn't enough room to roll over. The washrooms and heads were impossible, made worse by inadequate and poorly functioning plumbing. Of course there was no air conditioning and damn little fresh air ventilation. It was just god-awful—made even worse because half the troops were seasick.

One major event occurred on that outward-bound voyage. We crossed the equator and we had a rousing "Shellback Ceremony" to commemorate that important event. King Neptune and his court held hearings on all of us Pollywogs and, of course, we were found to be guilty of all manner of nefarious offenses. The punishments were bizarre but non-lethal, and in the end we were inducted into The Ancient Order of Shellbacks.

Our first port of call was in Finchaven on the northern coast of New Guinea, then Holandia, and then Biak, a small island off the western tip of New Guinea. We put our combat unit ashore there, as reinforcements for the Army division that was engaging the enemy on that island. Then on the 22nd of October, we dropped anchor in Ulithi Lagoon. There were a few Navy ships at anchor but none to which any of us had been assigned. We went to bed that night disappointed. I turned out the following morning at about 5 a.m. and went on deck. The first signs of dawn were breaking in the east. I saw a sight that I shall never forget. The entire Task Force 38 was at anchor. Sixteen fast carriers, nine fast battleships, twenty-four cruisers and, it seemed, hundreds of destroyers. They had just returned from the great battles off Formosa. Among those ships was the *U.S.S. Massachusetts* (BB59), my ship! Finally, I had joined the battle.

Later that morning, we were transported to our new ships in an LCVP that had been ordered alongside for that purpose. We made the side of the *Massachusetts* and I went up the accommodation ladder with all the smartness that I could muster. I had rehearsed a hundred times saluting the colors aft, saluting the officer of the deck and saying "Sir, I am reporting on board for duty."

The officer of the deck was polite enough but he informed me that there was no room in officers' quarters for me and he had the quarterdeck messenger escort me the chief petty officers quarters.

I didn't know it that morning but the *Massachusetts* already had 134 officers on board and they were not exactly holding their breath for the arrival of Ensign Slaff. Nor were the chiefs overwhelmed to have me billeted in their quarters. They didn't exactly send out the "welcome wagon" to greet me. The chiefs' quarters had to be two miles from the officers' wardroom, at least it seemed that far away to me. Finding my way there and back was an adventure.

That first night I recall being in my bunk and not feeling very happy or very secure. At about 2330 all hell broke loose. The general alarm sounded and the bugler sounded "general quarters." The bos'nmate's call echoed through the ship, calling all hands to battle stations for an emergency night sortie. Of course, all the chiefs, who were well schooled in such procedures, were out of bed, dressed in battle gear and up the ladders in record time. I was out of my bunk in a flash as well and I dressed as fast as anyone, but I didn't know where to go. I had not been assigned a battle station nor did I have any battle gear. Even if I had a battle station I wouldn't have had the foggiest notion how to get to it. I sort of ran around chiefs' quarters trying to look engaged. While I was trying to decide what to do, down came the armored hatches and out went the lights. I was locked in chief's quarters for my first battle evolution! How ignominious! The next day we were on our way to the battle of Leyte Gulf.

I never forgot that lonely first night on board the *Massachusetts*. In later years, when I rose to command, I took special pains to ensure that every young officer who reported to my ships was properly welcomed and made to feel that he was to be an important member of the ship's company. I had a standing order with the executive officers that I wanted the newly arrived officers to call on me as soon as they reported. I made sure to tell them how important their arrival was to the ship, even though it wasn't always the case. In *Albany* we had eighty-six officers, and were never really holding our breath for the arrival of a new ensign.

On the *Massachusetts*, I was almost immediately transferred to the wardroom lounge, where, along with several other junior ensigns, I resided for the next few months. The lounge was under two twin 5´ mounts. When the watch fired, it sounded like the inside of an enormous base drum. I was so tired that if I was not at the guns I had no trouble sleeping through that awful din.

The day after our emergency sortie I was assigned to the Third Division. The third was a gunnery division, which manned the ship's after 16-inch turret. As a Third Division junior officer I was also assigned to a bridge watch team. Each team stood a watch in three. Initially, there were four officers on watch on the bridge: the officer of the deck, the junior officer of the deck, the officer of the watch, and the gentleman of the watch. I, of course, started out as the gentleman of the watch. It sounded great, but essentially I was under instruction. In addition to our regular four hours on and eight off, our division manned the after fueling station, which had to fuel three destroyers every morning. We were also obliged to go to general quarters one hour before sunrise and one hour after sunset, as this was a favorite time for the Japanese to attack. When in the forward areas where the attacks were more or less constant, when the ship was not at battle stations, we doubled the steaming watch, which meant that when we were relieved on the bridge, we manned a gunnery station for an additional two hours. Add to this the requirements to administer a division, its personnel, and its equipment and it is quite obvious that we got damned little sleep. For weeks on end we could expect about four hours in twenty-four and that was all. It's amazing that we all more or less flourished. I guess it was youth that got us through. To make matters even worse, the captain knew that I had been editor in chief of the *Log* and so I was immediately appointed to be editor of the *Bay Stater*, the ship's newspaper. I was plagued with that job in every ship in which I served until I got senior enough to tell them to sit on it.

Massachusetts was a unit of Task Force 38. She was assigned to Task Group 38.1 along with *Indiana* her sister ship. The task groups, of which there were four, were the primary tactical entities of the great Fast Carrier Task Force. They operated under the Task Force Commander Admiral McCain and in turn were under the tactical command of Admiral "Bull" Halsey who was commander third fleet.

The Fast Carrier Task Force was designated 38 when Admiral Halsey commanded the fleet and Admiral McCain commanded the force. When it passed to the operational control of Commander Fifth Fleet Admiral Spruance, its designation was changed to Task Force 58 and it came under the direct command of Admiral Mitscher. This confused everyone at home because they never really knew that these two famous task forces were made up of exactly the same ships. One fleet commander would carry out the operations that he and his staff had planned during the time that the other fleet commander was carrying the fight to the enemy.

The landings at Leyte Gulf were the most powerful assaults mounted in the Pacific War to that date. The forces were not as large as those at Normandy in the ETO but they were nevertheless tremendous. My small part in the engagement was insignificant. The Japanese strategy was to draw our powerful force away from the landing assault area. This they did by a feint from the north with carriers and cruisers commanded by Admiral Ozawa. Admiral Halsey very unwisely went for the feint and we steamed north at full speed to attack this northern force.

The main strength of the Japanese fleet was divided into two forces. One, designated the central force, was to steam through San Bernardino Force and the other was to steam through Surigo Strait. These two forces were to put a mighty pincer on our amphibious forces and fire-support ships in Leyte Gulf. The Japanese strategy very nearly worked, with Halsey uncovering the amphibs. With only the small jeep carriers and fire-support ships to protect against the central and southern Japanese forces, the allied situation in Leyte Gulf without our force there became enormously precarious. It was only the extreme heroism of those small carriers and the cruisers and destroyers in the fire-support groups that saved the day. They were, of course, helped by the indecisiveness of the Japanese admirals. Admiral Halsey was ordered back to Leyte Gulf and we returned to lend our support at flank speed.

We didn't know all of this on the 24th of October 1944. We were steaming north to engage the enemy, which we did, but should not have. This terrible mistake by Admiral Halsey was indicative of his lack of brilliance through the entire time I served in his fleet.

But those were the good times. When we were in heavy action, such as at Okinawa, we sometimes stayed at battle stations for days on end. Only standing easy to eat K rations and go to the head between attacks—but more about that later.

The Fast Carrier Task Force operated in Philippine Waters for the balance of 1944 and for January and February of 1945. We supported the landings at Mindoro, Leyte Gulf, Lingayan Gulf and on Luzon with almost constant attacks on Japanese shipping and airfields. A task force attack on Formosa in January resulted in heavy damage to our force, as the Japanese committed large numbers of kamikazes for the first time.

For rest after each operation—which lasted from four to six weeks—we would anchor in Ulithi Lagoon, a hugh anchorage almost surrounded by coral islands and reefs. A fleet recreation center, which included a so-called officers' club, was established on Mog Mog Island. The club consisted of a thatched-roof bar and picnic benches and dispensed refreshments at an incredible price. Premier bourbon went for 25 cents a shot. The enlisted area on Mog Mog had similar facilities including some primitive ball fields and, of course, a beach.

The *Massachusetts* sailors hated the Japanese, but if anything they hated the sailors on the *Massachusetts'* sister ship *South Dakota* even more. *South Dakota* participated in much the same operations as did the *Massachusetts* but somehow or other she got most of the publicity, principally because she took a large number of hits from the Japanese. She had become known to the American public as "Battleship X." There was a very practical reason for the animosity directed at the *South Dakota*. *Massachusetts* was scheduled to return to the States ahead of the *South Dakota* for repairs and overhaul. There wasn't a man on board *Massachusetts*, including the captain, that didn't believe that *South Dakota* purposely tried to get under the bombs so that she could return to the States ahead of us. To the world she may have been known as Battleship X but to the *Massachusetts* sailors she was universally known as the Shitty Dick.

During the long and arduous war operations against the Japanese, our crew carefully planned for their next meeting with the hated *South Dakota* sailors on Mog Mog Island. They lovingly made brass knuckles; they sewed heavy bolts and nuts into the toes of socks and endlessly plotted their next encounter with the hated publicity hounds. And then, inevitably, came the big day. An LCI would come alongside to transport a liberty section to Mog Mog Island for a two-hour stay. On arrival at Mog Mog, all hands would be issued two cans of warm beer; no whiskey here. The warriors collected the unwanted beer rations from the youngsters who didn't want theirs. The tropical sun, the copious warm beer and the terrible tensions of battle would then take over and the war would begin.

The shore patrol of which I was often a member was instructed not to try to stop the fights but to do what we could to keep anyone from getting killed. Liberty was, mercifully, for only two hours, and the bloodied *Massachusetts* sailors, uniforms in shreds, would be somehow loaded back on board the LCI for the trip back to the ship.

After everyone got the first aid that was necessary, and a sobering shower and clean uniform, they invariably would recount with admirable exaggeration the mayhem which they had visited on the cowards from the Shitty Dick. Their hard-to-believe stories of victories became even more incredible as plans for the next glorious liberty on Mog Mog Island moved ahead.

It was while operating off the Philippines in December of 1944 that a natural disaster hit our force. As we proceeded to rendezvous with our logistic support force, the weather began to deteriorate. Instead of taking evasive action, Admiral Halsey tried to keep to his replenishment plan. He ordered the destroyers, who were very low on fuel, to pump the salt-water ballast that they took on to replace the fuel, which they had used in order to maintain proper stability. A vicious typhoon struck the force in this condition on the 18th of December. The winds exceeded 130 knots. Not only was it impossible to fuel, but it was impossible to even maintain station. Disaster struck when three of our destroyers, the *Hull*, the *Spence* and the *Monihan*, who had pumped ballast, capsized, with terrible loss of life. In excess of 1000 officers and men were lost. About thirty were picked up, in spite of an exhaustive search of the operating area. One of the survivors proved to be the commanding officer of one of the lost destroyers. A court of inquiry, convened in late December, placed full responsibility for the storm damage suffered by the ships and the terrible loss of life squarely on the shoulders of Admiral Halsey.

In mid-January, Admiral Halsey moved our fleet into the South China seas. We entered through the Luzon Straits on the 10th of January. Our objective was the Japanese bases at Singapore and at Camranh Bay in French Indochina. Although we expected to surprise a large force of Japanese warships in Camranh Bay, no warships were sighted there. There were however, very large numbers of Japanese merchantmen in Camranh Bay, in Saigon, and along the coast from Saigon to Hanoi. All together our forces sank about 45 ships, including several small naval escorts. In one stroke we had severed the vital Japanese supply routes from Singapore, Malaya, Burma and the Dutch East Indies. When I went to fight in Vietnam in 1967, the hulks of the ships that we had sank there in early 1945 were still visible in the Long Tau River.

Tokyo Rose was very much aware of our operations, of course.

She tried to taunt us by announcing that we were able to enter the South China seas but we were never going to be able to leave alive. In spite of Japanese air attacks we exited as we came, through the Straits of Luzon.

Every ship has its special characters and *Massachusetts* was no exception. Our executive officer, Commander O'Mally filled the bill. In the intense and dangerous environment in which we lived and fought, having a bit of comic relief helped greatly and our exec unknowingly supplied that. I was always amazed and proud of how well our bluejackets and officers held up under damn near impossible living conditions and under the constant tension of battle with practically no real rest. The resilience of our ship's company and by extrapolation our American fighting men were nothing short of outstanding, and a little humor helped a great deal.

The exec's nickname was "Jungle Jim." He got his nickname because he was a squared away officer who was dedicated to setting a proper example for all hands. As the war moved forward and many of our ships were inevitably damaged or sunk, the Navy developed more and more devices and equipments in its attempt to reduce casualties. By 1945, when general quarters sounded we were obliged to carry a life jacket, a gas mask, a side arm with ammunition, morphine surettes, a helmet, flash gloves, a flash hood, flash cream and night adapting goggles to our battle stations. The exec assigned this burden to his marine orderly who, of course had to carry his own as well. The exec, steaming through the ship at a near trot with his marine bearer close behind, reminded all hands of Jungle Jim, a fictitious big game hunter who was well known at the time.

There are many great stories about Jungle Jim. One of them that I particularly like happened while *Massachusetts* was sortieing from Ulithi en route to another combat operation. Our ship was the third battleship in a column of five. The exec came on the bridge and, apparently trying to impress the captain with his knowledge of the operation order, grabbed the officer of the deck's arm and exclaimed, "Mister, there are supposed to be five battleships in this sortie. There are two up there and there are two back there. Where the hell is the fifth one?" I would not have believed it either had I not been on the bridge at the time.

Another of my favorite stories about "Jungle Jim" occurred later in the war off the Japanese home islands. The Japanese were very big on mine warfare and had sown thousands of mines in the approaches to the home islands. Inevitably many of the moored mines broke loose from their anchors and drifted on the surface of the sea. The winds and currents carried many of them into our operating areas. Standard operating procedure was, when one of them was sighted, a screening destroyer would be designated to sink or detonate it by gunfire. If a mine got through the screen undetected, a heavy ship nearest to it would throw a smoke bomb to mark its position and a destroyer would be designated to destroy it.

One sunny afternoon a mine was sighted by our lookouts. It was coming down our starboard side. Before the signal bridge could activate a smoke bomb, the exec, who happened to be on the bridge, took charge. He grabbed a smoke bomb out of a locker and started to activate it. The little bombs were made of wood and had stabilizing fins fixed to them. There was a metal diaphragm in the nose, which had to be pierced before it was thrown over the side so that the seawater could interact with the chemicals inside. Well the exec pounded the nose of the bomb against a marlinspike and finally succeeded in punching through the metal membrane. It was defective, and started to smoke in the exec's hands. He tried to give it to the officer of the deck who was not having anything to do with it, and after several other unsuccessful attempts to hand it off to a member of the watch, he gave it his best shot and tried to heave it over the side. From the wing of the bridge to the side of the ship is a pretty good distance in a wide-beamed battleship and his smoke bomb didn't make it. It landed in a marine five-inch mount a few decks below the bridge.

A battleship bridge is very formal, especially when the captain is present, which he was on that occasion. No one said a word until a young telephone talker couldn't stand it another second and blurted out, "Oh shit." That got the captain and he had a hearty laugh, which, of course, was the signal for all hands to crack up.

The exec succeeded in exasperating the captain on a fairly routine basis. Our wonderfully patient commanding officer, when he just could not stand it another second, would say, "God damn it, God damn it, McNally!

When the *Massachusetts* went into action she showed what a formidable warship she was. She had her nine 16-inch, 30-caliber guns for offensive fire, but on defense she put up an enormous cone of fire. When we were fully engaged we could utilize our 20 five-inch guns, 80 40mm and 120 20mm antiaircraft weapons. During action the exec's battle station was in Battle Two. It was a full-ship control station to be utilized if the bridge got knocked out. Not to be left out of anything, Jungle Jim insisted on bringing a marine carbine to Battle Two which was located aft of the main mast. During an attack we would be blasting away and you could hear the sharp crack of a carbine being fired. We had 18 quad 40 mm mounts on board. When the Jungle Jim opened up with his carbine, the gunnery control officer would announce on his control circuit that quad 19 had commenced fire. The exec, of course, couldn't hope to hit anything with his little rifle but it must have made him feel that he was making a contribution.

After the South China Seas Operation—where we steamed for ten days and logged over 4,000 miles—we once again returned to Ulithi Lagoon for a much needed rest and ship maintenance. In early January 1945, the ship, along with the Task Force, sortied from Ulithi to support the amphibious landings on Luzon, which delivered the final coup de grâce to the Japanese Philippine occupation.

After reprovisioning once again, we were underway, but this time we sailed as Task Force 58, as Admiral Spruance relieved Admiral Halsey as fleet commander and Admiral Mitcher relieved Admiral McCain as task force commander. While the Army, supported by the Seventh Fleet, was securing the Philippines, we were on our way to support the epic battle for Iwo Jima. Arriving several days before D-Day, our forces conducted continuous strikes on the island in preparation for the landings.

On the 18th of January '45 our Task Group 58.1 was detached to make the first carrier strikes on the home islands. I had the watch on the bridge as we launched our strikes on Tokyo. The weather was terrible, with heavy seas and driving snow. Our planes met little resistance but were unable to hit their primary targets due to the weather.

I recognized the historical significance of our strikes and asked the ship's navigator, Commander Savidge, whom I knew well as an executive department officer in Bancroft Hall during my midshipman days, if I might have the battle flag that we were flying at the time. He very obligingly had the quartermaster of the watch replace it with a new one and gave it to me. I kept that national ensign until 1990, when I presented it to the battleship *Massachusetts*, which is now the state of Massachusetts' war memorial, berthed in Fall River Massachusetts.

We returned to the waters off of Honshu during the week of 25 February. The weather was still terrible and therefore strikes were not attempted against Tokyo, but our aircraft struck targets in the vicinity of Nagoya. Later in that same operation, we moved south and started the initial offensive operations against Okinawa. Little did we know at the time that the bloodiest naval battle in the history of the world would be fought there in the ensuing months.

Once again we returned to Ulithi to prepare for the Battle of Okinawa and sortied on the 12th of March. Our first operations were against Japanese naval units in the Inland Sea. These operations were heavily resisted. The Japanese defense was notably stiffening as we started to press in earnest against the home islands and we started to take serious casualties. The carrier *Franklin* was badly damaged and almost sank, with over a 1000 officers and men killed in action.

Our task force arrived off Okinawa on the 23rd of March and on the 24th, *Massachusetts* joined with other fast battleships of the force for the opening bombardment along the southern shores of the island. Thus began an incredible test of fortitude, stamina and bravery for our ship, which was to last for 40 days.

A week after our initial bombardment, the amphibious forces started moving troops ashore. It was Easter Sunday, the first of April 1945. The Japanese anticipated our invasion and had developed the Japanese war plan *Ten-Go*, envisioning a major defense of the Ryukus using thousands of suicide planes and Baku bombs, along with an elaborate army defense. Designed to slow down and, if possible, turn back our advance towards the home islands, it was to be the major Japanese effort to hold off the United States forces.

The Japanese naval counterattack started in earnest on the seventh of April. From that day on we were under almost continuous air attack by either kamikazes, manned Baku bombs or by conventional aircraft. The toll was staggering. But we had come to stay and stay we did.

In an effort to give our main force as much early warning as possible, each evening two of our screening destroyers were detailed to take a position between our main force and the Japanese air bases from whence the attacks came. At first the Japanese ignored them, to their great disadvantage, because with that early warning we were ready for their attacks. Then they changed tactics and went after the pickets first. After that, each evening two destroyers would leave our screen, many never to be seen by us again.

During one four-day period we stayed at battle stations continually, sleeping while sitting on our helmets during lulls in the action. We just couldn't keep that up indefinitely, so we went to a system of modified battle conditions which called for additional manning of antiaircraft guns after we were relieved of our normal condition three watch (a four-hour watch with eight hours off).

The reader might be interested in what a typical day was like during that long battle. An hour before dawn the entire ship went to battle stations. It was called "dawn alert." Immediately after securing, if there were no attacks, we would fuel three destroyers. I was in charge of the after fueling detail, and that consumed another hour and a half to two hours. We then went on our normal condition three watch, mine being on the bridge. After relief, four hours later, we manned a gun station for two additional hours on a split-watch basis. If the attacks were relatively light, this reinforced watch fought the ship while the off watch rested. At dusk we went back to battle stations for dusk stand-to, and then back on our regular watch. That was pretty much the routine that we followed on good days. On many of them, however, we just stayed more or less at general quarters. We also tried to administer our divisions, censor mail, get something to eat and keep ourselves clean. For weeks we got practically no sleep. The danger kept the adrenalin flowing and we performed amazingly well. And during all those 40 days we were taking a pasting. In the end, the fleet lost 84 destroyers either badly damaged or sunk, 16 cruisers and nine carriers. In total we took over 10,000 naval casualties—but we hung in there and we won.

One important episode in the battle was the result of the Japanese decision to dispatch their powerful new battleship *Yamato*, together with six cruisers and a squadron of destroyers, to engage us in a last-ditch battle. Yamato mounted nine 18-inch guns, far larger than the 16-inch guns in our battleships. The Japanese had no air cover except what could be supplied by their air force. On the 7th of April, Admiral Mitcher committed our entire strength to the attack on this force as it moved south in the Inland Sea. Two-hundred and eighty of our aircraft took part in the battle. With our powerful force and without effective air cover of their own, the Japanese were doomed. The entire Japanese force, including their mighty battleship, was sunk in one afternoon engagement.

We did not return to Ulithi after the battle. Instead we put into Samar in Leyte Gulf, where we rested and began preparations for the final battle for the homeland—Operation Olympic. Okinawa was a preview of what was ahead for us. While we had damned near sunk the entire Japanese fleet, the Imperial Army was very much intact, and intelligence indicated that there were thousands of kamikaze planes being readied for the final showdown.

In June, operating off the Japanese home islands, we again were devastated by a killer typhoon. Halsey, who had resumed command of the fleet was so damned anxious to kill "Japs" that he drove us all over the ocean and largely ignored warnings from our task group commander, Admiral Jocko Clark, that he was running us into a typhoon, and so he did. As a matter of fact, our Task Group 38.1 ran right into the eye of the typhoon. The seas were in excess of 80 feet and were crashing down on the ships with hundreds of tons of water. Our anemometers were carried away when the wind reached 158 knots. At that wind velocity there is no clear division between air and water. The air is literally filled with water, making visibility practically zero and making it impossible to use our radars with any effectiveness.

Maintaining station, which is so vital to safe maneuvering at sea, was essentially impossible. I was proud that I had recently been qualified by our captain as a senior officer of the deck. But as the junior top watch stander, I was ordered up to spot one—the highest point in the mast—to try to use our fire-control radars to assist the bridge in avoiding collision. Spot one was about 120 feet above the waterline. We were rolling 35 degrees to a side. Thus I was literally on the end of a 120-foot pendulum swinging through a 70-degree arc. The ship's bow plunged deeply into the seas and when it came up it lifted hundred of tons of green water over the ship. I actually took green water over spot one. I spent years at sea subsequent to that storm but I never experienced anything like it again.

The cruiser *Pittsburgh* operating in our formation lost 120 feet of her bow. Neither the ship nor her bow sank, and our lookouts sighted the bow after the storm was over. A fleet tug took it in tow and took it all the way to Guam, where it was reinstalled on the *Pittsburgh,* well enough to permit her to steam to the United States.

After the storm was over, there wasn't a gun that could fire or an aircraft that could fly in our entire task group. The carrier flight decks were crushed around their bows, like wrapping paper. Why Halsey was not summarily court-martialed for his incredible stupidity was mystifying to all hands, especially since he had done it before, off the Philippines, with enormous loss of life.

I must add parenthetically that the difference between the ability of Admiral Spruance and Admiral Halsey was evident to every officer and man in the fleet. Halsey was flashy, impetuous and reckless. He did have a great fighting spirit, which was valuable in the dark early days of the war but was largely counterproductive later, at least in the way he performed when we were a mighty fleet. Spruance, on the other hand was brilliant, methodical and businesslike. It was no wonder to us that he performed so brilliantly at Midway. He handled us like a pro and we all admired and respected him enormously.

In early July we were underway for the final showdown. On the 15th of July, the battleships *South Dakota, Indiana* and *Massachusetts,* the cruisers *Quincy* and *Chicago* and a squadron of screening destroyers took the home islands under gunfire for the first time. Our target was the Kamaishi Iron and Steel Works. We poured our 16-inch shells into the facility, leaving it in complete ruin. We continued to bombard and our carrier aircraft flew almost at will against Japanese targets. Our Army Air Corps operating from Guam and using Iwo Jima as an emergency landing field flew thousands of missions with their new B-29s. They flew a few over our formations so that we could see what they looked like.

On the 6th of August we had completed a bombardment of Hamamatsu and were busily engaged in equalizing turret ammunition in preparation for our next action. It was back-breaking work, as each shell—weighing either 2800 or 2300 pounds, depending on the type—had to be hoisted out of the barbette of one turret, placed on a wheeled dolly and mule-hauled up the deck to the turret that it was assigned. We were in the midst of this exercise when word was passed that the B-29s had just dropped a bomb on Hiroshima with the force of 20,000 tons of TNT. It made our effort seem a bit meager. This was quickly followed by another atomic bomb drop, this time on Nagasaki. On the 15th of August, the Japanese agreed to unconditional surrender. I was on watch on the bridge when the ship received a message from the fleet commander announcing that the Japanese had surrendered. Admiral Halsey added that if any Japanese aircraft flew over any of our formations they were to be shot down in a friendly manner.

That atomic bomb undoubtedly saved our lives because we were scheduled to steam into Sagami Wan (Tokyo Bay) on the following week to take Tokyo under fire with our 16-inch guns. We did enter Sagami Wan as part of the victorious fleet. The fleet commander had ordered the Japanese to put white sheets over all of their gun emplacements on the headlands guarding the entrance to the bay. As we steamed through the headlands we counted literally hundreds of bedsheets—guns that could bear on us had we had to force an entry into the bay. It would have been bloody.

We took a position of honor very close to *Missouri* where the surrender was to take place. When the ceremony concluded, *Massachusetts*, the light AA cruiser *Santa Fe* and a few escort destroyers were immediately detached to proceed to Uncle Sugar. We steamed through the entire fleet at anchor, streaming a 735-foot homeward-bound pennant—one foot for every plank-owner left on board. The war was over; we had made it and we were homeward bound.

⚓

Chapter 4

The Early Postwar Years

THE COMMANDING OFFICER of *Massachusetts* was officer in tactical command for the trip home. That meant that *Massachusetts* was the guide. We set a great circle course for Seattle, Washington, where we were to undergo a much-delayed yard availability at the naval shipyard in Bremerton, Washington.

After sortieing from Sagami Wan, the light cruiser *San Juan* and *Massachusetts* were joined by two destroyers who would act as our screen for the homeward-bound voyage. It would be impossible to describe the elation in the ship's company. We had made it safely through the war and, of equal importance, we were homeward bound to our families and friends. It really took a little while for those incredible facts to become a personal reality.

A 17-knot speed limit was immediately placed on the fleet to conserve fuel. There was to be no more routine steaming at 27 knots. How frustrating to have to limp along when we were going home! We officers of the decks solved that one in quick order. We would relieve the watch with the task force steaming at 17 knots. With absolutely no complaints from the other ships in the formation, we would gradually increase the engine turns until we were steaming along at well over 20 knots. Just before our watch was to be relieved we would reduce our speed to 17 knots so that we could report to the oncoming officer of the deck that we were in fact making turns for 17 knots and we could write that in our log. Looking back, I'm dead sure the captain and the navigator knew what we were doing but no one said anything. We just chalked it up to favorable currents.

Since we no longer were required to stand our normal war cruising watch and since we conducted almost no drills, all hands were able to relax. Now that we had all that free time, the problem was how we were going to occupy ourselves. What a luxury—free time! Well we soon started a poker game in junior officers' quarters, which we kept going almost continuously during the 11-day voyage home. Not the same players, of course, but we had lots of junior officers who were anxious to join the game. We had a great trip, although it seemed like 11 weeks rather than 11 days.

I had the mid-watch on the bridge when we made our first landfall on "Uncle Sugar." Our watch sighted some flashes on the starboard bow and I immediately notified the captain, reporting that they appeared to be gun flashes. The navigator and the captain came to the bridge and identified my gunfire as lights from flashing navigational lights. In the hundreds of watches I had stood on the bridge I had never seen a lighted navigational aid. They, of course, had all been extinguished during the war.

We entered the Straits of Juan de Fuca in an absolute dead fog. It was cold and it was fairly rough. Combat Information Center reported a contact that was on a collision course with us and the bridge maneuvered to stay clear. But each time we would come to a safe course the contact would alter course to close us again. This went on for over an hour when out of the mist the pilot boat from Port Angeles finally appeared. It had been chasing us all over the straits and when the bar pilot finally came on board he looked like he was half drowned.

We were moved into the ammunition piers in Bremerton to unload our ammunition before going into our berth in the yard. The word was passed that no one would be permitted to leave the ship until all ammunition was safely off the ship—an absolutely tremendous job. We all worked for 24 hours straight unloading the 16-inch shells and powder, the 5-inch fixed ammunition, the 40 mm, the 20 mm and small arms ammunition, and we finally got the job done with no mishaps. We were then allowed ashore. As I recall the date was 17 September 1945.

The first thing I did was to call my mother and dad to let them know that I had reached home safely. That telephone call was full of emotion for them and I guess for me as well. So many of us didn't make it.

We had a pleasant six months in Bremerton. I tried skiing several times in the Cascades, with no notable success, met some girls, and carried out my divisional duties incident to the yard overhaul. I was working on the ship's history and had to go ashore often to arrange for a printer, or for other business. It was a cold and uncomfortable winter in the ship, but because of my special assignment to get the history done I was given a rather spacious commander's cabin up in the superstructure.

My dear friend Hal Stewart and I got leave in the second leave group and flew to the East Coast together. It was my first experience in an airliner. It was a DC-3, which had to stop every few hundred miles, but we thought that it was grand.

After three weeks at home, we met at LaGuardia Airport for the flight back to Seattle. A dense fog had settled in and we could not get out of New York for several days. Through family friends we got railroad berths on the 20th Century Limited to Chicago but we were going to be late. Hal and I ginned up a message to the captain, which as I remember went something like this:

> *Chicago by train,*
> *Seattle by plane,*
> *Hope to hell it doesn't rain.*
> *We'll not make it on time,*
> *But we're not to blame.*
> *Feeling fine,*
> *Hope you're the same.*

We were late but no one ever mentioned it to us.

In early April, we finished our overhaul and got the ship underway for sea trials. We had a new captain, Huber H. McClain, but we were down to only three qualified officers of the deck, me being one of them. The captain conducted a man overboard drill by having the after watch throw a dummy named "Oscar" over the fantail. The lookouts duly sighted the "man overboard" and the ship went into its drill, which is fairly complex and includes mustering all hands to find out who the poor victim is. The captain brought the ship around to recover Oscar but missed him by at least a hundred yards. He tried again with similar results. He then told me to try it.

Having spent literally thousands of hours on that bridge, I knew my ship. I brought her around in a Williamson Turn, and asked the captain on which side he wished me to make the recovery. He thought that I was kidding but when he said, "port," I had the ship dead in the water with Oscar close enough to pick him up with a grappling hook just under the port bow. After that morning our new captain and I were good friends.

Soon after sea trials I received my orders from the Bureau of Naval Personnel. The captain was horrified and immediately tried to have the orders canceled, with no success. My orders were to the precommissioning detail of the light cruiser U.S.S. *Galveston*. I was ordered to join the precommissioning detail in Newport, Rhode Island.

After mooring in Long Beach California for a few days, we steamed to San Francisco where I was detached. I left *Massachusetts* with great sadness, as I loved that ship and my shipmates who had fought her with so much gallantry, dedication and good humor. I have visited on board her several times since she became the war memorial for the state of Massachusetts. As a matter of fact, in May of 2002, I was invited to be a guest of honor and speaker at ceremonies on board commemorating the sixtieth anniversary of her commissioning.

After several weeks of leave, I reported to Newport but was only there for a very few weeks when the Navy Department decided not to commission *Galveston* and I received a new set of orders to the light cruiser *Houston* which had just departed for England to serve as the flagship of Commander Naval Forces, Europe.

I embarked for England in the Coast Guard transport *General Muir*. She was carrying a few thousand German P.O.Ws. It was a pleasant enough crossing and we got pretty used to hearing most of the words that came over the general announcing system in German. We entered the port of Liverpool, which had taken a terrible pounding from the Luftwaffe. The Germans were disembarked first and turned over to a few companies of British M.Ps. We watched as they lined up the Germans and had them empty all their gear on the pier. All candy, cigarettes, soap and other painfully scarce items in England were systematically liberated and there was a lot of it. We loved the whole thing.

I traveled to London with a few other officers en route to *Houston*. After a night in the Grosvenor House, we went to Southampton and joined the ship there. I was delighted to find my old friend, Carol Turner on board as the gunnery officer. He was in the class of '42, was in my company my plebe year and married my roommate's sister, Polly. I was assigned as the ship's radio officer and took over the C Division.

There then began one of the most interesting and delightful nine months that anyone could possibly imagine. Admiral Kent Hewitt was not only the senior naval officer in Europe but was also a U.S. delegate to the Satellite Peace Conference, which was then underway. Thus he had enormous prestige.

We spent nine months either operating with the British Home Fleet or conducting a full dress goodwill cruise all over Europe and North Africa. It was truly like a storybook. We made that cruise when the United States' prestige was at it, absolute zenith and most Europeans and citizens of North African countries had never seen a U. S. cruiser.

While on the goodwill phase of our operations we would typically stand into a port for five days and would be entertained at several parties each day. In reciprocation we would give a great reception on board during the last afternoon of our visit, to repay all the hospitality that we had received. As soon as our guests were safely off the ship we would get underway for our next port of call. In that way we visited Bergin, Oslo, Stockholm, Copenhagen, Antwerp, Amsterdam, Rotterdam, LeHarve, Lisbon, Gibraltar, Tangier, Oran, Port Said, Nice, Naples, Genoa, Athens and other cities, which I probably have forgotten.

This entire cruise took place in 1946 at the very height of the precipitous demobilization of our forces. Ships in full commission were being left literally without sufficient manpower to get them underway. The only way *Houston* was able to deploy was that they fleshed out her crew with 300 prisoners from Portsmouth Naval Prison. The deal was that if the prisoners behaved themselves on the cruise they would be restored to full duty and given an honorable discharge. Most of them did very well but one of the convicts murdered an English girl in a bomb shelter in Southampton.

It would be difficult to recount even part of the incredible experiences we had on that cruise. We were routinely entertained at palaces, embassies and at other exciting venues. We almost came to grief in Stockholm Harbor. We were to moor fore and aft to mooring buoys in the old harbor of Stockholm in echelon with the flagship of the Swedish fleet, *Three Crowns*. We had a Swedish docking pilot on board and we secured tugs to both our bow and stern. There was a very strong wind abeam that was putting enormous pressure on the *Houston*, to such a degree that the tugs could not hold her up. In spite of the tugs' best efforts we were being slowly set down on the Swedish flagship. All hands on *Houston* were at quarters as were the Swedes on *Three Crowns*. The Swedish boat booms were rigged out and their boats were secured to them. They were between *Houston* and *Three Crowns*. No one moved until we were no more than 50 feet away. All of a sudden their boatswain pipe sounded. Swedish sailors made a dash for the booms, manned their boats and got them out from between us in the nick of time. At that moment additional tugs arrived to avert a disaster and we finally were able to pick up our mooring buoys.

But we were not done yet. As soon as we were safely moored, we began a series of gun salutes that eventually numbered about 135. At that time our standard one-pounder saluting batteries had not yet been reinstalled so we fired short charges out of our 5-inch batteries. The old harbor in Stockholm is surrounded by a most picturesque port with ancient buildings literally coming down to the water's edge. The concussions from our saluting charges blew out a great majority of the windows in those old buildings! How embarrassing!

One of our most spectacular visits was to Lisbon. We were joined there by the light cruiser *Little Rock* and her two destroyer escorts. The Portuguese put on an old-fashioned bullfight in our honor. It was an extravaganza, with golden carriages, beautifully costumed bullfighters riding their horses (the Portuguese fight the bull from the back of a horse) and their numerous attendants. All hands, including our bluejackets, were invited. Thus about thirty percent of the crowd was American. The Portuguese, of course, rooted for the bullfighters but all the Americans, especially the bluejackets, rooted like hell for the bull.

The highlight of the entire afternoon was a team of six amateur bullfighters made up of Portuguese nobility who, with no weapons at all, took on a very ferocious bull. They lined up in a single file and the leader—wearing a very wide red sash indeed—got the bull to charge. His job was to try to get between the bull's horns while his teammates tried to grab an assigned leg or the tail of the beast. That bull knocked that team captain ten feet up in the air. It was a hell of a fight but the Portuguese finally got control. It was the fairest fight of the day and we all enjoyed it immensely.

The next evening the Portuguese opened the Summer Palace, which had been closed during the war, and gave a great fête in our honor. It was like a Cecil B. De Mille movie. When we arrived that evening there were three companies of the Portuguese palace guards in beautiful full-dress uniforms lined up as a guard of honor. The scene was made even more glamorous by a score of high-powered search lights stabbing the night sky.

Inside, the long hallway leading to the reception rooms was lined with beautifully turned out footmen in satin coats and silk knee britches, holding halberds. The banquet hall was lighted with thousands of glass bejeweled candles. It was beautiful, but that damned wax dripped all over our shoulder boards. A string orchestra in colonial dress and wigs played music. At about 11:30 p.m. we had dinner. We ate off of golden plates, standing up!

At about 1 a.m. we departed, but not to go back to the ship. We went to the famous casino at Estorille where we played roulette. I was ahead about $150, which was a lot of money in 1946, at least to me. At this point I believe that they threw in the magnets, because I lost my $150 plus nearly all the money in my wallet. We had just enough for the cab ride back to the ship. We arrived alongside just as the bugler was sounding "officer call" for morning quarters. It had been a great and memorable night.

Our visit to Port Said at Suez occupies a very pleasant place in my memories. Port Said was and still is one of the toughest ports in the world. When we stood in there in 1946 the Brits were still masters of Egypt and King Farouk was still on the throne.

As I recall, Port Said had about five or six major items for sale: girls or boys, whichever was your preference, dirty pictures, smutty books, Spanish fly, and daggers, with a brisk trade in camel saddles made of poorly cured camels' hides. The Brits entertained us in their mess and then we all went down to see the local belly dancers. While we were in Port Said, most of us went up to Cairo to see the pyramids.

And so the nine months went, one interesting experience after another. It was during this cruise that I got to know many British naval officers. We operated with the British Home Fleet out of their bases in Northern Scotland at Scapa Flow and Invergordon. The British cruiser *Frobisher* and carrier *Illustrious* also followed us on portions of our goodwill cruise.

I found the British a great deal more relaxed about going to sea than we are. My British friends would often say if they ever got into a war with us, they would stay in port and let us go out and exercise ourselves to death. We spent a great deal of time socializing with them. If a foreign officer visits a British navy wardroom, he can "open the bottle on the queen." Thus we often went to their ships for cocktails and since the food in their wardrooms was universally awful, they would often come to our wardroom for dinner.

During our time in England, I was designated as the ship's top-secret courier, which meant that I frequently had to go up to London to pick up cryptographic material for both the ship and the Flag. I got along famously with the Flag and as a matter of fact, the Admiral's chief of staff tried to get me transferred to ComNavEu in London. The captain wasn't buying that, however.

One of the curses of being a writer and editor of the midshipmen publications was that I was again destined to be the editor of the ship's newspaper and cruise book. Our exec, Commander Miller, whom we called "Bird Dog" when he was a D.O. in the executive department at the Naval Academy, wouldn't let me up. He proclaimed that if I didn't make sufficient progress on the cruise book I couldn't go ashore. Since we needed all the officers we could muster to go to all those parties every day, he would go through the motion of mustering me at the party. Actually we were great friends and our friendship grew stronger through our many years of service together.

We returned to our homeport in Newport, Rhode Island just before Christmas of 1946 and, in January, I was picked by our cruiser division commander, Rear Admiral Burroughs, to join his staff in the cruiser *Huntington*. In March, we were on our way back to Europe.

I left *Houston* with great sadness. Captain McManes, later Admiral McManes, became a dear friend and, although he died many years ago, I still see his son and feel very close to him.

I was the staff navigator and assistant operations officer. The chief of staff was Nev Schafer, who was to become one of my closest friends and with whom I was to serve together in the future.

Our cruise in Europe this time was confined to the Mediterranean. We spent four months there and, since there was not yet a Sixth Fleet, it was essentially a pleasure cruise. We moored for almost two months in Rapallo on the Italian Riviera. We became very familiar with Rapallo, Porto Fino and Santa Margarita, charming and beautiful little ports. We also visited other Italian cities, including Genoa and Venice. Our admiral was designated Commander Naval Forces Adriatic at the time the Yugoslavs were putting enormous military pressure on the Trust Territory around Trieste. We and our escort destroyers moved up the Adriatic towards Trieste when it was still heavily mined. One of our escorts, the destroyer *Fox*, hit a mine off of Spilt and damned near sank.

We entered our berth in Trieste and prepared to use our guns to support the 82nd Airborne which was manning the Morgan Line on the perimeter of the Trust Territories. The Communists in Trieste had a fit, as they claimed we had trained our guns on their headquarters. We hadn't, but there is an optical illusion associated with major calibre guns. They always seem to be pointing at you. At a time when our garrison troops in Europe were going to hell, the troops of the 82nd Airborne were the finest I had ever seen. Every one of them looked like a West Pointer. Their commanding general, Maxwell Taylor, was truly a great Army officer and he would rise to considerable prominence in later years. The Yugoslavs never did get up enough courage to test the Morgan Line. The 82nd would have clobbered them if they had.

During that cruise we had a most interesting visit in Tangier. It was at the time the Istiqual Party was agitating to free Tangier and Morocco from the French. The Pasha of Tangier, in an attempt to ingratiate himself with the U.S., laid on an Arab *diffa* in our honor. It was held in his palace that looked like something out of the *Arabian Nights.* Mosaics everywhere, with beautiful intricate carving and elegant oriental rugs. We sat at round tables on cushions arranged on the carpets. There was an Arab host between each of us. The food was delicious and incredibly plentiful. As I recall, we had about ten courses. We could only eat a little from the dishes set in the middle of the table. They were carried away with most of the food still on them. Our host told us that not a scrap would be wasted. After we finished, the women and the children ate, then the servants and finally anything left over went to the poor. Of course, the Arabs don't drink alcoholic beverages. Instead they served almond milk, which is made by squeezing almonds. It tasted like Hind's Honey and Almond Cream smells. Not bad!

It was in mid-summer 1947 that the staff complement of officers was reduced and my billet was eliminated and I was ordered detached upon our return from Europe. My orders to my first shore duty were awaiting us on our arrival in Newport in the summer of 1947. After an appropriate leave I was ordered to report to the Office of the Chief of Naval Operations in Washington. I was on my way to a tour that was to change my life.

Chapter 5

My First Tours Ashore

A FTER SEVERAL WEEKS leave, I reported to OPNAV for duty and was assigned to OP 202, Communications Supplementary Activities, Washington. This, I soon found out, was a cover name for the Navy's cryptanalysis efforts, which were intense, especially against the Soviet Union, who had become the number one nemesis of the United States. It was this activity in the very same buildings—which originally was Mount Vernon Seminary, a prestigious Washington school for girls—where the Navy attacked and broke the Japanese naval and diplomatic codes. These enormous intelligence successes enabled the Navy to fight the Japanese Navy on the most favorable strategic and tactical terms. The activity was located at the confluence of Massachusetts and Nebraska Avenue and was a most pleasant venue.

Working with this super-secret activity required a full background investigation, which took about five months. Apparently, the FBI looked into my background with enormous diligence, even interviewing various neighbors in various neighborhoods where I had lived even prior to entering the Navy. During this time I was held in sort of an isolation status and occupied my time by taking several courses in cryptanalysis. When I was eventually cleared, I was assigned to the estimates branch, probably because my records indicated that I was a writer and editor. This outfit took the raw intelligence generated by our cryptanalysis effort and combined it with other intelligence which was called "collateral intelligence," and produced estimates with the highest security classifications in the government. This enormous effort, later to be folded into a super intelligence outfit known as the National Security Agency, has an entire set of laws governing every aspect of the effort.

At any rate, I found my new duties enormously interesting. Although very junior in rank, a JG, I undertook the very first full-blown intelligence estimate of the formidable Soviet Submarine Service. It took me about six months of intense work. It was a great success and was used as the bible in the Navy for Soviet submarine intelligence. This great success was to have very important consequences for my later assignments.

After a few weeks of backing and filling in Washington, I joined forces with two other classmates, Steve McClintic and Louis Knudsen, plus a fellow out of '46, Ted Hartley. We rented a house on 26th Street in Georgetown, hired a couple of maids, Minnie and Beulah, who lived across the street, and settled in for a pleasant tour ashore.

Ted Hartley I knew well at the Naval Academy. He came aboard our table as a plebe and was in our company for two years. He also was elected editor in chief of the the *Log* when I graduated. In addition, we served together in the cruiser *Houston*. He was a man about town and thus our social life prospered almost immediately. We quickly got to know a lot of people and started to receive some invitations to some very nice parties. Hartley, by the way, eventually married Dinah Merrill and became a Hollywood mogul.

We gave a party of our own in early November that was to change my life. Ted had invited a young lady by the name of Mary Stewart Price. She accepted and asked if she could bring a close friend and her friend's date. Her friend's name was Mary Lee Schaeffer. Well I thought that she was an absolute knockout, a strawberry blond and beautiful. Fortunately for me, her date had too much to drink and went to sleep. I asked her for her telephone number, which she gave me, and I told her that I intended to call for a date.

In due course I telephoned her and she gave me a date. When I went to pick her up, there was some confusion. She thought that I was Louis Knudsen when I called and was a bit surprised to find me at the door. Oh well, I guess she figured, "What the hell" and went out with me. I thought that she was terrific. I knew after only a few dates that she was the girl that I wanted to marry.

Her father was a naval aviator, Valentine H. Schaeffer. She was born in San Diego and lived the life of a Navy Junior. She graduated from Holton Arms School in Washington and spent two years at Smith College. When the war came she withdrew. While her father was at sea, she and her mother went to live in Mexico City, where she attended the University of Mexico City. In later years she convinced her parents to allow her to join the American Red Cross for duty in the E.T.O. where she served from 1945 to 1947. I met her soon after her return from Europe.

I went to visit my mother and dad for Christmas of 1947 and told them that I had found an absolutely wonderful girl. They both were very pleased for me. Apparently she found me to be okay, because our romance blossomed. Our courtship was not to be an easy one however, as her mother took a very serious dislike of me. At first we tried to overcome it, but Mary Lee, who had trouble with her mother for her entire life, decided that she had to get away if she was to have any happiness or freedom. In May of 1948 she moved to New York and obtained a position as a secretary at Bonwit Teller on Fifth Avenue. June, July and August found me driving to New York to be with Mary Lee on the weekends and then driving home on Sunday night. That I didn't kill myself on the road was a miracle. I'd inevitably be tired and sleepy on the trip back to Washington; I had all sorts of schemes designed to keep me awake.

We had wonderful weekends together in New York. I used the car my dad had given me for winning the war. I tried to tell him that I got a little help from Nimitz, Halsey and Spruance, among others, but it didn't seem to matter to him. It was a blue Studebaker. That little car enabled us to go where we wished, up to Westchester for dinner or summer theater or out to Long Island to a special restaurant. If it weren't for that damn drive it would have been just wonderful.

Mary Lee set our wedding date for the 10th of September 1948.

Because of the attitude of her mother, we decided to have a very small private wedding at the Little Church around the Corner in Lower Manhattan. I asked my classmate, good friend and house-mate, Steve McClintic, to be my best man and Mary Lee asked her very close friend from American Red Cross days in the E.T.O., Adele Range, to be her maid of honor. We had a great dinner and were off to Bermuda for our honeymoon.

Ted Hartley had arranged for us to stay at the beautiful Coral Beach Club, which had opened a year earlier. We arrived about midnight and everyone except the night watchman had already retired.

He was expecting us however, and deposited us in our room. What a wonderful and romantic place! We have been back several times since and love it as much now as we did then. Our stay at the Coral Beach Club was somewhat marred by a powerful hurricane which hit the island. The storm did great damage to much of the flora for which Bermuda is famous. It particularly ravaged the cedar trees which had previously grown copiously all over the island and which were used extensively for architectural details in home design and construction.

We found our first home in Washington at the very fashionable address of 2100 Connecticut Avenue. It was really only a one-room efficiency but it was located in one of the most prestigious areas of the city. It had a kitchenette and a bath and we thought that it was grand. It cost an arm and a leg. As I recall, it was $110 a month plus $35 for parking in the garage. After a year there, Mary Lee found a one-bedroom apartment in Fairlington, Virginia for $68 dollars a month, and we moved there in 1949.

I had become very enamored with naval intelligence and thought very seriously of shifting to Special Duty Only (Intelligence). After much thought I decided against it, because I really aspired to command at sea. However, I did apply for the postgraduate course in naval intelligence, international relations and foreign languages and was duly accepted for the class entering in 1949.

I thoroughly enjoyed the Intelligence and foreign relations part of the curriculum, but had a terrible time at the French language school. Never being very good at foreign languages, (I was in section Dix C at Annapolis), I never worked harder to master anything in my life. It was a fourteen-hour-a-day effort. We spent six hours in class and I spent another eight hours trying to absorb the incredible workload that the professor heaped on us. Our professor, Monsieur Pulver, was quite a character, given to heavy drinking. Often he would show up a bit tipsy and would become hilarious as he recounted many great tales, mostly in French. We had to learn about 150 new vocabulary words per night. Mary Lee helped enormously by making cards for me; on one side she would write the English word and write the French translation on the other. Since there were only five of us in the class there was nowhere to hide.

My plan was to be an attaché in a French speaking country, if I was able to pass the course successfully. A week before the final examination to qualify as a naval interpreter in French, however, Mary Lee and I were at a Saturday night dance at the Army-Navy Country Club. At about 11 o'clock, we noticed that many of the oriental attachés left rather hurriedly. The next morning, the *Sunday New York Times* reported that the North Koreans had invaded South Korea. I really wasn't too sure exactly where Korea was.

I was soon to find out. On Monday morning, Captain Layton, the director of the school, called me to his office and told me that the director of naval intelligence had ordered that I was to depart for the Far East on Wednesday and that I was going to be given my final seven-hour French exam on Tuesday. I was to go immediately to get all of my shots.

That night, feeling terrible from a series of shots that always made me sick, I stayed up most of the night with my Annapolis and French school classmate, Julien Le Bourgeoise. He tutored me for the exam to come, and miracles of miracles, I passed. I always suspected that there was a bit of charity there. On Wednesday, Mary Lee drove me to the airport to begin my trip to Japan, via California. And so the Korean War had started and I was off to do my bit.

But why was I chosen? Because, it later turned out, I was the foremost expert on the Soviet Submarine Service. One of the most important "Essential Elements of Information" placed on the intelligence service was, "Will the Soviets enter the war on the side of North Korea?" One major indicator under this EEI was the forward deployment of the Soviet Far Eastern Submarine Forces into our theater of naval operations in the Sea of Japan and the Yellow Sea. There were several squadrons of soviet submarines in the Soviet Pacific Fleet, which were based in Vladivostok and Petropavlosk. My job, among others, would be to try to know where those submarines were at all times.

⚓

Chapter 6

The Korean War

W
HEN I ARRIVED in California, I met three other naval intelligence officers who had been ordered to the new war
on the same emergency basis as I was: Jack Wohler, Bill
"Tubby" Doyle and Cal Calhoun. We flew to Tokyo together, where
we reported to the staff of Commander Naval Forces, Far East. The
staff had just taken over the Tokyo Stock Exchange building for its
headquarters. We were definitely going to need a lot more space if
Admiral Joy was to command naval operations associated with the
war, and the new headquarters building promised to serve the Navy
very well.

A Commander Art Johnson whom I knew slightly from my intelligence duties in Washington then headed the intelligence section.
Captain Eddie Layton, who had been the director of the Naval Intelligence School, would soon relieve him. Captain Layton was soon
to make admiral, and Captain Murt Stone in turn relieved him. The
staff already had a handful of intelligence officers, but they were completely swamped and it was my impression that they were not particularly sharp. To say that our outfit was initially confused would be
a bit of an understatement. We had to get organized, and quickly, because we not only had to support our admiral, we also had to develop
a coherent naval intelligence effort for the entire war theater.

As expected, I was designated as the underseas warfare intelligence officer and the special security officer. The latter position was
associated with control of all special intelligence matters for the Navy
with respect to the war. I was given almost total responsibility for
organizing the special intelligence effort. I immediately set about organizing a secure office on the flag deck. It was really just a walled off
passageway. I had bars installed on the windows and a jimmy-proof
steel door with a speakeasy style sliding panel so that I could see who

was knocking on my door. I set up my Soviet submarine files and covered the walls with area charts so that I could plot Soviet submarine movements on a daily basis.

I was also assigned as mine warfare intelligence officer. Here I was truly at sea. I didn't know anything about Soviet mines, but neither did anyone else. One day, soon after I moved into my cell-like office, a cleared British liaison officer, a Commander Grey, came to me to seek information on enemy mine activity off Songjin. My desk was covered with agent reports, dispatches, photographs and generally was in much disarray. I was truly in doubt just where Songjin was located, but I plunged right in. He waited until I ran down, and then in that laconic manner the British use so effectively, he said, "Lieutenant Slaff, I have asked a simple question and you have given a simple answer; you simply don't know." He was right, of course, but I never liked him much after that.

I was also designated as the theater submarine contact evaluation officer. It was my responsibility to evaluate all reported undersea contacts, and there were eventually lots of them, as our anti-submarine forces dramatically built up in the Sea of Japan and the Yellow Sea. I not only had special intelligence to help me with my evaluations but all other collateral intelligence as well. I also used careful plotting, and oceanographic information, such as depths, currents, and plotted wrecks. Admiral Joy insisted that I be the only one on the staff authorized to evaluate these contacts. I was flattered, but it meant that, in addition to my regular long hours, and my intelligence duty officer watches, I was continuously on call at any hour of the day or night to come to headquarters to make a COMNAVFE evaluation on a reported submarine contact. These evaluations were of critical importance to the fleet and task force commanders as well as to Washington. A high evaluation of "confirmed" or "probable" would immediately warn our ships of potential danger and have a dramatic impact on possible Soviet intentions.

During the year and a half that I carried out that evaluation role I must have evaluated well over a hundred submarine contacts. In no case were any of them Soviet submarines. I generally knew where the Soviet submarines in the Far Eastern Fleet were on a daily basis and I don't believe that any of them ever entered our area of operations.

My very conservative evaluations aggravated the destroyers enormously. In many cases, the skippers would have bet their last dollar that they had made and developed a bona fide contact. I remember one case in the Yellow Sea. The destroyer *Renshaw* tracked a contact for almost two days. They had a course and speed and doppler effects. In addition, when they fired their depth charges they got oil bubbles rising to the surface. They really had a submarine, so they thought. What they had was a World War II hulk in a current of about five knots which, on their dead reckoning tracer, gave them a course and speed opposite to the current which was moving them along, not the hulk. The depth charges merely released oil that had been trapped in the hull. The commander in chief of the Pacific Fleet, as well as the Office of Naval Intelligence in Washington concurred in my evaluation. Interestingly, almost fifty years after this incident, members of the ship's company of the *Renshaw*, still infuriated by my evaluation, actually wrote a book trying to refute it. They were certain then as they are now that I was just plain wrong. The negative intelligence that I was able to supply helped enormously in planning and executing our naval operations.

I don't believe that we were in the staff for more than three weeks when the Inchon Operation was conceived by General MacArthur. All hands immediately turned to this enormous intelligence project. The more we looked at the proposed landing area the more we were convinced that it couldn't be done. The tides in the Yellow Sea were huge. At Inchon there was a 34-foot rise and fall of the tide. At low water, three miles of mud flats were uncovered. A small, heavily fortified island, called Wolmi-Do flanked the so-called landing beach at Inchon. Not only did the landing force have to time their assault so that they could make the beach at high tide but also an assault party would have to take Wolmi-Do before the main landings could be undertaken. An additional problem with Wolmi-Do was that it had no beach at all. To assault the island the Marines would have to use scaling ladders to go over a high sea wall, which faced the approach.

The more we looked the more we were absolutely convinced that it just couldn't be done. Admiral Joy and all of the senior Navy officers agreed. The disagreement with General MacArthur became so great that Chief of Naval Operations Admiral Forrest Sherman flew out to Tokyo to try to dissuade General MacArthur. The general stood his ground, however. At an intelligence briefing at which I was present he told Admiral Sherman that he alone in the history of Army warfare had entrusted his armies to the Navy on countless occasions and the Navy had never let him down. We were going to make the landings at Inchon, period!

On the 10th of September 1950, the First Marine Division, reinforced as part of the Tenth Army Corps, landed at Inchon as if they were following a textbook case. It was a near perfect execution of a very complex plan and caught the North Koreans completely by surprise. The Tenth Corp drove east at a lightning clip and trapped the great preponderance of the North Korean Army to the south, cutting off all hope of an orderly withdrawal. What had been an incredibly precarious position for us in the Pusan Perimeter turned in just a few days into an enormous military victory. From that moment, I never doubted the military genius of General MacArthur.

A few days after our landings, I had a call from our deputy chief of staff, Rear Admiral Arleigh Burke. When I reported to his office, he instructed me to be at Haneda Airport at 2300 that night. He would not tell me where we were going. This was about ten in the morning, so for the next 13 hours I was on pins and needles. I was at the airport promptly and was overwhelmed to find that I had been selected to go with General MacArthur and his party to Seoul to participate in a ceremony officially giving South Korea back to the South Koreans. We left Haneda Airport around midnight and flew to Kimpo Airport outside of Seoul. The Tenth Corps was still fighting in Seoul when we arrived, and our vehicles were escorted into the city by a squadron of tanks. Apparently, that's the way General MacArthur liked to operate.

The ceremony was held in the Diet Building, which had been severely damaged by shells. President Sigmund Rhee represented the South Korean government and it was a dramatic moment, punctuated by pieces of the glass skylight falling on us every time a shell exploded near the building. I sat next to a female war correspondent. Even though she was filthy, it was evident that she was a very attractive woman. She was Maggie Higgins, the first full-blown female war correspondent, working for the *New York Herald Tribune*. She, tragically, later died of a liver parasite infection in Vietnam.

The entire trip was of enormous interest to me and it signaled the admiral's appreciation for my efforts. I was working my butt off on a 24–7 basis and that my efforts were recognized made it all more than worthwhile.

During those hectic times in Tokyo, I essentially worked all the time, with no time off at all. I didn't mind, because what I was doing was important to the war effort and, besides, Mary Lee was not there. I had no interest in sitting around the officers' club or in fooling with the Department of Army civilian women, who were much in evidence in Tokyo. I lived at company-grade billet, the Yuroku Hotel, in downtown Tokyo. I shared a room with two other officers, one of whom was the commander of General MacArthur's honor guard, while the other was the CINCFE bandmaster. The food in our mess ranged from poor to awful, so I did try to go to other messes for dinner. My favorite was the Australian Army Club, where they served huge steaks. Looking back on it, I am not at all certain that they weren't derived from horsemeat. Cal Calhoun was promoted to lieutenant commander soon after we arrived and he would often invite me to dinner at the field-grade mess, which was much better.

After about six months of those 12 to 14 hour days, my boss, Captain Murt Stone, insisted that I take a few days off. I needed the rest badly. I selected a beautiful Army R and R resort in the mountains north of Tokyo. It had a golf course and a practice range. I didn't play, but I did practice until I got great blisters on my hands. I came back to Tokyo much refreshed.

Later in the winter of '51 I went away again, this time to a beautiful Japanese ski resort in the north, near Sapporo. My skiing was no better than my golf, but I had a fine time in the beautiful Japanese mountains. I was amazed how much the Japanese loved skiing. Even in 1950 and '51, when they were still almost flat from the pasting we gave them, the railroad station would be jammed with skiers on a Friday afternoon.

I never doubted that the Japanese would recover from the war. Their industry was truly amazing. They worked with an enthusiasm and will that was wonderful and, even during the relatively short time

I was there, they made great progress in putting their country back together. I came to Japan with a smoldering hatred for the Japanese. I had seen too much death in the great battles of World War II and learned too much of their unbelievable cruelty to their prisoners and to the subjugated people in the territory they conquered to have any warm feeling for them. I was very surprised to find that there were many facets to their character that I grew to admire. I found them personally very honest. The young Japanese girl who took care of my quarters earned about five dollars a month. I never bothered to lock up my money or my valuables and I never lost a thing. In addition, she would from time to time leave a little "presento" for me. The Japanese were great at giving gifts. It was and is a part of their culture

I learned to admire and love the Japanese sense of beauty and their architecture, which melded with nature in a most delightful way. Unlike today, in the early '50s everything in Japan was dirt cheap. I didn't buy much, because at that time Mary Lee was into a French period.

Soon after our return to Tokyo from Seoul, I had a night intelligence watch when a very attractive Department of Army civilian came to the intelligence office. She asked to speak to me in private. She told me that ever since our landings at Inchon she had been very upset and this evening she decided that she had to do something. She told me that about a week before the landing she had a date with a young naval aviator. In order to induce her to have sex with him he told her that he was soon to go into battle at Inchon. When we actually landed there she recognized that he had committed a very serious breach of security and she felt that it was her duty to report him. Well it wasn't long before that young lieutenant was called before the admiral. He was summarily relieved and sent back to the states. His career was over.

Everyone on the staff was optimistic that the war would soon be over. The Eighth Army and the Tenth Corps were pursuing the remnants of the North Korean army well north of the 38th parallel and it looked like we would have the entire peninsula secured by Christmas. It was not to be. While intelligence carried a powerful Chinese Communist order of battle on the northern border of Korea, there were no indications that they intended to enter the war. Unfortunately, the decision to do something like that in a dictatorship resides in the mind of the dictator. Unless you can look inside his mind you have no way of knowing what his decision might be. They had the capability, but their intentions were largely unknown to Army intelligence.

In November, they struck with great force and caught the Eighth Army by complete surprise. The Army's retreat turned into a rout. Entire artillery battalions left their artillery pieces and literally bugged out. It was a disgraceful page in Army military history. The Marines, however, were another story. They were way up on the Chosen Reservoir when the Chinese struck. Seven Chinese divisions got between the Marines and their escape route to Hungnam. The winter had set in. It was bitterly cold and the snows were deep. The Marines, under General Smith, didn't panic. They maintained their integrity and fought their way through those seven divisions, carrying their dead and wounded as well as all of their equipment with them. They arrived at the port of Hungnam intact and the Navy evacuated them to Wonsan.

It was a tough winter. General Walton Walker, the Eighth Army commander, did a terrible job in rallying his troops. Unfortunately for him, but fortunately for the Eighth Army, he was killed in a jeep accident and was replaced by General Matthew Ridgeway. From the first day that General Ridgeway arrived the Eighth Army started to improve. He issued an order that there would be no further retreat and there was none. The Eighth Army quickly regained its composure and its fighting efficiency. Intelligence learned that because of the very unsatisfactory logistics system in the Chinese Army it could only sustain an attack for four days. At the end of that period the Chinese would be out of rice balls, ammunition and fuel. The Eighth Army withdrew for those four days and then counterattacked with great results. They began to drive the Chinese north with enormous effectiveness.

It was at about this time that General MacArthur was summarily relieved by President Truman for insubordination. He came to our headquarters to say goodbye. During his remarks he predicted that if we didn't defeat the Chinese in Korea we would be fighting in Southeast Asia within fifteen years. He proved to be prophetic.

We settled into a routine at our headquarters, with little respite in our workload. I got a few assistants and set up my own Commint Unit in our headquarters, and on we went.

In May of 1950, a copy of a memorandum from our deputy chief of staff, Rear Admiral Arleigh Burke to the staff intelligence officer was delivered to my office. I found that memo in my files and it read as follows:

Memorandum for: Intelligence Officer

1. In order to preserve the sanity of one of our younger officers, it is suggested that you take this one back as aide, with the understanding that his daytime hours are completely devoted to hard work.

Respectfully,
Arleigh A. Burke
Rear Admiral USN
Deputy Chief of Staff

I was going to Washington with our staff intelligence officer! I couldn't believe it, but go I did. Mary Lee and I had a wonderful reunion and the chief of operational intelligence at the Office of Naval Intelligence told me that he didn't want to see me for even ten minutes at the Navy Department. We had the entire time for ourselves. I was, of course, indebted to Admiral Burke. I didn't know then that he was to rise to be our greatest contemporary naval officer, nor did I dream that I would be associated with him so closely in the future.

Our forces were becoming so effective that political overtures, encouraged enormously by the British, met with positive signals from the North Koreans and Chinese. By the fall of 1951, negotiations were underway to start a truce discussion with the enemy. By that time our forces were pushing the enemy steadily north. To prevent us moving too far north, however, the politicians directed the Army to slow down. They did this by prohibiting corps-size attacks. When that didn't slow the Army enough they prohibited division-size attacks and eventually got down to battalion-size attacks. Militarily, we had the Chinese beaten, but politically, our national leadership wanted to stabilize the line in the vicinity of the 38th parallel. The Brits were pushing hard for this because the Chinese had warned them that if we didn't stop they were going to take Hong Kong.

In October, Admiral Joy was designated as the chief negotiator for the United Nations Command. He formed a negotiating team and moved it to Munsan-Ni, about ten kilometers from Panmunjon, where the negotiations were to take place. I could not join the team on a permanent basis because we could not hazard me or my intelligence briefs that close to the front line. I did fly to Korea weekly to brief the admiral and his team. I flew from Haneda to Kimpo and then went by jeep with an Army escort to Munsan-Ni. I would stay overnight in an Army tent and return to Tokyo the next day. Damn, it was cold up there. We had a wooden floor in our tent and a big potbelly stove to keep us warm. They could have Army living as far as I was concerned, but to the Army this was as good as it got.

In late October, my detachment orders arrived! I couldn't believe it. I was to be detached in December and report to San Francisco for further orders. Unbeknownst to me, the chief of staff laid on a ceremony on the day of my detachment to express the command's appreciation for my performance. At that ceremony I was awarded a Bronze Star, the only such award given to staff officers up to that time. I was enormously proud, but also thrilled that I was on my way home and to Mary Lee.

Chapter 7

Back to Sea in Destroyers

M Y DETAILER ASSURED me that I would get four weeks leave before I had to execute my new orders. On the strength of that assurance, Mary Lee made plans to meet me in San Francisco, where we planned a wonderful reunion and an opportunity to get to know one another after a year and a half separation. She reached San Francisco by train from Washington and was waiting for me there on my arrival. It was a joyous reunion.

I reported in to Commander 12th Naval District as ordered, only to find that the plans for me had been changed. Instead of the leave that I had been promised, I was ordered to the U.S.S. *Holder* (DDE 819) based in Norfolk, Virginia. Prior to reporting, I was ordered to the Navy's antisubmarine school in Key West and its C.I.C. School in Boston. So instead of our much-contemplated leave, we were soon on our way across the country on the *City of San Francisco*, a beautiful train that ran between San Francisco and Chicago.

In due course we arrived in Key West to enroll in my ASW course. It was pleasant enough there, and since this was my first real introduction to antisubmarine warfare I found the course work very interesting. President Harry Truman used a house on the Key West base as his vacation home. By coincidence, he and many of his advisors and poker-playing buddies were in residence during the time we were there. One evening, Mary Lee and I sat in the row right behind him at the station movie. It was all very relaxed and informal. The president and his pals all wore loud Hawaiian shirts and there didn't seem to be much, if any, special security in evidence.

Mary Lee and I went from Key West to Boston and arrived in early January, 1952. Since we were scheduled to be there for a month we had to find suitable quarters. We lucked out by finding a rather beautiful furnished apartment on Commonwealth Avenue. A delightful couple by the name of Ellis owned it. Although they rented us a very inexpensive apartment in the basement they insisted that we actually occupy one of their nicest. We had a very pleasant stay in Boston and came away with a great fondness for the place.

In early February 1952, I reported for duty on board the *Holder*. She was under Commander George Street, a Congressional Medal of Honor winner. He had taken his submarine through the Japanese mine fields and submarine nets into Tokyo Bay and sank several ships, including a large tanker as it slid down the launching ways. Not a bad exploit!

George Street was a fine submariner but not a very good destroyer commander. I thought that *Holder* was mediocre in many ways. Not long after reporting, Captain Street was taken seriously ill and had to be summarily relieved by Commander Robert Merritt. Captain Merritt was a better skipper and the ship started to prosper.

Mary Lee and I had found a small rental apartment in Norfolk, which we did our best to fix up. It was about this time that Mary Lee found that she was pregnant and we started our long and anxious wait for our first child. As best Mary Lee could calculate, our baby was due in mid-August.

For the first several months on board *Holder*, we participated in local exercises, which permitted me to be home with Mary Lee for a reasonable period of time. In early summer, we learned that we were scheduled to deploy to Europe around the 15th of September. We were not concerned, because that would give us about a month after our baby was born before I had to depart for distant service.

During those months, I learned a great deal of the art of being a destroyerman. As operations officer, I was very much involved with the tactics and procedures that had been developed to fight the submarines of that day. Our capability was not very great even though we had been specially configured to maximize our ASW (antisubmarine warfare) capability. Our QHBa sonar operated at about 24 KCS, which was too high to permit much penetration of the inevitable thermocline that exists in the Atlantic. Our weapons systems were not much better. We had the standard array of depth charges and a forward array of hedgehogs, which were really a cluster of mortars that could be fired ahead in a pattern. Their range was about 100 or so yards, but they did permit us to fire while we still held contact. This was not the case with depth charges, since the ship had to essentially pass over the target before it could fire, thus forcing the ship to lose contact.

The summer of 1952 in Norfolk was as hot as the devil. We, like all of our contemporaries, did not have air conditioning, so we just had to bear the awful heat, which made Mary Lee even more uncomfortable. It was early in the summer that we learned that our deployment schedule had been changed from mid-September to the 25th of August, which still gave us time for our baby to be born and get everything squared away before my departure.

This was not to be. The 15th of August arrived and Mary Lee was not ready to give birth. The day of our departure came closer and closer and still nothing. Finally, two days before we were to part, I gave Mary Lee a mink stole which I had purchased for her as a baby present. She got so excited on seeing it that she immediately went into labor and we were off to the Naval Hospital in Portsmouth, Virginia. It was Sunday, the 24th of August. I sat with Mary Lee for a few hours and then went off for lunch. When I returned, Mary Lee was in the labor room and shortly thereafter gave birth to our son, Randolph Eliott Slaff. He was beautiful from the first day, with his blue eyes and golden hair.

On Monday we departed, along with the rest of our squadron, for European waters. We operated with some units of the British fleet out of bases in Britain. We enjoyed the warm hospitality of our British counterparts. We left northern European waters and headed for the Mediterranean in mid-October. One of our first ports of call was Tangier, where my classmate Julien LeBourgeois was the assistant Naval attaché. Julien made my visit there very pleasant. I remember seeing my first Spanish-style bullfight, which I found not terribly appealing. Using Julien's position, he and I purchased a great assortment of French liquors, which we smuggled on board *Holder*. There must have been ten different varieties. That was in 1952. In 2003, I still have the great majority of those liquors, which we have been hauling around the country for these many years. I'd have gotten rid of them a long time ago but they are really part of our family.

It was while moored in Oran Harbor that an event occurred

that had an important impact on the development of my philosophy relating to standards in our ships. It was a beautiful November day and I was on deck. I noticed on the horizon a group of small specks. As I watched them they grew closer and I was able to identify them as a division of U.S. destroyers. I watched them enter the harbor through the breakwater and as they got closer I observed that their sides were streaked with rust. Their brightwork was not shined. Their crews were at quarters but were unmilitary and not well turned out. Their bridges were manned by officers and men in foul-weather jackets and generally had a slovenly appearance. I noted that there were several hundred Arabs watching them enter port. The ships finally made their moorings alongside one of the moles. The shift of colors was not smart and the details that came ashore were still in working uniforms. I was embarrassed.

Not more than a few minutes after the U. S. destroyers made their moorings I noticed a single ship on the horizon also making for Oran. As it came through the breakwater I identified it as a British minesweeper. That little ship couldn't lick its way out of a paper bag, but she was beautiful. Her sides were clean. Her brightwork gleamed in the morning sun. A beautiful gold British crest adorned the bulkhead amidships just under the bridge. Her bunting was clean and her bridge was smartly turned out. Her skipper was on the wing wearing one of those large floppy caps, which the British favor. Its white cover was dazzling in the bright sun. Her tiny crew was drawn up at a smart attention in its best dress blue uniforms. She made her landing smartly and a British sailor stamped down the gangway and took his position as gangway sentry, which would have done the guards at Buckingham Palace proud.

Those hundreds of Arabs watching these ships had no idea that the little minesweeper was really inconsequential as far as any naval capability was concerned. That ship represented to them the power and prestige of the British navy and England. They could not help but be impressed nor was the lesson lost on me. It shaped my view of the importance of high standards of military smartness and cleanliness in the ships of the fleet and had a major impact on my approach to this vitally important aspect of my seagoing life.

Our deployment was only to last a merciful three and a half

months and we were on our way home, scheduled to arrive before Christmas. Mary Lee met the ship at the Destroyer Piers in Norfolk and brought our new son on board as soon as we moored. I was thrilled to see them both. Young Randy had developed very well and he lived up to his early promise of being a handsome young fellow. Mary Lee looked absolutely beautiful. She was glad that I was home so that she could hope to get a little help and some much needed rest from the constancy of being a new mother.

We operated in and around Norfolk for the rest of my tour, entering the Portsmouth Naval Shipyard for a much-needed overhaul in the spring of 1953. That meant that I could be with my little family almost every night for several months.

Before we emerged from overhaul, I received new orders, taking me ashore to Washington for a second time. I was to report as an instructor at the Naval Postgraduate School in Naval Intelligence from which I had graduated in 1950.

Chapter 8

Shore Duty, 1953–1955

B OTH MARY LEE and I looked forward to our first tour ashore since the arrival of Randy. We decided that this was the time to buy our first house, so when I was detached from *Holder* we headed to Washington to start house hunting for the first time. We didn't have much money but we were able to scrape up $4,000 for a down payment.

We found one house which we both liked very much. The owner was asking $33,000 and we offered $31,000, which was really more than we could afford. We had a rather sleepless night worrying about it but, fortunately for us, the owner rejected our offer. We found a wonderful little house, which we could afford in Brookdale, a small community of lovely homes at the confluence of River Road and Western Avenue in Bethesda. We had a little extra money to make some small changes in it to better suit our needs and we moved in with great pride and happiness.

The yard was beautiful and quite functional for our family. It had a marvelous azalea planting all around it. The back yard was fenced in so that Randy would have a safe place to play. The interior, although not very large, had a comfortable master bedroom and a room for Randy. Downstairs we had a small den, a living room, a dining room, a half bath, a kitchen and a small screened porch.

I reported to the intelligence school and was assigned to teach operational intelligence, a subject with which I was well acquainted, having recently spent that year and a half very much involved in it during the Korean War.

I also became enormously interested in guided missilery, a technology that was in it infancy. I taught a course in it and thus became very familiar with the principles of the various guidance systems that were being developed. While still a very distant possibility, I saw the potentially enormous impact that guided missiles were bound to have on naval warfare and the decisive impact that it was going to have on surface warfare. That early interest was to have an important impact on my development as a naval officer and my evolving understanding of the future of surface combatant ships in the fleet.

Now that I was in Washington I became interested in our Naval Academy class activities and attended our monthly class luncheons. We had been out of the Naval Academy for about nine years and it occurred to the class members on duty in Washington that the time was ripe to organize a permanent class association. I was elected the first president of the association and formed an executive committee to get us organized. My classmate and friend, Cal Cobb, who was a Washington lawyer, helped enormously in establishing us legally. We set about trying to differentiate our class and adopted a few themes that have carried forward until this day.

Prior to the war, a secret society existed in the fleet called the Green Bowlers. It was comprised of outstanding midshipmen selected from the regiment and inducted into the group, who were dedicated to looking after one another both socially and professionally for the remainder of our careers. In 1942, the society was disbanded by order of the Navy Department but its prior existence was still well known in the Navy. We decided that every member of the class of '45 was a Green Bowler and we adopted a green derby with a gold 45 numeral on it to identify our class at various class and Naval Academy functions. Our motto, "Look alive with '45" became well known throughout the Navy. At one football game at Annapolis we had an airplane fly a banner with our motto on it over the stadium. One non-'45er was overheard saying to his wife "My god, they even have an air force."

To commemorate the 10th anniversary of our graduation I put together a small *Ten Years After* book, in which I included biographical information on the first ten years of our life after graduation and compiled some interesting statistics about our class. It was a modest effort produced at no charge to our classmates. It was the genesis however, of much more elaborate books commemorating our twentieth, thirtieth, fortieth and fiftieth anniversaries. I take great pride in having had a direct hand in the development of our class association, which has prospered so well through the years.

We had not been ashore very long when Mary Lee found that she was again pregnant! What a surprise! Mary Lee felt the strong need for some domestic help but we couldn't afford the high prices prevailing in Washington. Mary Lee got the idea that there were plenty of young girls just dying to come to Washington to work for her in the black communities in Virginia. One Saturday we embarked on a maid hunting expedition. We got about 50 miles south of Washington and then turned off the main highway on to a dirt road to look for our domestic help. When Mary Lee spied a black girl walking along the dirt road that we were on we would stop and she would ask her prospect if she would like a job.

Eventually, one of her prospects suggested that her cousin who lived across a fordable stream might have such an interest. Following her directions, we came upon a clearing which contained a rough, unpainted cabin and had about ten small children running around the hard-packed earth yard. Mary Lee inquired about the more senior inhabitants. A black woman emerged from the cabin. The first thing she did was to spit. If there were a medal given at the Olympics for distance spitting, she would have undoubtedly brought home the gold. She had greased her hair so that it came to a point up front. She wore no shoes and her toes looked like a collection of small logs. While I was wondering what Mary Lee was thinking, she said, "Good morning, honey, can you cook?" Happily, she didn't want the job but she recommended another cousin who lived nearby. Here we struck pay dirt. We bundled our new employee into the car along with a cardboard box containing her worldly possessions and headed for home.

We had a little room in the basement of our house, which we had set up as a maid's quarters. We ensconced her in her room and soon thereafter we went to bed. Not long after turning in we heard a weird sound coming through the ventilation ducts. It sounded awfully spooky, something like a low wail. It continued all night. The next morning our new maid informed us that her dear dead Daddy had visited her during the night and told her to go home. I packed her into our car along with her cardboard box and took her to the bus station. So much for Mary Lee's big idea.

Valerie Ann Slaff was born on the 28th of April in the Bethesda Naval Medical Center. She was perfect. We set up a nursery in the downstairs den. Mother and Dad sent us a marvelous nurse that stayed with us for four weeks so that Mary Lee could rest and get her strength back. What a wonderful thing my folks did. We loved her. I don't recall her name but we called her Mrs. B. She got Valerie off to a great start and we never had a moment of trouble with her. Now we had our family, a boy and a girl. That's all we felt that we could manage in the Navy.

At about this time a defining event happened in my life. It centered on the aggressiveness of the Chinese Communist regime which took control of China in 1949. The Chinese Nationalists retreated to Formosa and the Chicoms became extremely aggressive, threatening an invasion. The Nationalists controlled two small islands in the Formosa Straits, Quemoy and Matsu. Naval intelligence indicated that the Communists were going to invade. This was at variance with the National Intelligence Estimate and the president ordered the Navy to get some highly qualified intelligence officers to Formosa immediately. On a Friday afternoon I received a telephone call from my old friend Jack Wholer who was heading up personnel at the Office of Naval Intelligence. He informed me that Director of Naval Intelligence Admiral Espy wanted me to go to Formosa immediately. I was shocked. I had recently spent a year and a half in the Korean War and then another two years in the fleet and I was enjoying a well earned and much needed shore duty with my little family.

That afternoon, Mary Lee and I had been invited to a very special party at the Shoreham Hotel. I was to meet her there. She knew something was amiss as soon as she saw me. We both stewed about it over the weekend and I finally decided to tell the director of Naval Intelligence that I wouldn't go, even if it meant resigning. I sought an appointment with Admiral Espy on Monday and told him of my decision. He said that my going was extremely important to the Navy and to the country and that he would put a letter to that effect in my personnel file. I replied that it couldn't be a very career-enhancing job if I needed a letter to protect me. We were old acquaintances, if not friends, so he took no offense. He said that he would think about it. The next day Jack Wohler called to say that I was off the hook. The crisis passed. There was no invasion and the officers that they did send may still be there for all I know. It was the one and only time that I demurred in taking a naval assignment. As it turned out my decision to resist was absolutely correct.

I was promoted to lieutenant commander and was ready to return to the fleet. I had learned that there was a billet for a destroyer executive officer opening in a squadron based in Hawaii. We very much wanted that job, but it was not to be. Instead, in the spring of 1955, I received orders back to the fleet as executive officer of the destroyer *Hazelwood*. She was in a squadron based in Newport, Rhode Island. We were very disappointed that we didn't get the job in Hawaii, but going to Newport was to turn out to be fortuitous. It opened an entire vista of wonderful career opportunities and we were to love our years in Newport. I was relieved at the Naval Intelligence School by my classmate and dear friend, Al Olsen.

Chapter 9

The Newport Adventure

M ARY LEE AND I had hoped to go to a destroyer based in Pearl Harbor. We had three squadrons there and my detailer thought that it was a good possibility. But it was not to be. We were somewhat disappointed. Being ordered to Hazelwood, however, was to prove to be a very lucky assignment indeed.

We were able to sell our little house in Brookdale without much trouble. We actually made a little on the deal. To permit us to house hunt with as little distraction as possible my mother and dad volunteered to take care of Randy and Valerie. We drove to Newport via Wilkes-Barre so that we could drop the children off. I had been in Newport briefly after I left *Massachusetts*. I was in the U.S.S. *Galveston* precommissioning detail. After a few weeks there the Navy decided not to commission the *Galveston* and I was ordered to the *Houston*. Because of that short stay there, I was some help in getting us oriented.

After a few days of house hunting we found a great little house on Victoria Avenue in the Ochre Point Area of Newport. It was truly the very nicest section of a generally beautiful small city. It was situated among the most beautiful of the Newport cottages. We were just one block from the magnificent Breakers mansion built by Commodore Vanderbilt around the turn of the century. And probably of even more delight to us, we were just one block from the Cliff Walk which went along the top of the bluffs facing the ocean. What a treat for us to be in that glorious setting! We were to take full advantage of our good fortune during the many years that we lived on Victoria Avenue.

We found our new home so quickly that we had a few free days before we had to pick up the children. We took advantage of the free time to tour Cape Cod. We went all the way to the end, visiting Provincetown and had a fine time exploring the quaint towns and beautiful beaches and sand dunes along the way.

After the usual hassles associated with taking ownership of a new home, we retrieved the children and moved in. While the house essentially suited us very well, we decided to enlarge it a bit by enclosing a breezeway between the living and dining rooms and the garage. It gave us a great family room which was to come in mighty handy as a wonderful place for our children to play and for the family to watch television.

I reported to the *Hazelwood* (DD531) in September of 1955. She was attached to Destroyer Squadron 34. Her captain was Commander Ed Forrest. He was a fine gentleman, a graduate of Yale but not a destroyer-captain type. As a matter of fact, after his *Hazelwood* tour he retired and became an Episcopal minister. He was a good enough seaman, but was overly gentle and not much of a disciplinarian. He needed me. We got along famously. Together we whipped the ship into shape and started to ready her for a Mediterranean deployment.

Hazelwood was a 2100-ton Fletcher Class destroyer. She had seen heavy action in the Pacific during World War II. At Okinawa she took two direct Kamikaze hits and was the most damaged ship in the fleet that didn't sink. Pictures of her after her battle damage were astounding. There didn't seem to be anything undamaged above the main deck.

The Fletcher Class destroyers were beautiful ships. They could make 34 knots, because they had a very high length to beam ratio. She mounted 5 single mount 5-inch 38-caliber guns, trainable torpedo tubes amidships, depth charges and two waist-mounted Mk. 35 antisubmarine torpedoes, plus waist-mounted 40mm antiaircraft guns.

Soon after Christmas, our squadron deployed to the Sixth Fleet. No sooner had we arrived in the Mediterranean than a major crisis erupted in the Middle East and our destroyer division of four ships was detached to form a Middle Eastern patrol force. It was really great duty. We were based in Beirut, Lebanon. Two of our ships were assigned to patrol the Egyptian coast and two the Israeli coast. We spent five days on patrol and five days in Beirut. Not bad duty.

Beirut in those days was a beautiful and very cosmopolitan city.

It had a splendid port and a truly beautiful European-style downtown. The French influence was extremely pronounced, Lebanon being a French protectorate between the end of World War I and the end of World War II. There were lovely hotels along the Mediterranean waterfront and smart shops along the wide boulevards. Of course it had the usual Arab quarter with its distinctive casbah, but the entire city was quite peaceful and the people were both friendly and hospitable. It was truly a great place to base.

We were at sea for one of our patrols off the Israeli coast when *Hazelwood* received orders to prepare to visit Haifa in Israel. We were the first U.S. man-of-war to be assigned to visit an Israeli port. There was a reason for our visit. The Commander Sixth Fleet had a NICR (Naval Intelligence Collection Requirement) on a new naval port that the Israelis were developing in Haifa and the Office of Naval Intelligence wanted some information on it. Since I was a trained intelligence officer, *Hazelwood* was the natural ship to visit Israel, so into Haifa we went.

In a man-of-war, other than to prepare the ship to enter port, the exec has little to do. He generally comes to the bridge where he administers the various standing into port routines. It's really the captain's show. The exec usually watches the captain maneuver the ship, secretly thinking to himself that he could do better, given the chance. Standing behind the captain on the starboard wing of the bridge as he made his landing approach, I noticed a very long automobile parked on the pier. I thought that it might be an official waiting to welcome our ship, perhaps the governor of the province or the mayor of Haifa. It was neither. It was a car owned by my old Annapolis classmate Paul Shulman who had learned of my visit and had sent his chauffeur down to deliver a letter to me welcoming me and my ship to Israel and to Haifa.

I think it important to digress briefly to tell our reader a little about my old friend, Paul Shulman. Paul and I became good friends during my stewardship as editor in chief of the *Log*. Because he knew more about the ships of the fleet than any other midshipman, he was a natural for the position of professional editor on my staff. He had an interesting background. His father had been chairman of the board of the Pepsi Cola Company. He reached that important position via the general counsel route. He had been the head lawyer of Pepsi during the famous Coca Cola–Pepsi Cola suit in which Coke sought to prevent Pepsi from using the word "cola." Winning that important suit must have been the impetus for his elevation to the chairmanship. The Shulmans were also avid Zionists.

I didn't see Paul after we graduated until I was in the Med, serving on the staff of Commander Cruiser Division Twelve. We were visiting Venice. The chief of staff, Captain Gentry, invited me to go ashore with him for lunch. We were on San Marcos Square when I ran smack into Paul. He promptly invited both of us to lunch at the elegant Danielli Hotel. At lunch he told us that he had resigned from the Navy and was running a small shipping company in the Mediterranean.

Some months later we found out that indeed Paul was running a shipping company. He had a group of merchantmen that were engaged in smuggling arms to the Israelis. It turned out that the British were after him for piracy and the U. S. Naval Reserve was just after him. We saw him in Venice in 1947. In 1948 Israel declared its independence, and who became the first commander and chief of the Israeli navy? My good friend Paul Shulman. He not only organized the navy but he became an important national hero by defeating the Egyptian navy in three successive naval battles. He didn't sink the Egyptian ships. He boarded them and then brought them into Haifa Harbor where he ran up the Israeli ensign and increased the strength of his fledgling navy appreciably.

In 1952 the United States Congress passed the McCarren Act, which made it illegal for U.S. citizens to serve in the armed forces of a foreign power. Paul was a great Zionist but he was no damned fool. Since he was not about to give up his U.S. citizenship he resigned from the Israeli navy. When we arrived in Haifa in 1955 he had organized an international construction company that was digging ditches in the Israeli deserts as well as in countries such as Ethiopia.

Paul was extremely glad to see me and the *Hazelwood*. He had a dinner in our honor at his beautiful home in Haifa overlooking the Mediterranean. Included in his guest list was the board of directors of his company. Every one of them was a U. S. Naval Reserve officer. Paul told us that he was not about to hire anyone who had not been in the U.S. Navy.

Then there came that very sensitive matter of the intelligence-gathering nature of our visit. After much soul searching, I finally took Paul into my confidence. He immediately became my co-conspirator. Together we put together an incredibly complete report on their new naval port—photographs, charts, the works. Com6thFlt was delighted with it as was the Office of Naval Intelligence.

After four months of steaming almost independently in Middle Eastern waters we rejoined the 6th Fleet, but not before we broke our anchor windlass shaft in Port Said, Egypt. Getting another shaft was an interesting, frustrating and time consuming adventure.

We returned to Newport in the fall of 1955 and operated with Atlantic Fleet units until the summer of 1956. In August of '56 I received a surprise set of orders to be the prospective commanding officer of the U.S. *Lester* (DE 1022). She was one of a new class of destroyer escorts presently being built to replace the World War II DEs. *Lester* was being built at the Defoe Shipbuilding Corporation in Bay City Michigan. To say that Mary Lee and I were thrilled would be an understatement. Getting my first command was exciting enough, but to be selected to command the newest and best to which a lieutenant commander could possibly aspire was an enormous source of pride.

I was detached from *Hazelwood* in time for me to reach the nucleus crew in Bay City on the first of October. The schedule called for us to depart Bay City for New Orleans on or about the first of November. Since this was 1956, the St. Lawrence Seaway was not yet completed, so it was necessary to take the ship through the Chicago Drainage Canal into the Illinois River and thence into the Mississippi. To do this, we had to unstep the mast, remove the sonar dome and her huge propeller and pontoon her up to a maximum draft of 13 feet.

The Defoe Yard looked like something that one might find in lower Slobovia. It was a mess, but somehow they built great ships. Tom Defoe, the son of the owner, had a dinner for me soon after I arrived. I saw then the tradeoff between a beautiful yard and personal gain. They had a house that wouldn't quit. The living room was 96 feet long with an indoor swimming pool at one end!

I hadn't been in Bay City more than a week when I had a letter from the Army Corps of Engineers advising me that, because of the very severe drought then being experienced in the Midwest, the water level in the Mississippi had fallen to an all-time low and it would not be possible to get my ship down the river until the spring runoff, which was expected the following April!

What to do? Happily ComDesLant and the Bureau of Naval Personnel decided to keep the nucleus crew intact and to use the months for additional schooling. I was ordered to the Naval Justice School in Newport for an eight-week course, something I found enormously interesting and extremely useful in the years in command that followed.

During my weeks in Newport, Mary Lee and I decided to find suitable housing in Bay City and to move the family there during the long winter months of 1957. I succeeded in finding a furnished rental which was quite suitable to our needs, and soon thereafter, Mary Lee, Randy, Valerie, our English nanny and our little dachshund Cartuffels arrived in Detroit by train. All but Nanny enjoyed our stay in Bay City. She hated it because there was no social life for her. So, soon after her arrival, we sent her back to England.

In due course the winter came to an end and *Lester* was sent on her way down the Mississippi. I didn't accompany her. Instead, I took the family to Charleston, South Carolina where she was eventually scheduled to be commissioned. We found a wonderful old Charleston house south of Broad and quickly became comfortable in our brand new surroundings.

I rejoined *Lester* at the Todd Shipbuilding Company in New Orleans where she was put back together after her trip down the river. A builder's crew sailed her from New Orleans to Charleston where the balance precommissioning crew joined us.

On June 14th, 1957, I proudly placed *Lester* in commission. My mother and dad came for the occasion. *Lester* might as well have been a battleship, I was so proud of her. I had a crew of about 280, with 11 officers. After the usual fitting out, trials and provisioning, punctuated by the usual material problems, we were finally ready for sea and we steamed out of Charleston en route to shakedown training at Guantanamo Bay, Cuba.

Shakedown training of a new ship at Guantanamo is quite an experience. The personnel of the underway training group there are handpicked for both their professional knowledge and their toughness. It was nine weeks of incredible blood, sweat and tears. During the first weeks we painfully learned how awful we were and then we slowly got it together. What frustration! I don't drink and really never have, but after being bloodied by the training group all day I would join the other skippers who were being similarly persecuted at the officers' club every evening and we would sit out under the palm trees overlooking the ocean and try to ease the pain by drinking rum punches.

We went through intensive underway training in damage control, gunnery, antisubmarine warfare, seamanship and engineering. During one underway exercise, a sister ship, the *Hartley*, while undergoing some emergency engineering drills, lost all power. Unfortunately, her operating area was close to shore and a strong onshore breeze was blowing her toward the cliffs lining the shore. *Lester* was ordered to take her in tow, a very complicated and delicate exercise, especially for a ship's company none of whom, including her captain, had ever done it. We got organized on the way to the rescue and succeeded in passing a towing rig just before she was blown into shoal waters. We got a 100 percent for the exercise and ended up our nine week ordeal with the highest mark ever made at Gtmo.

We left Gtmo in triumph on our way for a much deserved shakedown cruise to South America. To celebrate our great performance I decided to relax the crew by hoving to and having a swim call at sea. Very much the leader, I donned my bathing trunks and went aft to join the crew. We had a swimming bill which called for various details including manning a life boat with marksmen to guard against sharks, extra lookouts, extra telephone talkers, cargo nets over the side, and so on. I told the fantail talker to tell the bridge to let me know when we had lost all way. The message got confused and they let me know that the ship had stopped, at which time I dove into the sea followed by at least 75 others. When we came up the ship was moving away from us. It was definitely not dead in the water. I am and was a pretty good swimmer but I had never swum in the open sea. It was quickly exhausting and I just barely got back to the cargo net. I had absolutely nothing left to climb the net, so I just hung on making believe that I was enjoying being in the water. Damn, I nearly drowned! Most of the other swimmers were able to reach the ship safely. The few that were having trouble were picked up by the ship's whaleboat.

We had an absolutely delightful cruise to Columbia, Venezuela, and Trinidad. Our visit to Venezuela was particularly memorable. We moored in LaGuira, the port of Caracas, which is separated from Caracas by an enormously high mountain range. A delegation of Venezuelan naval officers came on board to welcome us. One of the officers was wearing dress augulettes and I was made to understand that he was to be my aide. They asked me to pack a bag and made it quite clear that I was to be their personal guest during our visit. They would escort me to my quarters in Caracas. Who was I to object?

We motored to Caracas and soon arrived at our destination, the Circulo Militaire or officers' club. But what an officers' club! At that time the military dictator Jimenez was running the country. This magnificent facility was apparently a payoff to the officers for their support of his regime. I had never been in a facility that was built with no budget control. Everything was luxurious, including my quarters, which were stocked with the finest liquors. The entertainment was equally elaborate. One evening we were entertained at the Humbolt Hotel at the top of the mountain separating the coast from Caracas. The only access to the place was via cable car. We ordered from an elaborate menu and I took pains to order the most expensive caviar. I wanted to let them know that I, too, was used to the finer things of life. While at the Humbolt we all went ice skating in our dress whites. It was quite a sight.

At the time of our visit the navy was commanded by a captain but the Circulo Militaire was run by a rear admiral, a man named Larazabal who had been a student at the Naval War College in Newport and had briefly been part of the junta that grabbed control of the country. He subsequently became suspect to Jimenez and was made officer in charge of the officers' club.

I noticed another interesting thing in Venezuela. There were three beautiful new destroyers moored in LaGuira. The U.S. Naval attaché told me that the destroyers were built for Venezuela by Sweden and had been delivered over two years prior to our visit. They had never been underway. They were regularly scheduled to get underway for operations at sea but on each occasion the commanding officer would report a serious engineering casualty. COs went through their entire tours without getting the ships underway at all.

We arrived back in Newport in late November and we had a wonderful reunion with our families. In mid-December another crisis arose in the Middle East and almost every destroyer in Newport was dispatched to the Med on an emergency basis. Since we had just arrived at our new home port we were exempt. At Christmas, Mary Lee and I located a Santa Claus suit. I got all dressed up in it and visited as many families as possible with small children whose daddies were deployed. My dad took me around on Christmas Eve and I had a wonderful time being Santa Claus. All of the children I visited were in absolute awe of Santa; that is all but my own. I arrived back at our house to find Valerie who was just three, having her bath. I ho ho hoed into the bathroom and found Valerie screaming. She hollered "Tell that stinky Santa Claus to go home." Randy was no better. He told Santa not to bring that naughty Freddie Heffernan any presents because he had been a bad boy all year. Freddie was Randy's very best friend. Nice son I had!

In late January, what ships in our squadron that were available went to the Jacksonville operating areas for some antisubmarine operations. On our way back in February we ran into a violent storm off Cape Hateras. At about 2000 the officer of the deck reported to me that our radio room had picked up an SOS from a ship that was in very serious trouble. I reported the intercept to the squadron commander, who detached *Hartley* and *Lester* to go to the rescue. The waves were about 50 feet and there was a blinding snowstorm. About 2130 we picked up the target on our radar. It was the Italian ore ship *Bonitas*. It was carrying ore from South America to Norfolk, Virginia; the cargo had shifted in the violent seas and she was sinking. As we closed our contact at about 2300 it disappeared from our radar. She had sunk. The visibility was zero in the snowstorm, so we were unable to even search for survivors. We stayed on scene with *Hartley* until it became light and we set up a search line downwind of the position of the sinking. At about 0900 our lookouts sighted some orange life jackets in the water. The visibility was still terrible because, while the snow had stopped, arctic mist covered the sea. It looked positively eerie.

With the wind still howling and the seas still mountainous, I closed the life jackets from upwind, stopped the ship as best I could and allowed the wind to set us down on them one at a time. There was a dead man in each jacket which we recovered by using grappling hooks. The ship had blown down on them. It wasn't very pretty but the men were dead anyway. All together we recovered 10 bodies. It was now rather late in the afternoon and it was starting to get dark. I decided to make one more pass to make sure we had recovered all that were possible. It was now about 1545 and twilight was setting in when the lookouts, whom I had stationed as far up in the mast as they could go, reported seeing what they thought was a piece of a boat and they thought that they saw some men holding on to the wreckage. With seas so high it was not possible to see what the lookouts were reporting, except very occasionally, we closed in the direction of the sighting.

Sure enough, we finally saw the wreckage and we identified three men waving to us. Having practiced all day picking up the dead I used the same tactics in my approach but instead of grappling hooks I had cargo nets rigged over the side and had swimmers placed in harnesses to assist as necessary. By the time I got the ship into position one of the men had drifted away never to be recovered. The ship was driven sideways into the wreckage and the rescue detail succeeded in grabbing one of the two remaining survivors. The other one was being driven under the ship. Really being keelhauled. I ordered the swimmers into the water and they dove under the ship. One of them miraculously found the man and grabbed him in a bear hug while the men on deck pulled them on board with the line attached to the swimming harness. We saved both of them!

Our ordeal was not quite over. Our type commander, Rear Admiral Espy was in the area on board *Norfolk* and they had recovered one of the dead. I was ordered alongside *Norfolk* to transfer the dead man from *Norfolk* to *Lester* preparatory to my being diverted into Norfolk to unload both the dead and the two survivors. The seas were still hellishly high and going alongside *Norfolk* was going to be one hazardous operation. With my heart in my mouth I made the approach and got our forecastle abeam of *Norfolk's* starboard quarter. As the type commander looked on we made the transfer without mishap! Whew!

We entered Norfolk as heroes, and were heavily covered by the local press as well as by the national media. One of our bluejackets took a picture just as the ship came down on the men in the water and *Life* magazine made a two-page spread of that spectacular photo. It was selected as the photograph of the week.

I had hoped to go to the Naval War College on completion of my tour in *Lester* but that was not to be. When we arrived in Newport, I invited Admiral Espy to lunch on board. He accepted and then had his aide call me to ask if he could bring his relief admiral, Whitey Taylor, along as well. Of course, I was delighted to have him. I was enormously proud of our ship and especially of our wardroom mess. We had a great lunch and a lot of good fellowship to boot. The admirals stayed on board for a couple of hours enjoying the whole thing and I enjoyed them as well.

A few days later I had a call from the force personnel officer asking me to call on him. I did so without much delay. He told me that Admiral Taylor wanted me to join his staff as aide and flag secretary. I told him that, while I was honored to be asked, I wanted to go to the Naval War College after leaving *Lester*. Then he invited Mary Lee and me to dinner at his home that night and, during the evening, he made it clear that I was coming to the staff, which I, of course, did. It turned out to be the most delightful tour of my long Navy career.

I was relieved as commanding officer of *Lester* by my dear friend and classmate Al Olsen and left my first command with both great regret and a sense of real accomplishment. I was to command other and much larger ships but *Lester* was and always will be special to me. I experimented with the ideas that I had formed through the years on how a Navy ship should be commanded. Those ideas were enormously successful.

In thinking about the motivation of seagoing personnel it became apparent to me that we were in competition in the U.S. manpower market, and not in a very enviable competitive position at that. We could not compete financially. Our pay scales, especially for our enlisted personnel, were much less than offered by industry for similar talent and abilities. This was particularly so in the technical ratings. Home life comparisons were even worse. Our ships were away a very good portion of the time. Those who put being with their families high on their priority list would not choose the Navy. Those who enjoy a great level of creature comfort would not be enthusiastic about berthing in a Navy man-of-war. Habitability standards of a U.S. bluejacket at sea, even in the most modern ships, were 50 percent of the habitability standards established for federal prisoners. Not only is space heavily constrained but human privacy is almost nonexistent.

Where we do have a competitive position is in pride of service in the greatest Navy in the world. But to maximize that competitive advantage it is absolutely necessary to establish and maintain the objects of pride in the fleet, and those are a beautifully maintained and operated man-of-war and well disciplined, well turned out men-of-war men. It means establishing and maintaining the highest possible standards of smartness and discipline. It's not easy, and there is a great deal of griping, but the end result is a ship's company that has enormous pride and a ship that stands out among all the rest. Thus the one competitive advantage that the Navy enjoys is maximized.

The *Lester* was such a ship. I had organized a military band on board which played during many all hands evolutions including standing in and out of port. That evolution I considered of great importance in reflecting the excellence to which we aspired. I believe a man stands up a little straighter to the tune of the "Stars and Stripes Forever." Our ship was meticulously maintained and our ship's company wore their uniforms with pride.

One day, after mooring alongside one of our sister ships, *Van-Vorhees*, I had retired to my cabin when our chief sonarman, named Surface, knocked on my cabin door. He said, "Captain, as we stood alongside of *VanVorhees* this morning with our band playing and the ship's company at careful attention, the chief sonarman on *VanVorhees* called over to me and said, 'Chief, thank God we still have a Navy.'" That meant everything to me. I couldn't have been more proud and it was just one more indication that I philosophically was on the right track. I continued to think about these matters in the years ahead and eventually I was able to extend my concepts to the entire force.

And so began a particularly wonderful tour with Admiral Whitey Taylor.

Chapter 10
Camelot

I REPORTED TO COMDESLANT on board his flagship, *Yosemite* in June of 1958. This was my first experience as an admiral's aide and I was a bit leery. The job of the flag secretary ostensibly is to ensure that all flag correspondence flows properly, is professionally drafted, and is carefully disseminated. The amount of paperwork necessary to command and administer a force of over 150 ships is huge indeed. I found that aspect of the job very easy and quite manageable. My experience as a writer and editor made it a natural for me. I set very high standards for the various divisions in the flag, much to the consternation of many of the staff officers, but Admiral Taylor was so delighted with the increased quality of his paperwork that the staff suffered in comparative silence.

One of the delightful privileges I had as a personal aide was that I immediately became a member of the admiral's mess. I took all my meals with him, and with the chief of staff and the captains in charge of the various flag divisions. What a treat! Admiral Taylor was an absolutely delightful man. He looked like a giant teddy bear. He enjoyed smoking his cigars. He enjoyed good food, but most importantly he enjoyed the fellowship of the officers that he had chosen to head his team. He had been captain of the Navy football team in 1923 and he loved talking about Navy football and its fortunes, but he wasn't an old jock who was living in his past glories. While he was full of good cheer, he also had a wonderful mind, coupled with an outstanding understanding of Navy high command politics and how to operate effectively in the Navy fleet game.

In 1958, the surface combatant forces were in desperate trouble. The battle for financial support among the three competing communities was devastating to the surface forces. The aviators were still enormously powerful from their great success in World War II. They literally had the Navy by the throat and the submarine community was not far behind. The surface combatant forces were getting the crumbs off the table. We had little military capability even in our newest ships, because our research and development funds were just not there. Since we were being starved by the aviators and submariners to the point of marginal capability, their argument was cyclical. Since destroyers can't do much, why waste money on them. We had to break that devastating and debilitating philosophy.

I had fired an opening salvo when I wrote an enormously controversial article in the *Naval Institute Proceeding* in 1955. My article entitled "Time for Decision," hypothesized that the tactical guided missile, even though it was in its infancy, was a potential competitor of the Navy's piloted aircraft in many of its roles and missions, such as fleet air defense, tactical air support, antishipping and the application of fleet offensive striking power against enemy targets both at sea and ashore.

I pointed out that the development of a true naval missile capability would multiply enormously the offensive hulls in the fleet, because all surface combatants could carry relatively long-range missiles capable of offensive operations against an enemy. I also pointed out in great detail that the enormous expenditures that the Navy was making to maintain a 15-carrier offensive capability could be substantially reduced, if the guided missile were permitted to develop with adequate R & D funding. No longer would we have to build and maintain as many huge and expensive carriers manned by upwards of 5,000 officers and bluejackets, and we also would not have the cost of building huge numbers of enormously expensive aircraft which were quickly worn out by constant flying or, equally quickly, became obsolete.

Frequent operational accidents, which were and are very numerous in the fleet, added still more to the enormous expense of manned aviation. The large shore establishment which was necessary to supply extensive logistics and maintenance support was still another significant cost factor. In addition, no longer would we have to select, train, pay, maintain, retire and bury huge numbers of naval aviators. The missile, while expensive, would essentially only be fired in anger from seagoing platforms that were much cheaper to build and to man. Such an advance would also greatly increase the number of offensive platforms in the fleet. It would permit the fleet to disperse over vast areas of the oceans and thus be in a far superior tactical disposition for atomic weapons defense.

As the fleet was presently deployed, the only tactical offensive capability resided in the carrier. Take out the carrier and the fleet became impotent offensively. To prevent such a catastrophe, tactical dispositions were drawn in relatively close to the carrier, making a far more inviting nuclear weapons target. If the carrier was taken out we had nothing left offensively. If a single missile ship was taken out or even if half or more were taken out, we still had a residual offensive capability in the hulls that remained.

All of this went down like ground glass in the aviation community. Its leaders did everything possible to discredit this line of reasoning and did all in their power to ensure that tactical missiles were brought along in the Navy at a snail's pace, except for those designed to be fired from manned aircraft. The Navy did support the Three T Program. This program was designed to bring three surface to air missiles, Tartar, a ten-mile bird, Terrier, a 20-mile bird, and Talas, a 100-mile bird to the fleet. All of these missiles were defensive in nature. They were really being developed to help protect the carrier, not to give the surface combatant an individual offensive capability.

In that article, I pointed out that the fast battleships built during World War II and decommissioned immediately after the war would be ideal hardened platforms for the missiles of the future. Some 20 years later, when I was a dean at the Harvard Business School, I had a call from the aide to the secretary of the Navy, Mr. Lehman, telling me that somehow the secretary had found a copy of my article and had built a speech around it which he delivered to the students of the Naval War College. In his speech he pointed out that I had the vision that was needed years ago to bring the important technology of viable missiles systems to the fleet and that the Navy ignored me to its great detriment. He also pointed out that the Navy needed officers with my kind of vision but had lost me to Harvard and to the business community. He said in his speech that the Navy could ill afford such losses.

Many years later, during the Gulf War against Iraq in 1991, I had the great thrill of seeing the U.S.S. *Wisconsin* fire the incredible surface-to-surface Tomahawk missiles against vital targets in Iraq with devastating accuracy. The wonderful capability which I predicted over 35 years earlier had come to pass.

But I have digressed. I hope the reader will forgive me, as I think it appropriate to describe the state of the surface combatants when I joined Admiral Taylor's staff. The admiral well knew the precarious predicament that we were in, not only vis-à-vis the aviation community but in relation to the submarine community as well. Here again we were being starved for research and development money in our efforts to come to grips with submarines possessing incredible new technologies and capabilities. Nuclear power had come to our submarine service as well as to the Soviet navy's submarines, which made our problem of fighting the submarine effectively damn near impossible. We had to break out of that box if we were to serve the Navy and our country effectively.

And that is what we spent our time during that incredible tour trying to do. We had some very good people on our staff, really the pick of the entire force. Our meals together in the flag mess were wonderful seminars on how we were going to bring our destroyers and cruisers into the modern age, and we began to make some progress. Admiral Taylor relished our conversations and truly loved the hard chargers which he had assembled.

I brought to the staff some other very basic convictions about the ships of the force. The average ship was poorly commanded. The general condition of the ships was slovenly and the ships' companies were largely sloppy. It was a disservice to the fleet, it was a disservice to the force and it was a disservice to the men who manned the ships. The essential ingredients of pride in the ship and pride in the individual, which were so important to human motivation in the fleet, were largely missing. We had a few good ships, but not very many. The great standards of smartness, cleanliness and military bearing that the fleet possessed in the prewar Navy were largely bred out of it during World War II and were never reintroduced. I made it my personal mission on that staff to do what I could to return the Destroyer Force Atlantic Fleet to a position of pride.

But how to go about it? I developed a broad plan which I had to first sell to the admiral. I talked with him about this vital problem on many occasions and I finally convinced him that it was something that we had to do and I set about doing it with enormous enthusiasm.

The very first thing I had to do was to establish comprehensive military standards of smartness and cleanliness for the force, which our officers and men could understand and to which they were going to be made to adhere. I convened a committee, with myself as chairman, and included two classmates, Al Olsen and Julien Le Bourgeois, who were serving in ships of the force at that time. Our group set about codifying a comprehensive set of military standards of smartness and cleanliness which we intended to insert into our force regulations. The job took several months, but we finished it and, after the usual "not invented here" attitudes of some of the staff, I presented it to the admiral. He loved it and told me to go full speed ahead. It was about a 30-page document which I promulgated to all the ships and commands of the force as Change #10 to our Force Regulations. It hit the force like a bomb. Predictably the flotilla and squadron commanders were something less than enthusiastic, especially when Admiral Taylor informed them that he held them fully responsible for implementing and enforcing the new regulations. And he did.

To make it easier to educate the officers and men of the force, I set about writing a small handbook that could be given to everyone who served in destroyers Atlantic. I called it *Destroyerman's Reefpoints*, after a similar little volume that each new plebe at the Naval Academy is issued. It not only contained the new regulations issued in Change #10 but I also included a great deal of information about destroyers, their glorious history in combat all over the world, and other such matters. The Commander in Chief U.S. Atlantic Fleet told Admiral Taylor that it was the best thing of its type that he had ever seen and he hoped other force commanders would produce something similar.

The enforcement was a tough job. It took awhile for all hands to find out that we were not joking. We intended to enforce what we had promulgated. I felt strongly about this, as I felt, and still feel, that an unenforced regulation is absolutely poisonous to good order and discipline. It creates important doubts in a destroyerman's mind about whether the command is serious or not. Boy, did we enforce it! A blizzard of messages pointing out noncompliance came out of the flagship and slowly the ships of the force responded. It was wonderful to see the improvement. The admiral and I often went on his veranda to observe morning colors and watch with pride as the ships held colors ceremonies as we had prescribed. It was not all angel cake and wine, however. Some of the squadron commanders felt that I was injuring their careers by addressing dispatches to them pointing out infractions on the part of their ships. There just was no other way to do it. We were either going to insist on compliance or we shouldn't have started the program in the first place.

To add to the military niceties, I built a ceremonial square between Pier One and Two at the Newport Naval Base. I installed a great naval-type flag pole as well as a fine monument to all destroyermen who had gone down to the sea in ships. I required that the force band parade the piers each morning and then lead the destroyers moored in Newport in morning colors. A rotating detail from the ships carried out the colors ceremony at the square. It was wonderful. I loved it and so did everyone else including, happily, the admiral.

On Memorial Day 1958, I organized a great Destroyer Force parade. Each of the thirty-odd destroyers in Newport trained a parade unit to represent their ship. I supplied guidons to each ship to identify them and after a great deal of rehearsing we held the parade. I led the parade with a staff just like in midshipman days. Admiral Taylor took the salute as each ship's detail marched by. It was just great! I loved it, as did all hands.

Not only was I enjoying my duties on the flag but my little family was prospering as well. Mary Lee was a wonderful strength to me in carrying out the responsibilities of an aide. She entertained beautifully and participated with grace in the varied social life that our job required. She was an enormous asset, not only to me but to the admiral as well. And the children were truly prospering. They were both attending Saint Michael's, a small but very good private school. We loved our little house on Victoria Avenue and we particularly loved our dachshund which my folks had given to us. We took full advantage of the beauty of Newport, including frequent walks on Cliff Walk, a public walk along the edges of the cliffs which overlooked the sea. The scenery was breathtaking and we never tired of it.

Then, early in 1959, something that was to prove truly wonderful happened. The Saint Lawrence Seaway was approaching completion after over ten years of major construction and the Navy was directed to participate in the ceremonies incident to its official opening, and then to bring a task force of Navy ships into the Great Lakes. Since there is much to tell about this great event I shall devote an entire chapter to it.

Chapter 11

The Navy Sails the Inland Sea

T HE OPERATIONS AND experiences that we were about to participate in were to be memorable indeed. The admiral was to command a 24-ship task force comprising destroyers, a heavy cruiser, an amphibious squadron and a few minesweepers. We were to organize a suitable international review to be held in Lake Saint Louis, just to the west of Montreal, to commemorate the opening of the seaway. Since President Eisenhower and Queen Elizabeth were to be on hand and were in fact going to review the assembled ships from the deck of the royal yacht *Britannia,* this aspect of the operation was going to require a considerable amount of planning. Upon completion of the International Fleet Review we were going to proceed through the seaway and conduct fleet visits in numerous Great Lake ports.

I was delighted to learn that the admiral wanted me to accompany him on this operation. He asked me to do what I could to ensure the destroyers assigned were brought to a peak of military smartness and readiness. I'd been working diligently on this project for many months and now I brought my principal focus on the two squadrons that were to be included in the force. The destroyer leader, *Willis A. Lee,* was to be our flagship and my focus included her as well.

The admiral intended to take his flag lieutenant, his public affairs officer, Ray Komorowski, his readiness officer, Emmett Bonner and, much to my surprise, an outsider as chief of staff, a Captain Ray Thompson.

We proceeded to organize the operation at a feverish pitch. There was an enormous amount of work to be done. I was put in charge of all port visit and ceremonial functions. We made preparations to embark the force band. We sought and received permission to issue special dress-white uniforms to the bluejackets in the flagship. We made preparations to embark the Third Class out of the Naval Academy in the ships of the force and we started detailed planning for the fleet review and the fleet visits to the ports in the Great Lakes. All together our plans included visits to 23 ports.

The logistics problems were daunting. In order for the cruiser *Macon* to be able to clear the bridges over the seaway, her radar, mounted on the foremast, and part of the foremast itself had to be removed. Rubbing timbers had to be fabricated to protect her sides in locks that could barely accommodate her. But one of the greatest problems was sanitation. At that time, ships of the fleet did not have sanitary holding tanks installed. Since many of the Great Lake cities take their drinking water from the lakes it was necessary to arrange for sanitation barges in all ports where the ships were not able to be accommodated alongside a pier. That was a very ticklish problem indeed.

We embarked in *Willis A. Lee* in late July and rendezvoused with the units of the task force north of the Nantucket Shoals Lightship. We entered the Gulf of Newfoundland and proceeded into the Gulf of Saint Lawrence preparatory to entering the Saint Lawrence River. All ships embarked river pilots and we began our long cruise up the river. We reached Montreal in good shape and the admiral and a few of the staff transferred to the Queen Elizabeth Hotel, newly opened for the occasion. Mary Lee was waiting for me at the hotel. The place was in a turmoil, because the queen and her party were expected there in late afternoon.

Mary Lee and I were scheduled to attend a party with Admiral and Mrs. Taylor at the U.S. embassy that evening, so I sent my evening dress uniform to the hotel's valet for pressing. We were to meet the admiral in the lobby at 6:15. When my uniform didn't arrive by 5:15, I called the valet to inquire. I was informed that the staff was not permitted to go through the lobby until the queen had arrived. At 5:45 I again called and explained that I had to have my uniform immediately. When nothing happened, I called the manager and told him that if he didn't get my uniform to me immediately, queen or no queen, I was coming down to the lobby in my skivvies to get it myself. I really think that he thought I might do it, because my uniform arrived within five minutes.

The next day the ships got underway and proceeded to their review moorings in Lake Saint Louis. We were joined there by the Canadian and British ships who were to participate with us. There were about thirty ships in all.

As an accommodation to the British, we agreed to adhere to the British table of naval honors. This involved cheering ship for a passing monarch, which is not in our table of honors. It involves manning the rail and, as the reviewing ship with the head of state embarks, all hands on signal raise their caps and shout "hooray." This is repeated three times.

Since I felt that it would be prudent to drill our ships in this procedure, I scheduled a rehearsal for that afternoon. At the appointed time I embarked in the admiral's barge and passed up the line of U.S. ships, who had manned the rail in preparation. As the barge drew abreast of the ship all hands cheered in more or less regulation fashion. I repeated the drill a few time and on the last time I gave each ship a queenly salute. Several of my friends in the various ships gave me a single-finger salute in return.

The next day dawned clear and bright and, during the late morning, our ladies came on board for a lunch on the admiral's verandah. Mary Lee was, of course, among the ladies, and as usual she was the most beautiful.

There was one major mishap that slightly marred an otherwise perfect evolution. When *Britannia* arrived in Montreal, instead of the captain or pilot making the landing, Prince Philip, an officer in the Royal Navy insisted on handling the ship. There is a horrendous current in the Saint Lawrence which he misjudged, and he scraped along the pier, succeeding in removing about 35 feet of beautiful blue cobalt lacquer from the side of *Britannia*. Since the lacquer can only be applied in dry-dock, *Britannia* had to steam the line with her damaged side in full view. Nonetheless, she looked quite beautiful, with her band playing for the queen and our president standing on the quarter-deck taking the salute of the ships as she passed. We received a fine "well done" from the president.

On the following morning, led by *Willis A. Lee,* the task force began its transit of the now officially opened Saint Lawrence Seaway. It was an historic event, not only because we were the first ships to pass through the seaway but because we were the first warships since the War of 1812 to enter the Great Lakes. To be allowed to do so required a special abrogation of a treaty with Canada that was signed after the War of 1812 that prohibited warships of either country to operate on the Great Lakes. The passage came off without a single hitch, but it contained some hairy moments. The seaway channel was deep enough, but it was quite narrow. If a ship got too close to the bank, the suction current generated by the propellers would draw it into the bank with disastrous consequences. Normally it was quite comfortable to stay in the middle of the channel, except, of course, when meeting a ship coming the other way. Then a game of "channel chicken" was played. Both ships maintained their position in the center of the channel until the very last possible moment when each changed course slightly to her right to avoid a collision. The proximity of the passing ship nullified the suction set up by the bank and each ship passed safely. It was thrilling, especially for the skippers.

Upon arrival in Lake Ontario, the ships were released to proceed to their various port destinations. Along with *Macon*, our first port of call was Chicago, where we rendezvoused with our amphibious squadron. The queen was also in Chicago and so there was much excitement. On the Sunday of our visit there, our marine battalion that was embarked in the amphibious squadron conducted a full-dress demonstration assault on the beaches just off Lake Shore Drive. The admiral and I were the guests of Mayor John Daly, the great machine boss of Chicago. The landings were truly spectacular, with explosions, vertical assaults, the whole thing. Mayor Daly told the admiral that the crowd of about a million people was the largest ever gathered in Chicago and it was the biggest traffic jam the city had ever experienced. It was a great day for the Navy.

Our next port of call was Milwaukee. Here we were received with enormous enthusiasm. Not only were the officers and midshipmen royally entertained, but so were our bluejackets. They had a series of block parties for them with lots of lovely girls and a generous amount of good old Milwaukee beer, especially from the Schlitz Brewery. The Elines, who owned Schlitz, were one of our official hosts and did their very best to ensure that we had a memorable visit.

At one luncheon held for us at the Schlitz executive dining

room, one of the officers present went up to the bar and asked the bartender for a Bud. Without blinking an eye the bartender filled a glass half full of Schlitz and then filled the remainder with water. He handed the glass to the wise guy officer saying, "Here's your Bud."

Our next port was Cleveland. I established visiting hours from 1000 until 1700. At the commencement of visiting, the line waiting to board *Willis A Lee* was a good five blocks long. At 1700 the lines would still be five blocks long. I extended general visiting until it got so dark that I felt it unsafe for the public to move around the ship. The enthusiasm of the people of the Midwest for their Navy was astonishing. There were hundreds of men who brought their children on board to show them what it was like for them when they served in the Navy during World War II. Their pride was touching, indeed.

In Detroit we hit our first bump in the road. Warner Brothers had finished the making of *John Paul Jones.* In an effort to publicize the new film, their publicity department decided to have the world premier in Detroit, coincidental with our visit. They contacted Ray Komorowski, our PAO, to seek our cooperation. Ray got the local naval station to send out a detachment of sailors to have an honor guard for the admiral and a public naval ceremony. We went to the theater in a convoy of cars with a police motorcycle escort, sirens screaming. That went over like a lead balloon with the admiral. Unfortunately, they didn't sell very many tickets. I don't believe there were more than fifty people other than the admiral and his staff and the bluejackets that were sent to give the event some color. It was damned embarrassing. Thank heavens we had a wonderfully human admiral. He wasn't thrilled with Ray but he overlooked it as best he could.

Leaving Detroit, we went to Put-in-Bay, an island in the lake very close to Detroit, that boasts a major U.S. monument commemorating Perry's great victory over the British in the War of 1812. The secretary of interior requested that the Navy conduct a commemoration ceremony incident to our cruise in the Great Lakes. That was in my area of responsibility and I early on started planning for the event. I invited the superintendent of the monument, one Sam Houston, to be the master of ceremonies and he accepted. He became my main point of contact. I organized a fine ceremony, including landing our band, along with a detachment of Marines, a detachment of midshipmen and a detachment of bluejackets. On dropping the anchor off Put-in-Bay, I landed the various detachments and then boarded the barge with the admiral for the trip to the landing. Sam was supposed to meet us there but he was nowhere in evidence. There was a large and rather beautiful old Packard Phaeton roadster to carry us to the monument. The monument, by the way, is very impressive. It is similar to the Washington Monument, but not as high. It overlooks a beautiful stone plaza of considerable size.

When we reached the foot of the plaza, we found Sam waiting for us there. He was in his park-ranger outfit, putties, Sam Brown belt and drill-instructor-type hat. He greeted us profusely, a little too profusely I thought at the time. There were about 8,000 people there to witness the ceremony, which was scheduled to start at 1400. To the absolute consternation of the television and radio stations, Sam started the ceremony 10 minutes early. He did just great, introducing all the V.I.Ps in attendance, which were quite a few indeed. He then went into a flowery introduction of the admiral. "Not bad," I thought. The admiral gave his five minute speech which I had prepared for him and retook his seat. Sam then introduced the second tier of V.I.Ps including the chief of police, the superintendent of schools, and so on, and then launched into another flowery introduction of the next speaker, who turned out finally to be Admiral Taylor again. Oh Lord, I was in trouble. The admiral graciously regained the podium and said what an honor it was to introduce Mr. Van Scoyen, the director of the national park service. Mr. Van Scoyen dutifully concluded his remarks, but Sam was now nowhere in evidence. I found him behind the monument taking care of the nervous condition that he was in. By this time his eyes looked like they had been varnished. With some difficulty I got him back to the lectern, whereupon he went into one of his now famous introductions, and damn if he didn't introduce the admiral again! This time the admiral told the audience that he was pleased to introduce his flag secretary who would carry on the ceremony. I did just that. We had the wreath-laying detail lay the wreath, the bugler sound taps and the Marines fire four volleys.

As all of us were standing there saluting, Sam regained the lectern and announced to everyone that the ceremony was over. Not quite! We still had about ten minutes to go. Well we finally struggled through to the end, whereupon Sam, now quite full of himself, went around thanking everyone for helping him put it over. He then sought out the admiral and said, "Admiral I'm going to take you up on top of the monument so that you can have a fine view of our island and then we have arranged a fine reception for you on the town square. We're going to have some champagne punch and some of them hoovary doovaries." Since that very day that's what they have been in our family. The reception wasn't quite ready when we reached the town square, so Sam enlisted the admiral's help in spreading the table cloths. Knowing that Sam was in great trouble, the admiral directed me to invite him on board the flagship to a reception that we had organized for the various V.I.Ps present. We did our best for Sam.

That night I wrote a dispatch to the Navy Department chronicling the events of the day. It has become a classic in the Navy and I quote it as written:

FROM; COMMANDER TASK FORCE 47
TO: CNO CINCLANTFLT

INLAND SEAS SITREP NO 31 201200R TO 211200R X COMMEMORATION OF BATTLE OF LAKE ERIE AT NATIONAL MONUMENT PUT-IN-BAY WENT OFF THIS AFTERNOON BUT NOT EXACTLY AS PLANNED X SAM (BLANK) CMA SUPERINTENDENT AT MONUMENT OVERCOME WITH GREAT EXCITEMENT AND IMPORTANCE OF OCCASION TOOK ABUNDANT PRECAUTIONS AGAINST POSSIBLE NERVOUSNESS X AFTER INFORMAL PRESENTATION FRIENDS RELATIONS AND DISTINGUISHED GUESTS SAM INTRODUCED TASK FORCE COMMANDER WHO MADE APPROPRIATE COMMENTS X SAM—REFORTIFIED AFTER SHORT EXCURSION BEHIND MONUMENT—INTRODUCED MORE DISTINGUISHED GUESTS AND THEN TO EVERYONE'S AMAZEMENT BUT HIS OWN INTRODUCED TASK FORCE COMMANDER AGAIN TO DELIVER ADDRESS X TF COMMANDER HOWEVER HAD THOUGHTLESSLY COME WITH ONLY ONE SPEECH X SPECTACULAR FIELDING PLAY SAVED THE GAME WHEN TASK FORCE COMMANDER INTRODUCED DIRECTOR OF NATIONAL PARK SERVICE—MR SCOYEN—WHO

DELIVERED APPROPRIATE REMARKS X AT THIS POINT SAM REINTRODUCED TASK FORCE COMMANDER ONCE AGAIN WHO GRACEFULLY TURNED PROCEEDINGS OVER TO FLAG SECRETARY WHO CARRIED ON THROUGH REMAINDER OF CEREMONY X SAM MADE ONE LAST ATTEMPT TO BE HELP-FUL BY PREMATURELY ANNOUNCING THAT THE CEREMONY WAS OVER X CONGRESSMAN KEARNS PRESENTLY ON BOARD LEE ASKED TO REPORT THAT STAR SPANGLED BANNER SAVED ONLY THROUGH HEROIC EFFORT TASK FORCE COMMANDER X BETTING ON FLAGSHIP THIS EVENING IS 10 TO 1 SAM WILL NEVER GET A MAJOR MONUMENT COMMAND X IN SPITE OF SAM'S BEST EFFORTS OVER ALL EFFECTS OF CEREMONY MOST IMPRESSIVE X

We received in reply the following dispatch from the Chief of Naval Operations:

CONGRATULATIONS ON THE NAVY'S SECOND GREAT VIC-TORY AT PUT-IN-BAY X NO MONUMENT WILL BE ERECTED TO THIS GREAT VICTORY BUT IT NONE THE LESS DEMON-STRATES THE NAVY'S RESOURCEFULNESS AND RESOLVE X WELL DONE X

ARLEIGH BURKE

The entire Navy was amused, but the same cannot be said for the Department of Interior. We had a formal apology from the sec-retary. Poor Sam, I am afraid our odds against his promotion as set forth in our dispatch were quite accurate.

While we steamed out of the Great Lakes we could look back on a magnificently successful cruise. Our ships visited 24 Great Lakes ports and we had over three million visitors board our ships. It was a tremendous Navy public relations triumph.

My relief, Bill Read was waiting for me on the *Yosemite* upon our return to Newport. After a very short turnover I was relieved of one of the most wonderful and enjoyable tours a naval officer could ever hope for. It was truly Camelot for Mary Lee and me.

Chapter 12

The Naval War College

W HAT A DELIGHT! After tour upon tour of challenging, but arduous assignments, I was about to be able to relax a bit. I had looked forward to attending the War College for several years and had, as a matter of fact, really hoped to be selected after the *Lester* tour, but my assignment as aide to Whitey Taylor had obviated that possibility. Now I was to enter the War College in September in the Naval Warfare Course. Although I was still a lieutenant commander, I had been selected for the senior course, which normally was for commanders and captains. How very nice for me! There were numerous officers from the other services as well as foreign service officers from the State Department included in the class.

Our course started in September 1959. It was interesting and stimulating. There was a good deal of reading required but I was delighted because, for the first time in many years, I had time to do some deep reading, and even some serious thinking.

The course consisted of daily lectures mostly by visiting high-ranking officers or senior civilian members of the Navy and Defense Departments. I found most of the presentations both pertinent and interesting. There was always a question period at the end of the presentation. It soon became evident that we had a few "Spring Butts" in the class. These fellows never lost an opportunity to ask a question. In many cases they just wanted to be heard or to favor us with their great insights.

We also met in small seminar sections to work on staff problems or to discuss various aspects of the subject matter that we were addressing. While we received no grades, most of us felt compelled to take the course material and requirements very seriously. Thus there was a great deal of reading that I had to accomplish at home. One evening I was reading my course material in our living room when I heard Mary Lee call from our bedroom to say that she thought that someone was looking into her window. I thought that it was probably her imagination, but to make her feel more secure I grabbed my flashlight and went out to our side yard. Young Randy, then about seven years old, went with me. I looked under a rather large weeping willow tree that occupied our side yard but saw nothing. Mary Lee was standing in her window pointing down. When Randy looked behind the foundation plantings where Mary Lee was pointing, a man jumped out at him. I immediately stepped between Randy and the man and started to defend our turf. I got socked in the left ear for my troubles and found myself on the ground. I picked myself off the ground and the man fled up the street with me in hot pursuit. I hollered for Mary Lee to call the police. Luckily for him and probably for me as well, he outran me. I was upset that he was looking in our windows at Mary Lee but I was even angrier that he had knocked me down.

After losing him I returned to our home just as two police cruisers rounded our corner. The police made notes on the incident, which I gave to them along with a description of the intruder. As I recall, I judged him to be about six foot four weighing about 250 pounds. He wore a red plaid mackinaw and had a black mask over his head. I got into one of the cruisers to help them look for the man. The other police stayed with Mary Lee as she needed some calming influence.

We hadn't been looking very long when the police spotted a rather large truck parked in a poorly lit street about a block and a half from our house. They brought me home and then returned to set up a surveillance of the truck. Sure enough, not much later the cruiser returned with a man in handcuffs roughly answering the description I had given. I had the dress right but instead of 6 foot 4, he was more like 5 foot 8, and instead of 250 pounds he was more like 150. Oh well, he looked big to me.

I accompanied the cops to the police station to sign a complaint and returned home somewhat a family hero! The next day the mayor of Newport called me to apologize for the incident. He told me that he was embarrassed that this could have happened to a War College student and his family. I waited for the other shoe to drop and drop it did. He told me that the man was married and that his wife was expecting a child. Also it turned out that his brother-in -law was a sergeant on the Newport police force. The mayor asked me if I wouldn't consider dropping the charges. If it had been a bluejacket that had been the peeping tom, this conversation would never have taken place, so I told the mayor that I intended to press charges. I never found out when the trail was to be held but I understand that the culprit got a suspended sentence with the understanding that he get psychiatric help.

One of the great joys of being at the War College was a chance to enjoy a wonderful social life. Mary Lee and I were really into it because there were so many congenial officers and their wives in our class.

But there was another requirement necessary to complete the course. All students had to write a lengthy thesis on a subject of their choice. I had written some articles on the relationship of technology to warship design and tactical deployment and was very interested in that subject. I therefore chose "The Influence of Technology on the Application of Naval Power," as my topic. Of course such a project required considerable research, since I intended to show that tactics, from the earliest days of the ram and Greek fire, were largely determined by the technology available at the time. As an example of this thesis, I wanted to put forth the proposition that if the French had only one modern destroyer at Trafalgar they would have blown the British out of the water regardless of the genius of Admiral Nelson. I also intended to show that the country that was slow to adopt and adapt to new and superior technologies historically lost the battles and ultimately the next war.

During the beautiful fall weather in Newport and with the distraction of our social life and our activities with our small children I had not done as much early research as I probably should have. Before we knew it, Christmas leave was upon us. We got two weeks off. During that period my conscience started to bother me a little about the lack of focus that I had applied to my research, and I resolved to go over to the War College library during our leave period to do a little catch-up. And over I went.

There was quite a collection of mail in my pigeonhole, which

I decided to go through before turning to my research. There was the usual collection of Christmas cards and other routine mailings. There was a rather fat letter from the Office of the Chief of Naval Operations which I immediately evaluated as a letter addressed to all officers about getting on with the leadership effort or some such thing, so I relegated that piece of mail to be read last.

I finally opened the letter and, after scanning it, all thought of research vanished. It was a letter from Admiral Arleigh Burke, our very famous Chief of Naval Operations, addressed to me personally. The first part of it described the terrible job, as he put it, of being his personal aide. The last part asked me if I was interested in being considered for it. I can still remember the shock that I felt. He could have had any officer in the Navy that he wanted, but for some reason was thinking about appointing me. My God! What to do? The postmark was ten days prior to the day that I was reading his letter!

I figured I needed big-time advice and, before even calling Mary Lee, I hightailed it over to the ComDesLant flagship to seek some counsel from my dear friend Admiral Taylor. Fortunately, he saw me immediately. He read the letter and told me that since Admiral Burke was not used to waiting for an answer to his letters for ten days from the likes of me, I had better call his office immediately and explain that I had just received his letter.

He had his writer call the CNO's office and I asked to speak with Bill Busik, his present aide, whom I had known slightly at the Naval Academy. He was an all-America running back, the best the Navy had had to that point. I had also known him slightly in the fleet. When he came on the line and I explained to him that I had just received Admiral Burke's letter about the possibility of being his relief, his response shocked me. "What relief?" He was being fired and didn't know it. How embarrassing for me! It turned out however, that he was delighted and relieved that he was being moved out, because he just was not fast enough for Admiral Burke. He disliked the admiral and the admiral disliked him. Although I had made an innocent mistake, our association through the years was not particularly cordial. After asking him to inform Admiral Burke that I had just received his letter I hung up and settled my emotions a bit over a cup of coffee with Admiral Taylor.

Mary Lee was equally excited and confused when I reached home and showed her the letter. There was nothing definite yet. We weren't even sure that we would hear anything more about the matter. We had not long to wait when the phone rang from Admiral Burke's office. It was the executive aide telling me that they were cutting orders for me to board the cruiser *Providence* in Boston where Admiral Burke was making a visit. I was to be interviewed by some senior members of his personal staff as well as by the great one himself. The three days that we had to wait to go to Boston seemed just under three years to us.

It was a beautiful day when Mary Lee and I headed up the highway towards Boston. She had not been invited on board *Providence* but she came on the trip anyway for moral support. All the way to Boston she gave me a short course on what to say and, probably more important, what not to say. Our plan was for me to drop her off at the Ritz while I went over to the Navy Yard.

Upon reaching the *Providence,* I talked to various staff officers for a total of about an hour and had a very short visit with Admiral Burke. Captain Larry Geise, his executive aide, saw me off the ship. He told me that they would not make a decision until their return to Washington and that they would be in touch.

Mary Lee and I had a very nice but nervous lunch at the Ritz and headed back to Newport. Naturally, our whole conversation centered on what happened, what I said, and what I should have said. That evening we were invited to the Beavers', a War College classmate, for a dinner party. We had just gone into the living room for after-dinner coffee when Jane Beaver returned from answering her phone to tell me that there was somebody calling from Washington for me. It was Larry Geise. He informed me that they had just landed at Anacostia and Admiral Burke had directed him to inform me that he had selected me for the job! For the rest of the evening that was pretty much anyone wanted to talk about. And this was the case at the War College where the word got around like wildfire.

Admiral Burke had called Admiral Ingersol, the president of the college to inform him that I was going to be withdrawn in ten days. The CNO wanted me to report as soon as possible so that I could get off to Europe for a few weeks of personal indoctrination before

I relieved. That ten days were more than hectic. We decided that we might as well sell our wonderful little home because we would, in all probability, never again return to Newport for duty. We did sell our house, but we didn't get all that we might have from it.

The War College surgeon decided that he had to get into the act because of the plan to send me to Europe immediately upon reaching Washington. Dr. MacGloughlin, or "Black Mac" as we called him, decided that I needed five booster shots, which he gave me all at once. That night we were invited to the Tazwell Shepherd's home for a farewell dinner in our honor. We weren't at the party very long when I began to feel terrible. I thought I was going to faint, which happily I didn't. I struggled through the evening as best I could and with relief returned home.

The next morning I awoke to find myself covered with a terrible rash and I had a high fever. I was terribly ill and started to go into shock. Mary Lee wanted to take me to the hospital, but I didn't want to turn in, because they would keep me there forever and I would be late reporting to Washington. We decided that the best thing to do was to call Admiral Taylor and ask him to help. Within 20 minutes his sedan was at our door and I was on my way to the sick bay on board his flagship, *Yosemite*. There they quickly diagnosed my problem as a severe allergic reaction to all of those shots and quickly gave me some adrenaline to counter the problem. They literally saved my life. That was the last immunization that I have ever had.

We were soon on our way to Washington and into a new arduous and exciting adventure.

Chapter 13

Aide to the CNO

WITH RANDY AND Valerie well ensconced at my folks' home in Pennsylvania, Mary Lee and I started our trip to Washington. In celebration of my good fortune in being picked out of the whole officer corps to be Admiral Burke's aide, we decided to stop in New York for a bit of a spree on the way south. We stayed at the elegant Plaza Hotel and had dinner at the world famous Four Seasons Restaurant.

Soon after arriving in Washington, Mary Lee found us a fine rental in Sumner, Maryland, a beautiful development off Massachusetts Avenue just over the Maryland line. It was only a few miles from the Naval Observatory, the site of the CNO's quarters at the time. In later years, these quarters were taken from the Navy and made the official residence of the vice president. Nelson Rockefeller was the first to occupy them, during the Ford administration. We were able to move into our home and get our children registered in private schools. Randy matriculated at Landon and Valerie entered Holton Arms, Mary Lee's old prep school.

I reported to the Pentagon and, as planned, I immediately got organized to go to Europe for a familiarization visit. The idea was for me to visit the major staffs in both London and Paris and get familiar enough with both the cities and the naval commands to permit me to function effectively there during Admiral Burke's frequent visits. Commander in Chief Naval Forces Europe and his extensive staff were located on beautiful Grosvenor Square, very close to the American Embassy. I was quite familiar with the facility, as I used to make frequent visits there as a top-secret courier during my tour in *Houston* many years before.

My reception, by everyone including the admiral, was warm and hospitable. After four days of indoctrination briefings and some very pleasant hospitality I left London for Paris. Here we had no U.S. Naval commands but we did have the major NATO command, Supreme Allied Command Europe. Located at this command was the NATO Military Standing Group, which hosted the NATO military commanders at their annual conference. I spent four days in Paris getting to know the personnel there and especially the U.S. Navy contingents. It was a very pleasant and relaxed visit, the pace quite unlike the one I would keep when later I accompanied Admiral Burke there. I learned a great deal in both capitols that was to stand me in good stead in the months ahead.

Upon my return to Washington, I set about the job of relieving Bill Busik. I must say that he was more than delighted to have me appear. He was a great football player but he was not fast enough for Admiral Burke. There appeared to be little love lost between them. Being fired by the CNO is not exactly like being fired from somewhere else. Busik left with an outstanding fitness report and command of the U.S. *Mahan*, one of our new class of guided missile destroyer leaders. It was an absolute plum assignment. Not bad for a guy who got the heave ho. In spite of that, my relations with Busik were never very cordial. I couldn't blame him much. I probably would have harbored some resentment or at least some embarrassment if the situation were reversed.

It was to be a 12-hour day, six days a week, plus at least four hours on Sunday. Admiral Burke was a great internationalist, a member of the Foreign Policy Council, and later he took over as acting chief of the Joint Chiefs of Staff when General Twinning went down with cancer. Because of his unique position, we were to travel a great deal internationally. In addition, because of his personal prestige and because he was a chief of a service, he received huge numbers of invitations to all matter of official, diplomatic and personal functions and entertainments.

Our office consisted of myself, a Marine Corps personal aide, a female officer for liaison with Mrs. Burke and two writers. On the other side of Admiral Burke's office resided the executive aide who handled the business side of the CNO's responsibilities.

I was the keeper of the door. All appointments to see Admiral Burke or for Admiral Burke to go anywhere were handled by me.

Thus I was in charge of the daily schedule, which I prepared the night before; at our early morning meeting I went over it with the admiral. Naturally more people wanted to see the CNO then could possibly be squeezed into his schedule. It was quite common to have two or three flag officers in my office trying to catch a word with him.

His duties as a member of the Joint Chiefs of Staff demanded a great deal of his focus and time. The issues that came before that august group were important and difficult. The military budget caused an enormous amount of infighting. Each service tried to maximize its share of the pie. The controlling factor in this division was the roles and missions assigned to each of the services. The force levels for each grew out of these assigned missions. Admiral Burke was in a constant state of tension with General Curtis LeMay who was then chief of staff of the Air Force.

There were, of course, many perks that went with the job of personal aide. One of the nicest was being a member of the CNO mess. It was restricted to flag officers and senior aides and was luxurious compared to the utilitarian food service available elsewhere in the Pentagon.

I quickly settled into a strenuous routine. Handling the personal affairs of Admiral Burke, including his finances, fell to the aide. In addition, the aide was responsible for organizing the numerous parties that the Burkes gave at Admiral's House. I assisted with the guest list, got the invitations out, organized the stewards at the quarters and even supplied the admiral with a list of conversation suggestions for the evening. For entertainments that he attended, I was responsible for giving him a written brief on when, where, and who, the dress, his dinner partners (if indeed it was a dinner), and insuring that his driver knew where he was to go and when he was to get there. The day after the party, I was responsible for writing the thank you note for the admiral.

Mary Lee and I received a great number of invitations to the many official parties in Washington. After Mary Lee went to a few, we decided that it was just not worth the effort. She had to go alone, find a place to park, which was frequently impossible, and largely fend for herself.

In addition to the bread and butter letters, I was responsible for drafting all of his private letters, which were numerous indeed. It was amazing how much mail he received. Each letter got a personal answer, which was written by me. There were numerous requests for photographs, which we were able to supply complete with inscription. Our chief petty officer writer could write like Admiral Burke, so accurately that we didn't even bother the admiral to sign banking documents. In all, I wrote more than 3,000 letters for Admiral Burke's signature during my tour with him.

I learned quickly that the job of CNO is a tough one. Problems arising in the Navy are generally solved at a lower command level. The ones that get to the CNO's desk are the ones that are not readily solvable, the tough ones that have no simple solution. Thus it is an enormously stressful job. The tension in the office was often palpable. The aides were the closest and most convenient people on whom the CNO could let off steam and he often did so.

Admiral Burke gained his wartime fame in destroyers. The Little Beaver Squadron (DESRON 24), which he commanded in the South Western Pacific, was probably the most famous destroyer squadron of World War II. He was truly beloved by destroyermen. In fact, however, he was a big carrier advocate. He placed enormous budgetary emphasis on the carrier and naval aviation, largely at the expense of the surface combatants. Under his command, surface combatant forces continued to decline in capability. No money meant no research and development which meant continued obsolescence of the surface forces. It was a vicious cycle; the surface combatants had minimal fighting capability, so why waste scarce funding on them? No funds, no improvement. As I had pointed out in many of my writings, the surface combatant potentially was the future strength of the fleet. The guided missile was going to gain the ascendancy but it wasn't to happen on Admiral Burke's watch.

The Albany Class heavy guided-missile cruiser was scheduled to receive the strategic Polaris missile when it was ready for service. The ships were configured, at great expense, to receive them. Mr. Gates, the secretary of defense, I am certain with prodding from the piloted aircraft community, decided to cancel this one important program that would bring the surface combatant into the future. When that happened with the concurrent cancellation of the Regulus II program, with no fight from Admiral Burke, I went into his office and, throwing caution to the wind, told him that his abandonment of that surface application program was going to set the surface forces back for years. I was unable to budge him.

Admiral Burke played a key role in bringing the Polaris Missile forward in the Navy. He nurtured, encouraged and put up with Admiral Rickover, as he developed the nuclear submarine that was to carry the missile. He supported the project officer, Vice Admiral Rayborn, with vigor and effectiveness. The day the first Polaris Missile was fired from the nuclear submarine *George Washington* was an emotional one for Admiral Burke. He was a little miffed because the kudos were going to everyone but him. He, in fact, should have received the lion's share of the credit.

The next submarine scheduled to test fire the Polaris was the *Patrick Henry* and nothing would do but for Admiral Burke to be on board for the event. He invited Mr. Gilpatrick the deputy secretary of defense to accompany him. In addition, the commander in chief Atlantic Fleet and commander submarine force Atlantic Fleet were invited to join us. We boarded the *Patrick Henry* at Cape Canaveral and almost immediately got underway for the missile range. Our schedule called for two Polaris firings, one in the morning and one in the afternoon.

The *Patrick Henry* took its position on the missile range and submerged in preparation for the firing. We went through a long and nerve-wracking countdown not unlike what is depicted in the movies. At last the order was given to fire. We could feel the missile being ejected from the submarine. Shortly thereafter we had a message from the range safety ship that the missile was motorboating, i.e. it was going around in a random fashion on the surface. It was destructed by the range safety ship before it could collide with anyone in the vicinity.

To say that this was an embarrassing setback would be somewhat of an understatement. We still had the afternoon firing to look forward to, however, which would undoubtedly put things to right. We had another long countdown with a final command to fire. The missile left the submarine. Shortly thereafter we heard a loud thud. I mused that it must be the missile doors closing. Very shortly after that the emergency sirens went off in the sub with an order passed for emergency surfacing. I figured that they were trying to get to the surface so that the VIPs could watch the missile go down range.

As soon as we surfaced, the entire party went topside. There we viewed a huge hole in the splinter deck. The missile had broken the surface but instead of igniting it had fallen back and hit the submarine. We came very close to having a king-sized disaster. To say that it was a quiet ride back to Washington would also be somewhat of an understatement.

The Polaris Missile was to play an even bigger role in the life of Admiral Burke. Under the Joint Chiefs of Staff's Roles and Missions Agreement, the Air Force was assigned responsibility for all strategic strike targets, weapons and weapons systems. Now along comes Polaris and its delivery system, the Polaris Missile Nuclear Submarine, and its associated support services. It's a strategic strike system, no argument. That is until General LeMay moved to get the system under the command of the Strategic Air Command. All hell broke loose.

There was absolutely no way that Admiral Burke was going to agree to that. After long and arduous and sometimes bitter fights in the JCS, the decision was bucked up to President Eisenhower. Admiral Burke decided to lay it on the line. He was going to resign if the decision went against the Navy. I called the limousine to carry us over to the White House so that Admiral Burke could inform the president of his decision. The old man was really steaming. We got into the car and as he leaned back in his seat he said, "You know Allan, you and I have the worst jobs in the Navy. I have the worst job and you have the next to worst job." I replied, "I agree with you Admiral, but I'd argue a little bit about the order." That got him to laughing and by the time we reached the White House he had relaxed a bit. The trip home was all merriment because the president supported the Navy's position.

Our trips abroad were always very interesting, but also hectic for me. I had all sorts of responsibilities, from selecting and having suitable engravings made for the official gifts, to firming the Admiral's schedule, to laying on our aircraft and to carrying out the schedule once we arrived. Wherever we went, the Admiral was received and entertained at the highest levels of the host government.

Admiral Burke told me, early on, that it was regrettable to be late, but it was unforgivable to be early in our aircraft arrival or at any official visit where extensive honors were involved. I was meticulous about it, including having the pilot slow down to ensure that we would not anticipate our official arrival time by even one minute.

Once we arrived, I was expected to go with the admiral on all of his official calls. My job was to remember all the substantive conversations that he had with various officials and especially any commitments that he made. I had to reduce these conversations to dispatches, which I sent to the Navy Department daily. In addition, I accompanied him and Mrs. Burke to all social events, which many times were pleasant enough, but after we returned to our hotel or to the embassy where we often stayed, I would have to prepare my dispatches as well as write bread-and-butter letters for the admiral to sign the next morning. I literally worked myself to a frazzle.

One South American trip brought us to Brasilia, at that time the brand new capital of Brazil. We called on President Kubitschek in his new presidential palace. During our visit, he remarked to Admiral Burke that he must be wondering why anyone would put a new capital so far out in the Brazilian wilderness. He told us that while Brazil had enormous natural wealth in the vast interior of the country he had found it impossible to make the Brazilians turn inward. He explained that the Brazilians were largely of Portuguese nationality and they were not happy unless they had one foot in the ocean. By putting the capital inland he was forcing them to look into the interior of their country.

Hailie Selassi, the emperor of Ethiopia, was visiting in Brasilia at the same time we were. He had his aide with him, who I am afraid outshone me in every way. He had a red tunic with a leopard skin over one shoulder, green trousers with an enormous gold stripe down each leg and a beautiful plumed headdress. It was during his time in Brazil, by the way, that the emperor was overthrown by a coup d'etat.

Admiral Burke was of Swedish origin and so he favored visiting Sweden. We went there a few times while I was his aide and had a very fine visit on each occasion. Coincident with one of our visits, final preparations were being made to surface the Swedish battleship

Vasa which had turned over on the day it was commissioned some 400 years previous. Apparently the reining Swedish King at the time insisted on adding another gun deck to the ship after construction had begun. He had little time for such niceties as stability, center of gravity, center of buoyancy, and so on. When completed, it was hopelessly unstable and thus turned over as soon as it left the construction yard. It lay on the bottom of Stockholm Harbor, largely intact because the water in the Baltic is too cold to permit the existence of sea worms. With a great deal of care the Swedes had raised the *Vasa* and we had one of the first looks at her.

They had completely covered the wood with a preparation of bee's wax, graphite and other preservatives, and kept sprays of water on her continuously to prevent her from turning to dust. It was wonderful to see that incredible relic that literally was suspended in time for 400 years. Subsequently they were able to stabilize the wood and build a suitable museum for her, which Mary Lee and I visited many years later at the invitation of our dear friend and Admiral Burke's ex local aide, Admiral Christer Kierkegaard. Admiral Kierkegaard eventually commanded the Swedish fleet.

Admiral Burke is the only naval officer to have been appointed to three two-year terms as CNO. We were coming to the end of his third tour when Jack Kennedy replaced Eisenhower as president. The attitude of the White House and the Cabinet towards Admiral Burke changed overnight to one of almost overt hostility. The whiz kids led by McNamara took over the Department of Defense and immediately started to treat the senior uniformed officers with contempt.

A very detailed plan was developed under the leadership of the CIA during the Eisenhower administration to mount a military campaign against Castro's Cuba. Of course the Navy was very much involved, including supplying absolutely essential air cover. The Kennedy administration, prompted by the damn fools that took over the military, continued to modulate the plan, eventually changing the target area to the Bay of Pigs. Instead of putting their collective feet down, much to their discredit, the uniformed heads of service continued to acquiesce in the constant changes.

When Admiral Burke left our office the night before the Bay of Pigs D-Day he was under the absolute impression that naval aviation would be committed to the battle the next day. That evening, Adlai Stevenson, the U.S. Ambassador to the United Nations, came down to Washington to dissuade the president from using U.S. naval forces in close support of the landings. With no reference to the commander of the Navy, the president directed the secretary of defense to issue orders through the Joint and Specified Command Structure to stand down naval aviation. Without it, the operation was absolutely doomed to failure and fail it did.

Kennedy made a statement—after he decided to stand down naval air, and thus made the success of the mission impossible—that he personally took the responsibility for the failure of his military commanders! The bastard! This was to be the way the Kennedy administration, followed by the Johnson administration, treated the uniformed services. It was an absolute disgrace and led to the disaster in Vietnam.

Soon after the episode at the Bay of Pigs, the president convened a board to inquire into the disaster. The board consisted of Alan Dulles, the director of the CIA, General Maxwell Taylor, the national security advisor to the president, Admiral Burke, and Robert Kennedy, the attorney general. It turned into a one-man court of inquiry with Kennedy acting as lord high prosecutor. I had the responsibility of meeting him when he came to the Pentagon for the meeting of the board. I found him to be arrogant, impolite and pushy. He thought nothing of going into the private offices of high-ranking department of defense officials when they were not in and reading correspondence on their desks. He was a swift pain in the ass and I wondered how those distinguished men could stand him.

As Admiral Burke approached his retirement date, he began to receive numerous job offers which I carefully catalogued. He had some great ones. The state of Colorado, his home state, offered him the job of Fishing Inspector. His duties were to fish in all the streams and lakes in Colorado and determine where the fish were biting best.

One day he had a call from Jimmy Roosevelt. Roosevelt was calling to ask him if he would consider becoming the president of the Roosevelt Raceway, a trotting track outside New York. When he hung up, the admiral buzzed for me. He said, "Allan, did you hear what that guy offered me? I don't know anything about horses." Then he leaned back in his chair and said," Well maybe I do. I've been dealing with horses' asses all my life."

The admiral directed me to lay on a huge retirement garden party at the Naval Observatory. I invited 1100 guests. Everyone who was anyone in Washington got an invitation. Senior Cabinet officials, senior members of the Congress, even the Supreme Court justices and their ladies were included. Incidentally, in all such parties I always included some of my personal friends. Why not? What are friends for? I added about 25 couples to my list.

One essential matter had to be satisfied before I selected a date. Mrs. Burke insisted that I check the *Farmers' Almanac* to ascertain the weather forecast for the date that I selected. I, of course, selected a date that the *Farmers' Almanac* predicted would be fair. But when I awoke the day of the party there was little doubt in my mind that it was going to pour all day. Admiral Burke wasn't mad at God—he was mad at me. I had two huge tents set up on the grounds, the Navy band, a couple of platoons of Marines to help park the cars and all sorts of food-service people. Using the tents was out of the question, so everyone crowded into the quarters, which fortunately had a huge verandah. I was confident that my friends, knowing that I was in trouble would not show up and thus take a little pressure off the crowd. Every one of the bastards showed up!

We had the retirement ceremony for the admiral at the Naval Academy. It was a beautiful ceremony and I was proud to be a part of this great tribute to a great warrior and great naval commander. On the way to Annapolis with the admiral and Mrs. Burke and Mary Lee we had a very pleasant time. Admiral Burke very graciously told me that I was the very best aide that he ever had and my fitness report and beautiful letter of commendation from him attested to that. While it was a tough and often frustrating job I never forgot the fact that having it was a great honor indeed.

I wasn't immediately detached. I stayed on as aide to the new CNO, Admiral George Anderson, for about three months, until the aide that he selected arrived on board. Commander Brian McCaulley, eventually reported on board and I was duly relieved. I had orders to the post-war destroyer *U.S.S. Davis* (DD 937) as her commanding officer. And where was she based? In Newport, Rhode Island, of course. I had, as the reader will recall, absolutely predicted that I would never return to Newport for duty. Why else would we have sold our house?

Chapter 14

Command of the *Davis* 1961—1962

T HE *DAVIS* WAS a post-war destroyer of the Forrest Sherman Class. Her hull number was 937. She was attached to Destroyer Squadron 34 and was the squadron flagship. That distinction was to play a very heavy role in my experience on board her.

Since we had sold our home in Newport we were obliged to find suitable housing. We knew that the ship was scheduled to depart for a nine month deployment in the Mediterranean in February of 1962. Since Randy and Valerie were still quite young, we decided that the family would move to Europe for the duration of our deployment; so we set out to find a furnished house for the five months prior to deployment.

We enlisted the assistance of Peter King, a delightful old gentleman who was very much part of the Newport scene. He almost immediately showed us one of the Newport cottages, Lily Pond House. It was a huge stone edifice standing high on a bluff overlooking the Atlantic. Eleven acres of land came with it, along with a pond and a resident flock of white swans. The house was owned by the distinguished dowager, Mrs. Whitehouse. She was the sister of Ambassador Aldrich, a member of the Rockefeller Family and our former ambassador to the Court of St. James.

Of course, it was necessary that we call on her, which we did in her mansion in downtown Newport. She took an immediate liking to Mary Lee and quickly approved the rental to us. What great fun! The center hall was big enough to hold a party of 200. The beautiful walnut-paneled dining room with its elegant fireplace looked like a setting for the liqueur advertisement, "A Man of Distinction." Mary Lee and I had a fine master suite overlooking the ocean and the children's accommodations were equally posh. The rent wasn't all that much but it was never built for Newport winter living, which made the fuel bill spectacular, to say the least. We used to say that we were the only family in Newport where the milkman came twice a week and the oil man came every day.

The grounds were beautifully maintained by a whole platoon of gardeners. At Mrs. Whitehouse's direction they frequently brought large bunches of flowers from her greenhouses to Mary Lee. We even had a colored cook by the name of Ethel. She really wasn't all that great a cook but she was a delight and we enjoyed having her immensely.

After settling in at Lily Pond House, I reported for duty on board *Davis* in late September. It was about ten o'clock in the morning and I tried to call on the squadron commander. When I was informed by his steward that Commodore Thomas had not yet risen, I was somewhat taken aback. I had heard only the most glowing things about Ned Thomas. He was a star man in the class of '38. He was the quarterback on the Navy varsity football team and a "Green Bowler." The Green Bowlers was a very secret society made up of the marked comers in the regiment. In 1943, it was declared an illegal society and was disbanded, but there were still Green Bowlers in the fleet and Ned was one of them.

He was an extremely popular officer and well regarded. He had served several years on the Navy staff in London where he acquired many of the mannerisms of the English upper class. He was a member of the New York Yacht Club, an expert on wines and a rather elegant and sophisticated officer. He had sufficient know-how and charm to be appointed as the local aide to Admiral Lord Mountbatten during his rather frequent visits to Washington.

When I finally was able to call on him I liked him immediately. He was friendly and charming. He had heard of me; apparently I had a good reputation in the force, as well as great prestige coming off the tour as Admiral Burke's aide.

I soon relieved and was on my way in my second combatant command. I immediately promulgated a letter to all hands laying out in detail how I planned to run the ship. I announced the same standards that had proved to be so effective in *Lester* and in the force as a whole. In addition, I immediately took steps to organize a standard military band. With some good luck we located sufficient talent in the officers and men, and the Bureau of Naval Personnel supplied all the instruments and military music that we requested. In addition, we organized several singing groups on board. One sang popular music. Another sang folk music and still another sang barbershop-type harmonies. Each of the groups were outfitted in a distinctive blazer. I planned to make good use of them in our people-to-people program when we went abroad. The *Davis* was off and running!

While the crew had to work harder than any other crew in the squadron, the payoff came our way almost immediately. The ship started to look great. It operated well and soon got the reputation as a winner. One day, the weapons officer came to see me in my cabin. He told me that he was on the forecastle when he noticed the captain from another of the destroyers in the squadron standing on the pier with the weapons officer from his ship. He was pointing at *Davis* and in a very loud voice was saying "Do you see that, Mister? That's what I want! Now damn it, get to work!" Word of episodes such as that go through the ship like wildfire and have an enormous influence on the ship's pride and morale.

Since we were to deploy in early February our operations were largely undertaken in waters close to Newport. We did go out on hunter-killer operations in December and put into Bermuda for a few days. But that was largely it. It enabled me to spend time with Mary Lee and the children and we truly had a great fall and early winter. We had a few large parties in Lily Pond House to which we invited our friends and fellow officers and their wives. It was during these parties that we began to notice a serious drinking problem in the commodore. When sober he was Joe Charm, but as he drank he got progressively less charming and on occasion he became downright rude to some of our guests, to the point where we actually stopped inviting him.

I started to worry about him deploying with the squadron. I am certain that Admiral Speck, the force commander, was aware of his growing problem but did nothing about it. It was a mistake that was to have tragic consequences. The commodore's wife was not in Newport. Coincidentally, she was a teacher at Holton Arms School in Washington where Valerie had just been a student. We didn't know it at the time but she was formally separated from the commodore.

In early February I took Mary Lee, the children and our beloved Cartuffels to New York where they were to embark in the SS *Constitution* for the voyage to Italy. My mother and dad met us in New York and put us up with them at the beautiful Waldorf Astoria. They had arranged for us to have excellent tickets to the Broadway hit *The Sound of Music*. We didn't know it at the time, of course, but this was the last time I was to see my mother alive. As we waited for the *Constitution* to get underway I noticed that my mother looked very tired and somewhat uncomfortable. I suggested that we leave before the ship got underway but she refused. We enjoyed the typical sailing of an ocean liner; lots of waving, the throwing of streamers and the ship's band playing gay music.

The remaining week before we got underway was filled with frantic preparations of all types but when the order came to "single up all lines" *Davis* was ready. With the band playing my favorite marching music we cast off for what was to be an amazingly successful and happy cruise.

Crossing the Atlantic in mid February was bound to be a rough ride and this was not to be an exception. On the first night underway we rendezvoused with a replenishment group that was scheduled to accompany us during the crossing. It was a terrible night. The seas were rough and it was snowing. To make matters worse I had somehow caught the flu bug and felt downright lousy. At about 2200 the *Davis* was ordered up alongside the oiler to take on fuel. I naturally took the con as going alongside at 12 knots on a black night in heavy seas was a job for the captain. It took us about an hour and a half to take station, go alongside, take on fuel, break away and resume our normal cruising station. My bridge coat became progressively wet and heavy and I felt worse and worse with a high fever and chills.

As soon as I got the ship snugged down in her night cruising station I turned over the con to the officer of the deck and went to my sea cabin. I had never been a drinker and certainly never on board ship but I figured that this was the time I really needed some of that medicinal brandy I had always heard about. I sent for the chief hospitalman and asked him if he could supply some for me. He was, of course, happy to oblige, and delivered four individual bottles to the sea cabin. I poured the contents of one of the bottles into a glass and took a mighty gulp. It was god awful. I damn near didn't get it down. When I was relieved well over a year later the other three bottles were still in my sea-cabin safe.

Other than battling the rough seas, we had no problems making the crossing. As usual we had a fleet rendezvous for the turnover. The carrier and destroyer squadron being relieved joined us at our anchorage for a round of briefings. The cruiser assigned to the Sixth Fleet stayed in the Med on a permanent basis. At the time it was the light cruiser *Springfield*. She was the flagship of the Sixth Fleet and was permanently based in Ville Franche, a delightful port along the French Riviera.

We operated with the Sixth Fleet for nine months and not once during that period were our operations or our schedule disrupted because of an international crisis. It must have been some kind of a record.

Very early in our cruise we put into Naples, Italy and I had a fine reunion with my family. They were well and happy. The children had been enrolled in the American School. Mary Lee had found a fine apartment on the Pocillipo overlooking beautiful Naples Bay and she had even found a pretty good maid. Through the Fleet Support Activity, which gave splendid support to Navy families living in and around Naples, I was able to purchase a Volkswagen Beetle. I think I paid around $850 for it. It was just what the family needed to get around and for most of the next several months they followed the ship around the Mediterranean. It was a delight to stand into a port and spy my little red-headed family standing on the pier, Cartuffles included. The children were old, and big enough to be able to be somewhat on their own, which made the problem of them being in the hotels and going to dinner by themselves fairly manageable.

In March the fleet moved to the eastern Mediterranean. We were ordered into Beirut for a fleet visit. The flagship carrying Com-SixthFlt was also there. The weather was perfect and Beirut, as it was during my previous visits, was an absolutely beautiful city and port.

The captains were invited for a reception at the Lebanese Army officers mess. We accepted and three of our captains and the commodore rode over together. After the reception, the commodore suggested that we stay ashore for lunch. We went to the brand new

Phoenicia Hotel. The bar there was unique. There was a very large plate glass window behind the bar that looked into the underwater portion of the hotel's beautiful swimming pool.

We noticed that the place was all set up with stage lighting and other paraphernalia that is associated with movie making. We also noticed some very attractive ladies in evening dresses. We were not at the bar long when a man representing the movie company introduced himself and asked if we would like to be in the bar scene, which was part of a film they were making on nightlife in the Middle East. We, of course, were happy to oblige and quickly joined the actresses at their tables. They were beautiful alright but we had one insurmountable problem. They didn't speak a word of English and we didn't speak a word of their language, which happened to be Spanish. It didn't matter. We smiled at each other a lot and toasted each other with champagne and the director seemed quite happy with our performance.

That evening the first indication that we were going to have trouble with the commodore became apparent. We were all invited to a lovely dinner party in honor of the fleet commander. All the senior officers were there in their dress whites and much of the society and diplomatic service stationed in Beirut were also in attendance. Ned had too much to drink and became overly enamored of some of the ladies present. As a matter of fact, he propositioned one of the ladies at his table and when he got up to leave, he fell down a rather prominent staircase.

The next morning I received a message to report to the fleet commander. He asked me to report on Ned's behavior. While certainly it hadn't been proper, I told the admiral that he was asking me to be disloyal to my commander and I just could not do it. He said that he understood but that he was concerned. He did let me off the hook, however.

Upon leaving Beirut, the *Davis* was ordered to the island of Lesbos. What a beautiful place! It is truly one of the loveliest of the Greek islands in the Aegean. Although it was a tight fit, I was able to moor the *Davis'* stern to the mole. Whenever I was the only Sixth Fleet ship in port I usually gave a reception on board. I would ask the U.S.

embassy in the country in which we were to visit to supply a guest list of about 75 people, representing the heads of the local government, military, service organizations and religious groups. I had a beautiful party deck on board *Davis* which had an awning and, when enclosed by signal flags secured from the awning housing line to the life line, made a wonderful, partially enclosed space, perfect for entertaining groups up to about 75.

My plan for Lesbos was no exception. Everyone that I invited through the embassy accepted. Included in the guest list was a woman by the name of Macaulay. Her father was the great British historian and was then the historian laureate of England. She was in Lesbos to erect a statue of her heroine, Sappho. She had given 20,000 pounds to have it made and erected. She was a nice woman but very much a lesbian, of which she was quite proud. She, like Sappho, was a poetess. She had an ancient coin with Sappho in profile on it and asked me if I saw a resemblance to her? Damn it if she didn't look like Sappho when she was in profile.

I tell the reader all of this because of what followed. Ned Thomas was heavily attracted to her and tried to get her to go to bed with him. She understandably declined and that should have been the end of it, but Ned persisted to the point that he made an ass of himself and upset her.

After a very pleasant visit in which we landed our band and our music of America groups and were well entertained by the locals, in reciprocation for my entertaining them, we left Lesbos. We next anchored at Piraeus, which is the port for Athens. As I let the anchor go, the signal light on the *Springfield* started to blink. It was a message from ComSixthFlt to the commodore to report on board. Ned came by my cabin and asked me to ride over to the flagship with him and I, of course, obliged. While Ned called on the admiral, I visited with friends on board the flagship. He looked pretty grim when I joined him for the boat ride back to the *Davis*.

What apparently had happened was that Macaulay was so upset by Ned that she reported his behavior to the embassy in Athens, who sent on her complaint to the State Department who, in turn, sent it on to the CNO. The CNO had directed ComSixthFlt to investigate it. The admiral told Ned that he was sending Admiral Hannifin to Lesbos to look into the complaint. Ned seemed worried and I, too, was very concerned.

After spending Easter moored in Piraeus, the fleet got underway for the western Mediterranean. We conducted some demonstration exercises just outside the harbor for the embarked Greek Imperial War College. After the demonstration, I was ordered up alongside of the carrier to take the Greek personnel on board and transport them back to port.

After disembarking them we rendezvoused with the fleet. As we started to form the screen around the carrier, the commodore came on the signal bridge, which in a flagship belongs to the embarked flag. He was drunk, and immediately started to put up tactical signals for the destroyers. Destroyer captains are very good at that sort of maneuvering but it is essential that the sequential signals make sense, one to the other. In this case they did not, and the destroyers started to mill around. How embarrassing! I immediately sent for the chief staff officer and ordered him to get the commodore off the bridge, which happily he was able to do. I sorted out the destroyers and got them formed up and we set our course for Barcelona, Spain.

Following two days in transit, a clear message appeared on the fleet broadcast radio schedule. It summarily relieved Ned of his command and ordered him to seek immediate return to the United States upon our arrival in Spain. What a disaster, and a humiliation! It went to all the ships in the fleet in plain language.

Mary Lee was waiting for the ship in Barcelona and she was shocked and saddened by Ned's downfall. We accompanied him to the airport and tried very hard to keep up his spirits.

The next day I had a dispatch from Congressman Flood, my dad's representative in Congress, informing me that my mother had died. I wanted very much to pay my last respects to that wonderful woman and asked the fleet commander whether I might go home on emergency leave. He was terrific about it, and allowed me to turn over the ship to my very fine and well qualified executive officer, Smoky Wentzel. I was on my way the next day and reached home in time for her funeral.

My dad drove me to Maguire Air Force Base in New Jersey to

The author admits that he was "never much of an athlete," but he did make the first team JVs at Wyoming Seminary. The varsity team played at the college freshman level. The author is in the left tackle position in this photo taken in the fall of 1939.

The author scrubs down fore and aft on board the old battleship Arkansas *during his Youngster Year Cruise during the summer of 1942.*

The author's plebe year photo was taken in front of the Academy's pulling cutters with which he got very familiar during Plebe Summer in 1941.

The author appears in full dress, in the fall of 1943.

The Regimental "march on" took place prior to the 1942 Army game played in Annapolis on Farragut Field. The field has long since been replaced by new Academy buildings.

The author's first ship, the U.S.S. Massachusetts, one of a class of four new fast battleships which steamed with the famed Fast Carrier Task Force in the Pacific Fleet.

A group of Massachusetts officers relax on Mog Mog Island in Ulithi Lagoon in early 1945. The "Officers' Club" consisted of a thatched roof hut that contained a bar—and little else.

The Massachusetts fires a nine-gun, 16-inch salvo with devastating accuracy against the huge Japanese Kamaishi Iron and Steel Works on Honshu Island. The bombardment took place on 14 July, 1945.

A gigantic wave hits the starboard bow of the Massachusetts *during a typhoon off Japan in June of 1945. Task Group 38.1, carrying out specific orders from Fleet Commander Admiral Halsey, steamed directly into the eye of the typhoon. The* Massachusetts' *anemometers were carried away when the wind reached 153 knots. The seas were in excess of 85 feet.*

Members of General MacArthur's party enter the Korean Diet Building in Seoul, South Korea, in September 1950. The occasion was the official return of the sovereignty of South Korea to its president, Syngman Rhee. The author is in the front row, coming down the stairs between Lieutenant General Stratemeyer (Commanding General Far East Air Force) and Rear Admiral George Henderson USN (Commander Naval Air Bases Japan). Behind them, from left to right, are Major General Lowe USA (Special Representative of President Truman), Vice Admiral Turner Joy USN (Commander Naval Forces Far East), Vice Admiral Sir William Andrews RN (Senior British Naval Officer Far East), and Lieutenant Duncan Joy USN, Admiral Joy's son.

The U.S.S. Lester (DE 1022) was the author's first command. She was a brand new post-war destroyer escort. Her top speed was 28 knots which, unfortunately, permitted her employment with carriers—albeit at full power—which shortened her life considerably.

The Lester *fuels at sea alongside a carrier. This was just one of approximately 350 times the author's ships were ordered alongside various ships. Although considered routine, a split-second error with the ships steaming about 85 feet apart could well spell disaster.*

The military band, drawn from the ship's company, poses on board the Lester. *The instruments were supplied by the Bureau of Naval Personnel. Because the* Lester *had a relatively small ship's company, the talent was a bit thin, but was nevertheless the pride of the ship. There were also ships' bands in* Davis, Luce *and* Albany. *As the ships grew larger, the talent got appreciably better.*

The smashed lifeboat of the sunken Italian ore ship Bonitos *is photographed as the* Lester *brought her alongside. Two survivors are visible, miraculously clinging to the wreckage. The incident occurred in February 1958 off Cape Hateras.*

The rescue detail succeeded in grabbing one of the survivors but the force of the wind and seas drove the Lester *over the second one. The survivor was literally keelhauled before a* Lester *swimmer dove under the ship and was able to save him.*

The author congratulates the two Italian seamen that were rescued by the Lester *for their great courage and extraordinary good luck.*

The author stands with Rear Admiral Edmund "Whitey" Taylor, Commander Destroyer Force Atlantic Fleet and Commander Task Force 63, on board his flagship Willis A. Lee. *The* Lee, *along with the destroyers and cruiser in the task force, were joined by ships of the Canadian and British navies in Lake St. Louis off Montreal for a formal fleet review. President Eisenhower and Queen Elizabeth II were on board the HMS* Britannia *as she steamed the line.*

Admiral Taylor invited the author's wife Mary Lee to come on board for a luncheon during the International Fleet Review. She is seen here with the author on board Willis A. Lee.

Admiral Taylor, commander of the first Navy task force to enter the Great Lakes since the War of 1812, incident to the celebration of the opening of the Saint Lawrence Seaway, is photographed being escorted by Sam Houston, the superintendent of the monument. Sam later became famous in the Navy for his hilarious performance at the ceremony.

The author organized "The Great Destroyermen's Parade" on Memorial Day 1959. Each ship landed a platoon under arms. Admiral "Whitey" Taylor, Commander Destroyer Force Atlantic Fleet was the reviewing officer. He took the salute at the Ceremonial Square, located between Destroyer Piers One and Two at the Naval Base in Newport, Rhode Island.

Admiral Arleigh Burke, the Chief of Naval Operations, reviewing a brigade full dress parade at the U.S. Naval Academy at Annapolis in 1960. Rear Admiral Davidson, the Superintendent of the Academy is in the foreground. The author is to the right of Admiral Davidson.

The U.S.S. Davis (DD937), a post-war destroyer of the Forrest Sherman Class, was the author's second combatant ship command.

The "E" plaque is presented to the author, when Davis won the Atlantic Fleet Battle Efficiency Excellence Award in 1963. Lieutenant Commander Wenzel, the ship's executive officer, is on the author's right.

Joaquin Balaguer, the president of the Dominican Republic, attends a luncheon in his honor on board the U.S.S. Davis. The Davis was ordered into Santo Domingo because hard intelligence indicated an imminent Communist coup. The Davis demonstrated strong U.S. support for the freely elected Balaguer government and the Communists backed down.

The author's third combatant command was the guided missile destroyer leader U.S.S. Luce (DLG 7).

The author relieves Commander Dave Bagley as commanding officer of the Luce *(DLG 7) in the Norfolk Naval Shipyard in 1963. The author (at podium) was* Luce's *second captain and* Luce *was his third combatant command. Commander Bagley is to the author's left.*

The ship's officers of the U.S.S. Luce (DLG 7) pose for a formal photograph. The ship's 5-inch 54-caliber gun is in the background.

Vietnamese President Lieutenant General Nguyen Van Thieu talks with Rear Admiral Kenneth Veth, Commander Naval Forces Vietnam, and the author at the Vietnamese Naval Academy graduation on 10 August 1967.

This photo was taken during a inspection visit to Coastal Group 34 at Tiem Ton, South Vietnam. Armed junks were used by these groups for coastal patrol and interdiction operations. The prominent eyes painted on all Vietnamese navy armed junks were there to ensure that the junk did not run into an evil spirit at sea.

During an inspection visit, the author talks to Lieutenant Le Van Qui, the commanding officer of the Vietnamese Coastal Group 36, at Long Phu, South Vietnam. A "GO NAVY" sign is proudly displayed on the roof of the advisor's "hootch."

This is a photo taken during an inspection visit to Coastal Group 11. It depicts the U.S. naval advisors assigned to the group as well as corps advisors who accompanied the author. It was this little group that fought to a standstill a North Vietnam main force battalion for six hours until relieved by a U.S. Marine battalion.

Admiral Tran Van Chon, the Chief of Naval Operations of the Vietnamese navy, is depicted presenting the author with the National Order of Vietnam, their highest award, incident to the author's impending detachment in late June 1968.

Rear Admiral Benson, the Commander of the First Naval District, is depicted presenting the author with the Legion of Merit for his service in Vietnam. Erasmus Corning, the long serving and distinguished Mayor of Albany, New York, looks on. Mayor Corning gave the principal address at the Albany commissioning ceremonies held in the Boston Naval shipyard on 9 November 1968.

The heavy guided missile cruiser Albany (CG 10) was the author's forth and last combatant command. She displaced 21,000 tons, was driven by four shafts generating 140,000 horsepower and could reach speeds of 32 knots. She was the first surface combatant to carry digital fire control systems.

The full Marine guard on board the Albany *(CG 10) stands before a Talos missile, during the* Albany's *commissioning ceremony on 9 November 1968.*

The author conducts a petty officer promotion ceremony on board the Albany (CG 10).

The author and his wife Mary Lee pose with their grandchildren in 1972. From left to right they are Randolph, Bradford, Tyler and Emily. As of 2004, all had graduated from college: Randolph from Annapolis, Bradford from Georgia Tech, Tyler from the Savannah School of Art and Design, and Emily from Vanderbilt.

A ceremony is held at Labsphere Inc. on the occasion of the opening of its first building in North Sutton, New Hampshire. Phil Lape, the company's founder, chief scientist and president, is at the microphone. Partners from left to right are Ed Pepper, Pete Fellows, George Peer, the author and Steve Howe.

The author poses with his wife Mary Lee in front of the Taj Mahal during a visit in February of 2001. They were on a four-month world cruise on board the Crystal Symphony.

The author and his wife share a thrilling ride down a narrow road in a basket cart in Madeira, where they visited during a round the world cruise in the Crystal Symphony.

The author's wife Mary Lee in 1998 takes pride in the Japanese water garden at their home in Port Royal, Naples, Florida.

The author and his wife, Mary Lee, celebrated their eightieth birthdays in Naples, Florida in 2003.

catch an Air Force flight back to Europe. Since I was to be the senior officer on board, I was invited to board early and to have my choice of seats. There was an Army major on board who was the officially designated commander of the passenger detail on board. He asked me to sit with him and immediately regaled me with a story. He said that he was in a plane flying from Frankfort to Maguire the previous week. A Navy captain boarded and was obviously drunk. During the early part of the flight he had more to drink and when the plane was well over the Atlantic he tried to force his way into the cockpit and insisted that the plane land in the ocean. It was obviously Ned!

The flight crew was able to subdue him and when they landed at Maguire at about midnight there were about twenty air police and the commanding general of Maguire on the tarmac when the plane came to a stop. He said that they put Ned under arrest and put him in the BOQ to sober him up. When they went for him in the morning he had disappeared!

I knew that Ned was in terrible trouble. I caught a plane from Frankfort to Naples where I planned to catch a COD aircraft to the carrier so that I could rejoin my ship. I was able to spend a little time with Mary Lee in Naples and, of course, told her what had happened. We agreed that I had to try to help Ned if I could.

When I landed on the carrier, the flag immediately had me transferred to the *Davis* by helo. The ship was in fine shape, and I lost no time in getting a letter written to Admiral Smedberg, the then Chief of Naval Personnel whom I knew quite well. I told him that I knew that Ned was in serious trouble but I asked him to consider his previous distinguished performance and to consider that he had a disease, such as cancer. He was not a bad man; he was just very sick. Two weeks later they caught up with Ned and, happily, Admiral Smedberg agreed with me. He had him admitted to Bethesda Naval Hospital. One week after his admission he died. It's a tragic story of the disintegration of a brilliant and charming man.

Not long after Ned's departure our new commodore, Captain Elwood Baldridge was waiting for the ship upon our arrival in Genoa, Italy. I had known Baldridge before. He and I had words during the Hazelwood tour. While on the Near Eastern patrol, ComSixthFlt had ordered the cruiser *Springfield* to deliver a much needed ship's jeep to us. When the jeep arrived in Beirut on board *Springfield*, I, as exec, went over to check it out. It was an absolute wreck and I refused to take custody of it. Baldridge was the exec of the *Springfield* and was not happy with me. I insisted that *Springfield* had an obligation to deliver a workable vehicle in reasonable condition. Much against his will he substituted a better jeep but the incident did not set well with him. Now he was to be my commodore. He knew that he was coming on board one of the best destroyers in the force and he acted accordingly. He never mentioned the jeep, nor did I.

In July, the ship was ordered into Cannes for almost the entire month. It was a great opportunity to be with my family in an absolutely beautiful port and I immediately made plans for Mary Lee and the children to join me there. I found a great apartment along La Croisette, the avenue in Cannes that runs along the entire bay. It was in a beautiful apartment house called *Le Admiral*. The plan was for me to have it for two weeks and then the commodore was going to take it over for the last two weeks. After a harrowing drive from Naples which lasted over ten hours, Mary Lee, the children and Cartuffels arrived. We had an absolutely wonderful time. As a matter of fact we had such a good time that the commodore relinquished his two weeks so that the family could stay on.

Mary Lee and I gave a small dinner on the party deck of the *Davis* on Bastille Day, the 15th of July, 1962. It was a glorious evening, and we were treated to the most wonderful display of synchronized fireworks that we had ever seen.

We completed our deployment in October. My family sailed for home on board the SS *Constellation* and we departed the Med for home soon thereafter.

We arrived off Newport, after an uneventful transit, in early November. It was a typical overcast November day in Newport, with a fresh wind coming out of the northeast at about 25 knots. *Davis* was assigned an inboard berth on the south side of Pier One. Thus we had a strong wind setting us off. I had my crew at quarters and my band playing its usual repertoire of martial music. There was a crowd of about 300 people on the pier including ComDesLant himself, as well as the force band. I made my approach and was able to get number one line over but I had fetched up too soon. Try as I might I was unable to twist the ship into the pier because of the heavy wind on my port side holding me off. Eventually my band ran out of numbers and so did the force band. I struggled for what seemed like a century and finally cast off to try again. On the bridge radio circuit I heard operations order a tug to assist *Davis* in her mooring. Destroyers don't generally need tugs and I was embarrassed and humiliated. I finally made the landing and reluctantly went down to the quarterdeck to welcome the force commander on board. He, of course, was too polite to say anything, but his chief of staff, Bob Guy after passing through the sideboys, whispered, "Nice landing, Allan." I never liked Guy much after that. For weeks after I would find myself remonstrating with myself over that seamanship disaster.

We were ordered to Boston to undergo an interim shipyard availability. It was a period of about six weeks for repairs and alterations and a very welcome rest for the ship's company. We arrived in Boston and immediately started the process of entering the yard, which meant taking off all of our ammunition and opening the ship for some strenuous repair and alteration work. The day after we discharged our ammunition, the electrifying news reached us that the president had demanded that the Soviet Union remove the intercontinental ballistic missiles that they had surreptitiously installed in Cuba. To enforce the United States demands he declared an immediate naval blockade of Cuba. Destroyers Atlantic were to be the principal blockade force. I immediately sent a dispatch to the force commander telling him that we could be ready for sea in 24 hours. By return dispatch he ordered me to return to full operational status and put to sea as soon as ready. In less than 24 hours *Davis* was underway for Cuban waters.

We were immediately assigned to a blockade station and our rules of engagement authorized the commanding officers to open fire on any vessel who, after being suitably warned, tried to run the blockade. We were on the brink of war with the Soviet Union. At the very last minute they blinked and ordered their ships to turn around for home. The entire First Marine Division, reinforced, was embarked in an amphibious lift with full battle equipment. That outfit was fully intending to land in Cuba, but the decision to land them had to be made fairly soon as they were starting to run out of beans.

While the issue was still in doubt, *Davis* received a top secret dispatch directly from commander in chief Atlantic Fleet. It directed *Davis* to proceed at best speed to Windward Passage and once there to await further orders. Man! We were going to lead the attack! At least that's what everyone on board thought. But that was not to be the case. While en route, the Soviets backed off and the landings were canceled.

When we arrived in Windward Passage we received another highly classified dispatch directing us into Santo Domingo, the capital of the Dominican Republic. The United States had received highly credible intelligence reports that the Communists were about to start a revolution against the freely elected Balaguer government and our job was to show immediate and strong U.S. support for Balaguer. Our arrival in the Dominican Republic was cheered by the democratic press and jeered by the Communists. I set about inviting the president to a dinner on board. We sent our various musical groups wherever we could get an invitation and we, along with the U.S. ambassador, did what we could to show U.S. support for the president. It apparently worked, because the Communists behaved themselves. They never did try to unseat Balaguer. We were able to chalk up another win for gunboat diplomacy.

On returning to Newport, I was delighted and thrilled to find orders there to report to the U.S.S. *Luce* as her commanding officer. *Luce* was one of nine new guided missile destroyer leaders and I was to be rewarded with command of one of them. What an absolute delight to contemplate! Before departing, I was informed that *Davis* had won the Atlantic Fleet Battle Efficiency Excellence Award for 1963. What a thrill for all hands!

A Commander Green was ordered in as my relief and he was not long in coming. My departure, however, was to again be marred by personal tragedy. I had always suspected that our new Commodore El Baldridge was gay. He, in addition to not being married, seemed to consort with men that were highly suspect. It never came up while I was on board. As a matter of fact he gave a lovely farewell dinner party for us at his rather attractive living quarters on Bellevue Avenue. Almost as soon as I left the ship, the news reached us that he was summarily marched off the *Davis* by agents of the Office of Naval Intelligence. Apparently he had tried to seduce the barber on the destroyer *Compton* and the commanding officer turned him in. He tried and failed to commit suicide in the Naval Hospital. He was asked to resign his commission, which he did, and thus forfeited all of his retirement pay and benefits—a very sad ending to a career that extended almost to thirty years.

Chapter 15

U.S.S. *Luce,* 1964–1965

INCE OUR QUARTERS on Jones Street went with command of the *Davis* it was necessary for us to find new quarters almost immediately. Peter King came to our rescue once again. He found a delightful furnished rental on Barclay Square, one of the loveliest areas in all of Newport. The home belonged to the Newbolds, who were summer residents. It was a fine house, beautifully situated with handsome grounds and a marvelous view of the ocean.

I left my little family there while I got underway for my new assignment. I didn't report directly to the ship as my orders took me to the Navy Guided Missile School at Dam Neck, Virginia. There I took several courses in preparation for taking command of my first missile ship. It was to be a fulfillment of a dream. I had talked about, taught, and written extensively about the future of missiles in the ships of the Navy and now I was to take an active part in that vitally important integration.

While *Luce* was homeported in Mayport, Florida, she was undergoing an interim availability in the Naval Shipyard at Portsmouth, Virginia. I relieved Commander Dave Bagley, her first commanding officer, while the ship was still in dry-dock. It wasn't much of a change of command ceremony, given that we were not in our home port, but my dad did manage to come down for it and I was delighted to have him.

I was quickly made to feel very welcome on board as the officers and men uniformly disliked Bagley. He was personally very tough and was, from my observations, solely interested in the operation of the ship. The crew was not smart and the ship-keeping was downright awful. It didn't take me long to issue my longstanding policies on standards and the balanced approach I intended to pursue as commanding officer. While I, of course, recognized the great importance of operational effectiveness, I stressed to the ship's company the importance of military standards of smartness and cleanliness as well as the absolute necessity of high standards of administration. I ensured that my policy statement was issued to every officer and man on board.

The ship's company soon learned that what I had promulgated to them in writing was the exact way I intended to run the ship. That took a lot of getting used to. The hallmark of my approach was absolute consistency, or as absolute as human nature can be consistent. If we had a rule, that rule was to be uniformly enforced, not enforced only when someone was looking or when someone felt out of sorts, but enforced all the time. That's hard to do, especially when you feel full of grace. But to be successful it is essential that the ship's company knows without question what is expected of it. That doesn't make the captain particularly beloved, but, on the other hand, I noted early on that if you show me a ship in which the captain is loved, I will show you a lousy ship.

I reported to Commander Destroyer Squadron 8, commanded by Captain Eli Vinock in Mayport. Since we were scheduled for local operations for the next several months after reporting, I was able to house hunt for my family. Fortunately, an old shipmate who served with me on DESLANT's staff came through for us. He owned a very nice, furnished home not far from the base, which he agreed to rent to me until we were able to find permanent quarters. I returned to Newport and packed up my family for the drive to Florida. Mary Lee and the children were delighted with the Zeni home and it made a fine base of operations for our search for permanent quarters.

Being in Mayport was an absolute delight. The weather was warm but pleasant. The base was small but quite adequate. There was a fine commissary, good medical support, a new officers' club and even a golf course. What was particularly nice was that the nearby Ponte Vedra Club invited the commanding officers to be honorary members at no cost to them.

The Ponte Vedra Club was beautiful. Mary Lee was delighted with the splendid golf course and made extensive use of it. It had a wonderful beach club associated with it and we rented a cabana so that we all could enjoy the beach and the club's many facilities to the fullest. It wasn't long before we made many friends among its members, which ensured that our tour in Mayport was going to be very pleasant.

Before long Mary Lee found a wonderful rental house in a subdivision in Atlantic Beach called Indian Woods. The house suited us perfectly and we moved in without delay.

We decided to put the children in a private Episcopal school about 45 minutes by car from our home. Mary Lee was willing to make the trip twice a day if it was truly superior to the public schools, but much to our disappointment, it proved not to be the case. We withdrew both of them and entered them in the local school system, which turned out to be more than adequate.

Randy joined the ship's little league team that was coached by our chief sonarman. He had a wonderful time playing baseball that season. Our normal routine was interrupted by the visit of a French navy guided missile destroyer. *Luce* was made the host ship and I spent considerable time arranging a full social and professional schedule for it. The visit, while a great success, didn't do much to endear the French officers to me. In all previous contacts that I had had with the French navy I found their officers to be somewhat arrogant, and this was no exception. I believe that they suffer from a collective inferiority complex. Soon after that visit our class went before the captain's selection board and happily my name was on the list of those selected.

We received orders to deploy to the Sixth Fleet with the nuclear powered aircraft carrier *Enterprise*. For more than a year prior to our scheduled deployment, the Soviets were sending out their long-range bombers, designated by us as Bears. Their mission was to shadow our ships in the Atlantic. To thwart their efforts the fleet commander ordered *Enterprise*, escorted by *Luce* and a sister ship *Farragut*, to make a high-speed transit from the United States to Gibraltar under conditions of strict radio silence. We were not even authorized to use our tactical radios.

The speed of advance was specified at an astounding 25 knots! Considering that we had to fuel frequently and also conduct flight operations, the ships would be required to steam at least 27 knots to meet our SOA requirements. For the first time in my long experience in the fleet, fueling speed was set at 27 knots. I considered it unacceptably dangerous. Our normal fleet replenishing speed was 12 knots. Even at that speed going up alongside another ship and conducting fueling or other transfers at about 80 feet between ships is hazardous at best. To more than double the speed amplified any steering error exponentially. We did it several times during the transit without mishap, but I was less than happy. The radio silence was also annoying, since the carrier conducted flight operations all the way across, which required that they use ship to air communications as well as Tacan. Tacan is a beacons system universally used in the fleet to give the aviators continuous information on the whereabouts of the carrier. Certainly any Bear aircraft would be able to intercept this electronic location information.

Because of our incredibly high speed we used an enormous amount of fuel, so much so that the *Enterprise* literally ran out as we approached Gibraltar. A fleet oiler had to get underway from the Sixth Fleet to rendezvous with us while still in the Atlantic, to supply fuel to *Farragut* and *Luce*.

The in-transit task group commander knew that we were damned unhappy with the entire transit. He tried to smooth it over at the Sixth Fleet turnover anchorage by recognizing the seamanship feat that we had accomplished and, with an air of levity, he presented both the skipper of *Farragut* and me with a rather elaborate scroll entitled " Sixth Fleet Pucker Factor Award." I failed to see the humor in hazarding the safety of our ships to conduct a stunt.

I should have known that this rather short deployment was not to be the smooth operation that we enjoyed in *Davis*. Mary Lee had such a good time on the *Davis'* deployment that we decided that she should come to the Med once again, as we had been scheduled for some very interesting ports of call. As we steamed trough the Straits of Gibraltar, we received word that the Turks had landed troops on Cyprus and the Greeks were preparing to go to war. *Luce* received a high priority message to precede at best speed to take over the job of Cyprus patrol commander. My job and that of the one other destroyer assigned was to literally steam between the Greek and Turkish naval forces to try to keep them from engaging. Of course, all of our port visits were canceled and I spent my time for three months either on patrol or in Suda Bay, not exactly the ideal liberty port.

Poor Mary Lee had to fend for herself for much of the time. Mary Lee and I did finally meet up in Nice but for only about a week. I was tired and Mary Lee was quite unwell so we did not have a great reunion. She returned home on the SS *France* and I followed soon after.

Operations in and around Mayport were routine and, on the whole, quite pleasant. We were scheduled for and received a board of inspection and survey inspection, which is conducted by a major off-ship team. It is rigorous, comprehensive, and mighty tough, extending over a few days. We were proud to be told by Admiral Reiter, the president of the board at the critique, that *Luce* was the all around best ship that his board had inspected to date. He gave us an enormously high mark, which gratified all hand and rewarded them for the great effort that they had expended getting ready for the inspection.

One local operation took us around Florida to Pensacola to plane guard for the *Lexington*, who had been assigned to the Naval Flight Training Center as the school carrier. It was nice to steam in company with a World War II heavy carrier. The old *Lex* was really on her last legs. The grand old ship that had steamed with us in the exciting campaigns in the Pacific was soon to go out of commission and be scrapped.

Another local exercise which was enormously interesting involved our operating with a Polaris submarine off Cape Canaveral. The U.S. was just getting into the development of a missile defense system. It was our job to try to pick up the Polaris missile as it breached the surface, lock on and track it down-range to the maximum capability of our tracking radars. We were pretty darn successful in picking them up and locking on. We couldn't hold on to them very long, however, because they were soon at our outermost tracking capability.

I embarked Randy for this short cruise as I thought he might enjoy going to sea with his dad. He had a fine time on board. On the way back to Mayport he asked me whether we might fire the *Luce's* five-inch guns. Since we had not exercised the guns for quite a while I thought it might be well to test fire them. At an appropriate time I put the ship at general quarters. Randy was on the bridge with me. We planned to fire the five-inch 54 just forward of the bridge, and set up to do so. I asked Randy whether he was ready and he indicated that he was. I gave the command to fire. The gun went off and when I looked around Randy had been knocked flat on his butt by the concussion of the rounds. Being used to the sound of gunfire in movies that he had seen, he never dreamed that the real concussion and noise of a five-inch shell was going to be so enormous.

Soon after our return to Mayport we were informed that *Luce* had been awarded the Atlantic Fleet Battle Efficiency Excellence Award for 1963. With our similar success in *Davis*, that made two in a row and seemed to ratify my approach to naval command. Of course, all hands were mighty proud and I was mighty proud of them for beating some enormously tough competition.

As summer approached fall in 1964, I received orders to go to Washington to report to the Chief of Naval Personnel. I was to head up a new activity that was to concentrate on our low reenlistment and retention rates.

Mary Lee and the children preceded me to Washington so that Mary Lee could enroll the children in Landon and Holton Arms before the academic year began. I joined her in Washington as soon as possible after I was relieved. She had been having a tough time physically, which necessitated her turning in to Bethesda Naval Hospital. By the time I arrived she had almost completely recovered and we both looked forward to being together after a very long period of fleet-enforced separations.

Chapter 16

Washington 1964–1967

I ARRIVED IN WASHINGTON in mid-September. Mary Lee had been discharged from the hospital and had taken temporary quarters at an apartment hotel at the junction of Wisconsin and Massachusetts Avenues. The children were already in school and so the important order of business was to find suitable housing.

We looked at various homes to buy in Bethesda and Potomac. We found a beautiful home in a lovely new residential area in Bethesda being developed by a local builder by the name of Spotswood Quinby. It would have been perfect for us, but it was priced at $84,000, which was pretty much out of our range. We went off to Wilkes Barre to visit my dad for a few days and to ask his advice. He encouraged us to stretch for it. On our return to Washington, we found, much to our disappointment, that the house had already been sold. We were, of course, disappointed, but Quinby offered to build a very similar house for about the same price on a still undeveloped lot.

We decided to go for it and signed a purchase and sales agreement. Mary Lee decided that she wanted French style architecture, and envisioned a slate mansard roof and white brick veneer siding. Spotswood estimated that the design and construction would take about eight months, which meant we had to find temporary quarters. We were able to get a furnished apartment at a lovely new complex at the intersection of Wisconsin Avenue and the Beltway. Pooks Hill was almost ideal for our purpose, except for one major drawback. The management would not let us have our beloved dachshund Cartuffels in the apartment. This necessitated our finding a suitable kennel for him. It broke our hearts to have to be separated from him for all those months but there just was no help for it. The separation was particularly hard on Cartuffels as he felt that we were deserting him.

I reported to Bupers (Bureau of Navy Personnel) in late October. I was to head up a new section, which was to focus on the Navy's retention problem, which in 1964 was becoming acute. All I had was an office and access to a secretary, which suited me fine since I had a great deal of thinking to do about how best to approach this extremely important, but chronically intractable, problem.

After thinking about it for several days I came to the conclusion that retention was a symptom. I reasoned it was not much different than a headache and fever which were symptoms of a disease. Our unacceptably low reenlistment rates and officer retention rates were symptomatic of all the facets of service in the Navy that directly or indirectly affected the lives, the well being, the morale and the personal lives of our personnel. If our enlistment and retention rates were unacceptably low, then this was symptomatic of too many adverse conditions of service that our personnel had to endure.

I further reasoned that if this problem was critical to the Navy's basic readiness, then the problem did not belong in Bupers. It belonged on the agenda of the very top leadership of the Navy, not only because of its importance, but also because it would require the support of that level of command to make the necessary changes.

Having drawn that basic conclusion, I spent the next few days preparing a paper putting forth my thesis. When I felt that I had it about right, I called Captain Elmo Zumwalt who was the aide to Mr. Paul Nitze, the secretary of the Navy. I told Zumwalt that I had a paper that I would like very much to show him. He invited me to the SecNav mess for lunch, and over to the Pentagon I went. During a very cordial lunch he took time to read my paper. He was impressed! He said that he would get back to me as soon as he could. I got back to my office about one thirty and at three o'clock Zumwalt called to say that he had shown my paper to the secretary and he had not only agreed with my thesis but that he was having Bupers order me to his immediate office that very afternoon.

Oh, oh! All of this without my boss, the Chief of Naval Personnel knowing about it. I waited for the explosion, and it wasn't a half hour before I had a call from the chief's aide asking me to see Vice Admiral Semmes as soon as possible. I expected the worst, but was delighted to find that Admiral Semmes had a copy of my paper, which the secretary had sent to him along with his desire that I immediately move to his office. I knew Admiral Semmes very well, as he was a destroyerman and he knew me as a destroyer captain, as an aide to Commander Destroyer Force U.S Atlantic Fleet and aide to the Chief of Naval Operations. He was not only extremely cordial but he also expressed his complete agreement with my conclusions. He wished me well and pledged the full support of the Bureau of Personnel in the long effort ahead.

Not only did the SecNav agree to mount the effort but he directed that the very best officers in the Navy be assembled to undertake the task. From myself the effort eventually grew to twenty-two officers headed by a Rear Admiral Alford. Just about everyone ordered to our new task force was senior to me, but in order for me to maintain a central focus on the effort I was named executive secretary. As soon as the Marine Corps heard about the establishment of our task force they wanted in as well, and ordered several marine officers to join us. By and large all of the officers selected to report to SecNav for this duty were among the best in both the Navy and Marine Corps.

In a memorandum of 22 December 1964, the secretary of the Navy set forth the charter of a policy board and a task force. The policy board was structured to advise him and the task force was to function as a working group. He charged them with two basic functions. First, to identify and examine the major factors bearing on retention of high quality officers and enlisted personnel. Second, to develop a plan for attacking these retention problems, which was to include specific recommendations, a program to implement the approved recommendations, and the identification of the specific government offices or activities which are presently empowered to implement such actions.

The secretary, in this same memorandum, outlined for the task force an unprecedented breadth for its study. He specifically charged that it must examine opportunities for education and training, as well as promotion and advancement; that it must study personnel distribution policies, the relationship between fleet manning and retention, sea/shore rotation policies including overseas duties, fringe benefits for both officers and enlisted personnel, habitability afloat, and personnel support facilities and housing ashore. He directed that it look into the Navy and Marine Corps' public images within, as well as outside the service, all aspects of compensation, working hours afloat and ashore, prerogatives of rank of officers and petty officers and their relationship to retention.

The policy board which he appointed to assist him in monitoring and evaluating the efforts of the task force consisted of the secretary as chairman, the under secretary, the Chief of Naval Operations, the Chief of Naval Personnel, the commandant of the Marine Corps, several other top military personnel in the Navy Department, three assistant secretaries of defense and two deputy assistants. Boy, when I held that the retention issue must be elevated to what amounted to the board of directors of the naval service I never envisioned that the secretary would have agreed so completely.

Thus we embarked on a year of monumental effort, an effort that was to produce 130 recommendations. Of these, 115 were recommended for approval by the policy board and subsequently approved by the secretary on 25 January 1966.

I had overall coordination of the effort, as well as responsibility for all recommendations affecting the surface line officer community. While it is not my intention to reproduce or comment on the broad range of recommendations that were approved, since I had both a special interest as well as specific responsibilities in regard to the surface line community, I will address the important recommendations which I brought forth in this area.

I found that the surface line community was the only officer community, not only in the Navy but also in the entire armed forces, that had no prereporting training. The lack of readiness to perform efficiently on board their fist ship had a serious adverse impact on the young surface officers' morale. Incident to my investigation, I undertook an analysis of the Naval Academy curriculum. Here I found that the Academy had almost completely eliminated such nuts and bolts training of the midshipmen in favor of "academic enrichment." I was so taken back by what I found that I wrote a letter to this effect to the president of the Naval Academy Alumni Association, Vice Admiral William Smedberg U.S.N. (Ret). Admiral Smedberg had been the Chief of Naval Personnel when I was with Admiral Burke as his aide. Admiral Smedberg was so taken by my letter that he ordered that it be published in its entirety in *Shipmate*, the magazine published by the alumni association. In order to try to soften the impact on the Naval Academy, he and I agreed that it would be published as a letter from me to the commandant of midshipmen. Because what I wrote in 1965 is even more true today, I include the entire text of the letter below, and a supporting letter from Real Admiral Kaufman:

Dear Captain Kinney,

I would like to follow up our talk on the Surface Combatant School with a few comments on the present drive of the Naval Academy towards academic enrichment.

While I, of course, believe it important to maintain high academic standards, I think that we must recognize that, unless we completely abrogate our responsibilities to our midshipmen to give them sufficient grounding in their chosen profession, we can never compete on a completely academic basis with other engineering schools that have the capability of concentrating solely on academic endeavors and, what's more, I don't think that we should.

The Naval Academy has served the Navy and the country magnificently during its long history. Its only pretense for existing has been that it has trained fine naval officers. Not fine engineers, not fine mathematicians, not fine scientists, but fine naval officers. The unrestricted line officer, which, of course, comprises our largest officer community, is essentially a manager. While he must be sufficiently grounded in engineering subjects to permit him to grasp technological fundamentals, I know of few if any URL officers who are in the business of direct engineering, nuclear or electronic design or who are scientists. At best, the seagoing officer is only a part-time specialist ashore and he invariably is cast as a manager of technological projects. It is in the management area that I feel our academic focus should be placed at the undergraduate level.

In my view, the most precious contribution that the Naval Academy has been able to make in the development of young officers is instilling in them a desire to serve. Other officer sources have been unable to come close. This intangible, indefinable, illusive attribute must be carefully protected and nurtured. If we lose this, no matter how fine a education we offer, it will do the Navy little good. While it is impossible to isolate this indefinable quality of Naval Academy life which engenders this desire to serve, I would suspect that it is the professional naval atmosphere, the professional indoctrination and the professional training gained in a tough military environment—an environment which is seeped in the traditions of the Navy—that contribute greatly to this element. I would look with infinite care at any change in the Naval Academy environment, regime or curriculum which might tend to upset this important quality.

It seems to me that the prestige throughout the country that the Naval Academy enjoys and thus one of its great attractions has been founded upon its reputation as an institution possessing extremely high standards, which require a real man to face its challenges and to succeed. If this challenge is removed I am afraid the great prestige that the Naval Academy enjoys will be seriously derogated and so will its ability to attract the kind of young men we so desperately need. The Naval Academy must remain a symbol of pride throughout the country and I believe that we must resist any action that would tend to tarnish the elements that comprise this symbol.

Again many thanks for your hospitality last week and warmest personal regards,

Sincerely
Allan P. Slaff Captain, U.S.N.

I have read Allan Slaff's letter to Sheldon Kinney and agree with it completely. In the process of markedly improving the academic program over the last eight years, the relative effectiveness of our professional education and training was somewhat reduced. Our major project this year on which we are now concentrating, is to bring this aspect of the Academy back to its former position of eminence. Further, we are convinced that we can do this while still pursuing the academic excellence so necessary in a highly complex and difficult world."

Draper Kaufman, Rear Admiral, U.S.N. Superintendent

The establishment of a surface officers prereporting school became one of my principal recommendations, which was approved and implemented.

The next major issue that I examined was who comprised the surface officer community? The submarine service had a discrete designator for submarine officers, the air Navy had a discrete designator or, more precisely, an entire family of designators for aviation officers of various types. A plethora of all kinds of officers, including Waves, also shared the 1100 designator assigned to surface officers. (The Navy used and still uses a 4-digit number to identify officers of the various officer communities.)

There just was no way to identify a surface warfare officer. Thus it was essential that a new designator discretely identifying this group of officers be developed and assigned. At the time, the 1100 designator was really used as the garbage can of the officer designation system. If, for instance, an aviation officer was drummed out of naval aviation, he wasn't called before the command to have his stripes ripped off; he was stripped of his 1300 aviation designator and was given an 1100 designator. What a disgrace! Thus, to differentiate the true going-to-sea surface warfare officer, a new distinct designator was recommended and approved.

Both the air and submarine service had qualification programs for their officers and enlisted men. In the case of aviation officers they won their wings. In the case of submarine officers they won their dolphin. In the case of the surface warfare officers they didn't have any qualification program and certainly no insignia. Thus I brought a recommendation forward, which was subsequently approved and implemented, to establish a surface warfare qualification program and a surface warfare device not unlike the aviation and submarine communities had long had.

During the implementation phase of the effort, I attended a meeting for this approved recommendation. Present at the meeting was an Admiral Bell, a fine submariner. He allowed as to his not understanding why our community should feel the need for such a device. Wasn't the fact that we wore a naval officer's uniform sufficient to satisfy our need for prestige? Admiral Bell was wearing civilian clothes. He had a miniature dolphin insignia carefully affixed to his buttonhole. I pointed out to him that he was sufficiently proud of being a submariner that he wore his insignia on his civilian jacket and that we too were proud of our surface warfare community. I embarrassed him but he remained very quiet for the remainder of the meeting. The surface warfare community got its qualification program and its surface warfare device.

Pursuant to the secretary's charge to us, we undertook an initiative to determine how the Navy and the Marine Corps were viewed by the U.S. public. We engaged the prestigious polling company of Louis Harris and Associates. They conducted a blind survey of a maximum sampling of 2200 people. I was interested to find that the cost of the survey was not primarily the size of the sample but how often the survey taker was required to try to interview the scientifically selected person to be surveyed. In our case we chose the maximum call back of four times.

What we found from this survey was that our image was much less than we would have hoped it would be. Our bluejackets were held to be women-chasing, happy-go-lucky men with little intellectual capacity. Our officers were seen as sort of fun-loving Rover Boys, again lacking in substance. Never mind that both were manning and operating ships of incredible complexity, that they worked 80 to 100 hours a week and that they sacrificed a normal home life to serve their country. Lou Harris' survey tried to determine how the perception of the U. S. public's image of the Navy personnel was formed. When asked if mass entertainment programs that ridiculed naval officers, such as "McHale's Navy," influenced their impression of naval personnel, most said that they didn't. However, questions buried in the interview revealed that that was exactly how the image of naval personnel was formed by a large segment of the U.S. population.

In discussing these findings with Lou Harris he cautioned us that we must ensure that the image we wanted to project reflected the true situation among our personnel. We could not fool the U.S. public by trying to project an image that was not true. We had a lot of work to do there.

Meanwhile, our new home was completed and we moved in on the 1st of July, 1965. We loved it. It was truly everything that we had wanted in a home and Mary Lee had us settled in in quick order. Randy had returned to the Landon School and Valerie to Holton Arms. Our home was perfectly situated between the two.

Valerie was now ten and enormously interested in being an actress. It was her custom to scan the audition notices in *The Washington Post*. She found one that interested her greatly. The American Light Opera Company was auditioning for a production of *The King and I* and she was determined to try out for one of the princess's roles. Mary Lee took her down to the audition and, although there was a huge turnout, our daughter won one of the roles! This was in mid-August. The company was to be in rehearsal until the show opened in mid-September and then they planned to give seventeen performances.

After the initial excitement about Valerie getting the part, reality set in. She had to be at rehearsal every evening at Listner Auditorium, which is located on the George Washington University campus in downtown Washington. It immediately became my job to take her to rehearsal. I was completely involved in the SecNav's office in the Pentagon. I got home just in time to grab a bite of supper and start for downtown. It was too far for me to return home, so I had to stay at the rehearsal.

The first evening there I sat in the back of the rehearsal hall reading my *Time* magazine. At the end of the first break one of the assistants came back to ask me what I was doing there. I explained that I was Valerie's daddy and that it was too far to go home. I offered to leave, however, if that was desired. He assured me that I could stay and left. At the second break he returned and asked me if I was an actor. I gave him a very positive no and went back to my magazine. After the last break he once again came to the back of the room and told me that the director had asked him to ask me if I wouldn't audition for the part of Captain Ortin, the skipper of the ship that carried Anna and her son, Louis, to Siam. I tried to decline, but Valerie was there then and she begged me to give it a try, so up to the audition room I went. I must have displayed some minor latent talent because they offered me the part. I quickly and emphatically declined, pointing out that I had never done any acting. It was Friday evening and they asked me to think about it over the weekend before I gave them a definite no.

Well I was subjected to a full-court press at home. Mary Lee pointed out that I had been away from my daughter for three years in *Davis* and *Luce*, and here was a wonderful chance to enjoy some togetherness with her, etc., etc. I finally caved in, and there began my career on the stage. My part was minimal. As I recall, I had 16 lines in three scenes. The leading lady was a very attractive British actress who spent considerable time teaching me to say my lines with a British accent. With a great deal of makeup, my ancient nautical uniform and my spiffy newly acquired British accent I was a completely new man. Half the Pentagon came to see me and many had to admit they didn't recognize me. What a ham!

To put it mildly, the show was a smash hit. The twenty-three-hundred seat theater was sold out quickly for all performances. To accommodate the demand, instead of 17 performances as advertised, we ended up giving 37. As for the togetherness with Valerie, it never happened. Even on the days we had a matinee and evening performance, I found myself having supper at the Hot Shop alone. Valerie was much too busy having supper with the princes! We even took the show to Baltimore and played to a sold out audience in the same theater Mr. Lincoln attended during his presidency. When they raised the possibility that we would also go to Richmond I told them that I was out. Fortunately, they didn't go. If they had, this Captain Orten would have been relieved.

I had so looked forward to coming ashore, especially so since it would be possible for Mary Lee and me to get down to the Naval Academy to see the Navy team play. That stint in the theater not only ruined my football season but it ruined my social life and sex life as well. Looking back on it now, I'm glad I did it, as we've had a lot of fun through the years talking about my short but hectic career on the stage. Valerie, by the way, was wonderful, and she had a super great time, much to the chagrin of the faculty at Holton Arms School.

As the show closed, coincidentally we entered the implementation phase of moving the approved recommendations into reality. The secretary was anxious that the entire Navy be briefed on the results of our efforts. He designated me and Tazewell Shepard to undertake an extensive speaking tour all over the Navy. Taz and I developed a presentation in which we spoke as a team, with rather extensive graphics. We had a fine time together until we reached San Diego. After our presentation to personnel at North Island we were returning to our room at the Hotel Del Coronado. We left our car and, as we were walking to the hotel, Taz froze. His back had gone into a tight spasm and he was just not able to take another step. With the aid of a few young boys who were playing on the hotel grounds I was able to get him to our room. I called the hospital and they picked him up in an ambulance. He suffered from a severe back problem for many years. When I was aide to Admiral Burke, Taz was also withdrawn for the War College to be the Naval aide to President Kennedy. His father-in-law, Senator Sparkman, was greatly responsible for his appointment. During his tenure as the president's aide he was able to avail himself of the services of Dr. Tavel, the president's personal physician. Through the use of heavy injections of Novocain she was able to keep the president functioning, and Taz as well. I, regretfully, had to leave Taz in San Diego and go on to Hawaii by myself.

Not long after my return to Washington I was summoned to Admiral Hyman Rickover's office. His office was in what was then called Main Navy, located on Constitution Avenue. It was a collection of temporary buildings from World War I that had not yet been torn down. They were collectively a public eyesore but were nevertheless still being utilized by the Navy. His office was a disgrace. His furniture was dilapidated and even his floor covering was worn out linoleum.

It wasn't long before I found out what he wanted of me. He, of course, knew about our Task Force and he wanted me to recommend that the Naval Academy be disestablished. I was incredulous. I told him that in my view the Naval Academy had traditionally served the Navy and the country with distinction and I wasn't about to recommend its disestablishment. I pointed out to him that the Academy was the prime source of regular officers, who had always been the nucleus upon which the Navy relied to expand in time of crisis and it was also the repository of much of the great traditions of the service. I asked him where he thought the Navy could find the nucleus of the regular officer corps if we didn't have the Academy. He responded by saying that we could get all the regulars we wanted from the enlisted ranks. When he determined that I wasn't going to budge, he unceremoniously threw me out of his office.

On the way back to the Pentagon I contemplated my fate. While generally held in low regard in the Navy, he was probably one of the most powerful admirals in Washington because of his incredible political support. Even Admiral Burke didn't want to tangle with him. I hadn't been back in my office more than a half an hour when my secretary told me that the Chief of Naval Personnel wanted to talk with me on the phone. Oh, oh! Admiral Semmes, after saying good morning, asked me what happened between Admiral Rickover and me. I told him what Admiral Rickover wanted and that I had refused and had essentially told him that he was full of hops. Semmes laughed and told me that he had just had a phone call from Admiral Rickover telling him what I fine officer I was.

In the fall of 1966, the major command board met on our year group. It is a board made up of line admirals who choose officers in the grade of captain for major commands. Admiral Chuck Nace in '39 was a member of the board and also a member of our task force. Upon completion of the board's work he very discretely told me that I was selected as number one on the surface line major command list. It wasn't a day later when I was summoned to Admiral Semmes office. I, of course, lost no time in getting over to Bupers to call on him. He seemed to be in an expansive mood. After greeting me, he told me that he had great news for me; I had been selected number one on the major command list. Since he could just as easily have told me this great news on the telephone I knew that another shoe was about to drop, and drop it did. He informed me that the Vice Chief of Naval Operations wanted me to go to Vietnam as senior naval advisor to straighten out and strengthen the naval advisory effort. He had a deal for me: I could have any major combatant ship in the fleet, and I could go to either the National War College or to the Harvard Business School if I would agree to go to Vietnam. Oh boy, how was I going to tell this to Mary Lee?

I asked him if I could discus it with Mary Lee before I gave him my answer. I should have known; my wonderful wife never even slightly stepped out of character. She encouraged me to do my duty and assured me that she would hold the fort at home. We decided that I was probably best advised to choose Harvard over the National War College since I was already a graduate of the Naval War College. That one decision was to have a major impact on the rest of my life.

The next day I informed Admiral Semmes of my decision and

he immediately arranged for me to enter the Advanced Management Program at the Harvard Business School in February of 1967.

To put my order to Vietnam in proper perspective, it was in late 1965 that President Johnson decided to send combat units to Vietnam in response to the near collapse of the South Vietnam armed forces. Like everything else he did, he allowed politics to get in the way of sound military advice and judgment. I personally saw a paper addressed to the secretary of the Navy and many other senior officials of the Department of Defense from the Joint Chiefs of Staff setting forth a force requirement of 750,000 troops to pursue a successful military campaign in Vietnam. Because that level of military effort would require calling up the reserves, Johnson got the civilians in the Pentagon, using then unfamiliar systems analysis, to come up with a force level of 250,000 troops. McNamara and his whiz kid Alan Enthoven, by programming the computers to pursue a graduated response strategy, gave Johnson what he wanted: he was going to pursue his guns and butter strategy. He was going to have his war and his great society as well and to hell with what his military advisors thought. Johnson was a damn fool, but McNamara was not only a fool but a criminal as well, as he sent young Americans to Vietnam completely under the domination of political expediency. At any rate the military buildup was underway in Vietnam and I was to be a part of it. Before I went, however, I was going to the Harvard Business School.

While I was waiting to travel to Boston I had a call from a good friend, Admiral Les Hubbell. He wanted to sound me out about taking command of the battleship *New Jersey* that was being reactivated for duty in Southeast Asia. She was to be manned as a gun ship, so that her heavy sixteen-inch guns could be brought to bear on the enemy in Vietnam. She was to have only 1400 men. Her regular complement was 2400, thus I would never be able to operate her as she was designed to be operated. In addition, I had already chosen the heavy guided missile cruiser *Albany*, which was going out of commission for a two-year modernization and would return to the fleet as our most powerful guided missile ship. I said no thanks to the *New Jersey* as I prepared to enter Harvard.

⚓

Chapter 17

The Harvard Business School

MY DECISION TO attend the Advanced Management Program at the Harvard Business School was to be one of the most important decisions of my life. I really didn't know much about the course but I chose Harvard over the National War College because I reasoned that I had already been to the senior course at the Naval War College and it seemed rather redundant to go to the National War College as well.

As it turned out, I almost lost my place at Harvard. Ray Peet found himself loose at the time and decided that he would like to go to Harvard. He was senior to me, but to Admiral Semmes credit, he refused to allow Peet to take my place. Peet and I were and are good friends. I have never mentioned the incident to him nor he to me, but it was a close thing.

I left our home and family in Bethesda in early February and set forth in my Volkswagen for Boston. I stopped en route to visit my cousin Jane Peck in Chapaqua New York. I had a delightful visit and was off bright and early the next morning for Boston.

I arrived in early afternoon and registered along with 159 other men for the 51st Advanced Management Program. I was assigned to Can 16. It was a fortuitous assignment, as the others assigned with me proved to be a most interesting group. The living quarters were in Hamilton Hall, one of the several resident halls at the Business School. Each Can consisted of four suites arranged around the heads and showers. Each suite accommodated two men. My roommate was Gordon Arquette, an executive with Airco. He was their chief scientist and an expert in cryogenics. He was a fine fellow but, like all scientists, he was more than a little absentminded.

After getting unpacked the first evening, we decided to get to know one another by going out to dinner. I drove my car and Gordon drove his. During the course of the evening he succeeded in losing three sets of car keys. This was not too unusual for him and he had several sets available in his car.

Our other Canmates consisted of an Englishman, David Alford, a retail executive, Phil Hawley, a Texas oilman, Ralph O'Connor, a banker, Bob Hutton, a General Motors executive Don Hart and a playboy, Fred Johnston. Fred actually came from Electric Bond and Share but he was only there because his uncle was the chairman. He proved to be a terrible student and a worse classmate. He bragged about his distinction of never reading a case and never having dinner in the Business School Faculty Club where we took our meals. Our acquaintance extended over several years. He never really improved, but he had an interesting, if not flawed, personality.

The makeup of the class was quite interesting. The attendees ranged in age from their early forties to the mid fifties. They essentially were the budding stars in their companies who were getting ready to move from functional management to general management. The cost of the program and the company's reputation kept them from sending anyone but their best. There were a good percentage of foreign students representing the UK, France, Norway, Sweden, India the Netherlands and others. The military at the time was also well represented. Each service sent five officers, again generally some of their best. They all were in the full colonel or captain grade. The Navy group included one fine marine officer.

It was both interesting and amazing how this nonhomogeneous group melded rapidly into a congenial and unified class. Of course, there were exceptions, but by and large, the men quickly made friends and got along wonderfully well.

The course extended over only a three-month period but the human interaction was intense. We lived together, we dined together, we studied together, we recited together and we went ashore together. We coalesced into a group, where friendships have endured through the many years since our Harvard experience. In later chapters, I shall describe the importance and delight of the wonderful human relationships that we established.

The curriculum embraced six areas of study: control, marketing, business policy, economics and finance, human behavior and decision making. We had three classes a day, each lasting for ninety minutes. Before the first class in the morning we met in discussion groups to go over the day's cases.

At the Harvard Business School, the core of the learning experience is the case. A case is an actual description of a problem facing a company from the perspective of one of the six areas enumerated above. The case researchers include every pertinent fact bearing on the case, including the personalities involved; thus the case material can and often is very lengthy and requires a great deal of preparation time, reading and then analyzing the issues contained in the case. Each student is supposed to come up with a viable solution to the issue or problem set forth in the case and must be prepared to defend his particular solution.

Because of the great importance the B School places on the program, it assigns its best professors in each area. Thus the students are treated to the school's superstars. They, as a group, play a class like an orchestra. They develop the case by leading the discussion and instructing and guiding just enough to keep the recitations focused on the issues in the case. It was often frustrating, because most of the men in attendance were conditioned to expect a right answer. The B-School from the get-go stoutly maintained that there was no correct or school solution. What the school did expect was that the individual student do his best to come up with a defendable approach.

Most of the students were thrilled and delighted to be there and did their very best to prepare their cases. I say most, because there were a few like Fred Johnston who refused to seriously participate. He would wing it in every class and it soon became obvious to not only the teachers but his classmates as well that he was not participating. It finally came to head one morning in a marketing class. Ted Leavitt, one of the great marketing experts in the United States, was teaching the case. He called on Johnston first. Fred had not read the case and tried to wing it to no avail. Instead of moving on, Leavitt kept after him, to Johnston's great embarrassment and discomfiture. After he had thoroughly destroyed Johnston he went on with the case. Johnston's reaction was truly amazing. Instead of licking his wounds he went to see the dean of the faculty, George Baker and demanded that Leavitt be fired. Of course that would never happen and Fred came damn close to being kicked out.

We had one long weekend break that permitted many of us to go home for a short visit. I invited my English classmate, David Alford to go to Washington with me to be our house guest. It was an opportunity for him to get away, since he obviously could not go back to England, and it afforded Mary Lee a chance to get to know one of my favorite Can mates.

Boston in wintertime is not the most hospitable city. It's cold and raw much of the time and all activities are confined to indoors. Several of us took up squash and availed ourselves of the Harvard Club squash facilities which the club very graciously made available to the AMP class. During the course of our time at Harvard several of our professors invited us to their homes for dinner, which was very pleasant and helped to break up our routine.

About midway through the program, my dear friend Jack Wohler, brought the *Albany* to Boston for its scheduled modernization. I was, of course, delighted to see Jack, but I was more delighted to see the ship which I was to command when she was recommissioned. I introduced Jack to many of my friends and they too enjoyed him. He invited me and some of them to visit the *Albany* which, of course, we did. They were damned impressed with her, but so was I. It was a fine introduction to the ship that was to be my capital ship command and she gave me much to think about.

The culmination of the course was the Big Case. Each Can competed with all the others in analyzing the case. Our Big Case concerned the Olivetti Company, an Italian manufacturer of office equipment. All of us, except Fred of course, worked for a week on our solution. The chairman of the company, Mr. Olivetti himself traveled from Italy to help judge the entrees. Regretfully we didn't win, but we gave it our best shot.

The culmination of the course was Wives' Week. Most of the students' wives came to Harvard for a week of class participation and a great round of social events. It was a delight. The school sent the wives a packet of cases, which they were to study before their arrival. Everyone, including Mary Lee, swore that they were not going to say anything in class. Boy were they wrong! Those professors had them on the edge of their chairs competing for speaking time. It was a wonderful experience for them, which I am certain, they have never forgotten.

The culmination of the week was graduation. We had become a well-integrated social as well as academic unit and we resolved to strengthen our social ties in the years ahead. We happily elected Bill Williams as our secretary. At the time, Bill was the district director of the Internal Revenue Service for New England. He destroyed my carefully constructed image of an IRS official: mean as hell, tough looking, abrupt, cold. Bill was the antithesis of that. He was a delightful warm guy who was a pleasure to have as a friend. He was to serve our class with distinction in the years ahead.

After our graduation exercises, we said goodbye to our faculty friends and to each other. Since I was off to the Vietnam War, I enjoyed a special status with my friends. I assured them that I would be back and would invite them to the commissioning of the *Albany*. Mary Lee and I headed for our home in Washington and to preparations for another long separation.

Chapter 18

Vietnam 1967–1968

I N THE THIRTY plus years that have passed since the Vietnam War I have thought deeply about it, about what happened subsequent to my tour, about the loss of our national will, about the incredible anti-U.S. bias which so distorted the media coverage of our operations, about the disgraceful behavior of the antiwar activists and radicals, the draft dodgers, including William Jefferson Clinton, about our abandonment of our gallant South Vietnamese allies and the effect of all of this on our national character.

Two articles which I published soon after my return from the war have served as contemporaneous notes and thus my writing about many of my experiences and observations does not suffer from the debilitating effect of trying to recollect accurately from a separation of over 30 years. A great deal, in addition, is based on numerous speeches which I have given about Vietnam in the years after my return and are conditioned by the years of pain that I have suffered and anger which I felt and still feel because of the shameless behavior of the media, the cowardly politicians and a small if vocal and vicious segment of our population.

But let's go back to the beginning of my Vietnam experience. After leaving Harvard and after enjoying a generous leave in which I was able to concentrate on my family from which I was again going to be separated—this time for an entire year—I reported to the State Department's Counterinsurgency School located in Washington. It was my first real look at Vietnam. It was an excellent familiarizing experience and a good general orientation of our political and military situation there. It gave me an excellent overview of the geography, history, demographics, politics and military situation, plus a very complete recitation of the problems that the U.S. faced, and those that I would soon be facing there myself. It was an intensive course, lasting about three weeks, and was well worth my time.

Prior to my agreeing to go to Vietnam I made one non-negotiable request. I was to be in military command of the naval advisory group in country. I was determined that I was not going to try to do my job as an officer on the staff of Commander Naval Forces Vietnam. I insisted on the title of "Senior Naval Advisor." I well understood that I reported to COMNAVFOR Vietnam but I reported as a subordinate commander. The Chief of Naval Personnel sought and received the concurrence of the Vice Chief of Naval Operation, Admiral Horatio Rivera, and I was well satisfied.

In the many years that I served in the Navy I had developed a serious medical problem which now had to be squarely faced. The innumerable immunization shots which all of us who served were obliged to take had built up in me a sensitivity to them that eventually almost resulted in my death. Years earlier, the War College's surgeon, Black Mac, had insisted on giving me a series of five immunization shots to prepare me for the world travels which lay ahead with Admiral Burke. He gave them all to me in one day because of my imminent departure. I had a terrible reaction, which sent me into shock, and I damned near didn't make it. That was to be my last immunization forever. The problem was that diseases such as malaria, yellow fever, cholera, dengue fever, diphtheria and several they hadn't written down yet were all prevalent in Vietnam.

To investigate the problem thoroughly I was ordered before the Immunization Board at the Naval Medical Center in Bethesda. I underwent three days of a huge battery of sensitivity tests. In the end, I appeared before the full board and was informed that it was the board's expert opinion that I was far safer taking my chances in Vietnam than participating in the Navy's immunization program.

During those weeks I spent as much time as possible with Mary Lee and the children. It was tough on me contemplating a year away from them and it was equally tough on them, especially Mary Lee, getting ready to tell me goodbye. I was headed into a hell of a war. Mary Lee, as always, was superb. She was proud of me and was fully supportive of what I was about to do. She prepared for our separation with good cheer and courage.

On the 3rd of July of 1967 she took me to the Washington airport to catch my plane to California. From California I flew to Vietnam on a chartered World Airways flight. On the morning of the 5th of July, I, along with a planeload of replacements, landed at Tan San Nhut Airport, outside of Saigon. Steve Rusk, the officer I was to relieve, was at the airport to meet me. Seeing him was not very reassuring, as he looked awful. I later learned that he had suffered a series of medical problems including some mental difficulties. It was my conclusion that he had just lost his nerve. He had apparently become ineffective and my arrival was indeed very welcome, not only by him but also by Rear Admiral Kenneth Veth, Commander Naval Forces, Vietnam.

I was taken to Admiral Veth's quarters where I was to be billeted. The senior advisor had his own little building separated from, but attached to, the main quarters.

The admiral gave a luncheon in my honor on the day of my arrival. Until Rusk left, I was assigned to a guest room in the main house. That night, my first in Vietnam, I became violently ill. Fortunately, there was a telephone and a directory in my room, so I was able to reach the staff duty officer, who promptly sent a staff car which took me to the hospital. I spent my first night in Vietnam in the Army hospital suffering from food poisoning. Apparently the chicken salad which was served at lunch was the culprit. That was not a very propitious beginning but I am happy to be able to record that that one episode was the only time during my entire tour that I was to become ill.

When I was discharged from the hospital after a two-day stay, I reported to my headquarters, which was located in the Vietnamese Navy compound. It was a typical French colonial structure, essentially comprised of a series of two-story whitewashed buildings with tiled roofs and huge windows with large green awning shutters. There was little air conditioning in spite of the beastly hot weather. There were ceiling fans everywhere and the thick walls and very high ceilings tended to make the facilities bearable if not comfortable. The entire facility was surrounded by a very high wall with its entrances carefully patrolled by sentries.

I immediately started the detailed process of digging in. I had two principal responsibilities. My first was to be in command of all the Navy advisors in country, and the second was to be the chief U.S.

Navy advisor to the Vietnamese chief of naval operations, Commodore Tran Van Chon.

A little background on Commodore Chon's position will be both of interest and useful in understanding the situation in which I found the Vietnamese navy. Commodore Chon had been in command for less than a year. He had assumed command of the navy almost by default. The navy had been in existence for about 14 years and had been in very heavy weather since the git-go. It had expanded rapidly, far too rapidly for its fragile and ineffective logistic support system. It lacked qualified commissioned officers and enlisted petty officers with sufficient experience to adequately man and command a navy that had grown seven-fold in just a few years.

In the years preceding my arrival, one CNO had been murdered, one was removed by an armed mutiny of senior officers, and Commodore Chon's predecessor lost his job as the result of a character assassination campaign mounted by dissident officers. Thus Commodore Chon's appointment was a dubious honor, to say the least.

Commodore Chon was a southerner, a devout Buddhist and completely apolitical. A graduate of the Foreign Officers' Course at the U.S. Naval War College at Newport he was strongly pro-American and completely U.S. Navy oriented.

Initially I spent a great deal of time with him, as I recognized that we not only had to get to know each other well but he had to develop both respect and confidence in me if I were going to be able to help his navy. All initiatives had to stem from him and not me. He had been informed of the change in the status of the senior advisor as a separate commander and he was both impressed and intrigued with this development.

Rusk had occupied a small, cluttered and inefficient office. With absolutely no representation on my part, Commodore Chon moved his vice chief of naval operations to a different suite of offices and assigned his office to me. It was a commodious office with high ceilings and huge windows, which made it quite comfortable even though it was not air-conditioned. The Army, at my request, sent over some prestige furniture and carpeting and the Navy Department sent me handsome portraits of the ships that I had commanded, as well as one of the *Albany* that I was scheduled to command. They were not only handsome but they also established my bona fides for all who visited me. Parenthetically, the Army very kindly refitted my quarters, complete with a new air conditioner.

I'll have a good deal more to say about Commodore Chon and our intense interpersonal relationship, which soon developed. Now, however, a brief description of the Vietnamese navy, which had evolved over the past few years. It consisted of about 18,000 officers and men. Although not very combat effective at the beginning of my tour, it was one of the largest navies in Asia.

Its 61 ships and 500-plus craft were divided into three principal forces. All of its ships and mine craft were concentrated in Fleet Command with its main base located in Saigon. The river assault craft, which numbered about 260, were organized into groups based on Mekong Delta. Most of the rest of the craft, numbering about 250, were essentially armed junks organized into coastal patrol groups and deployed all along the coastal lateral of South Vietnam.

The Fleet Command included 41 patrol types, 19 amphibious types, essentially utilized for logistics lift, and 16 small mine countermeasures craft. The patrol types included gun boats, patrol escorts, coastal minesweepers and shallow draft flat-bottomed LSIL/LSSL landing ships which were admirably suited for river patrol and gunfire support assignments.

The amphibious lift was largely centered in three LSTs and 16 LSMs, while its mine sweeping capabilities were contained in ten motor launch minesweepers and six specially configured LCMMs which had recently been transferred from the U.S. Navy.

The navy's operations were essentially concentrated in the Mekong Delta. It was in this strategically important area that the navy's first sign of its growing effectiveness began to manifest itself. The fighting effectiveness of the riverine forces was already being noticed before my arrival.

These forces were organized into 13 River Assault Groups. Inheriting the concept of amphibious river assault operations as well as many of the specially configured craft from the French, the Vietnamese navy was becoming particularly adept in this unique application of naval power. The Mekong Delta with its thousands of miles of waterways was ideally suited to river assault operations.

Each river assault group, or RAG as they were popularly known, had sufficient craft assigned to lift one Vietnamese army battalion. The typical Vietnamese troop only weighed 80 pounds so the need for an amphibious lift for a battalion was far less than that required by U.S. forces. They utilized heavily armed LCMs for their troop lift. In addition, each RAG had a French commandament for command and control, a few monitors for fire power support and various escort and patrol craft for mine sweeping and bank security missions. It was an efficient, self contained package that worked wonderfully well in its assigned environment.

If copying is the highest form of flattery, then the RAGs could be proud indeed, because the U.S. Mobile Riverine Forces which evolved in the Mekong Delta closely resembled the RAGs. The U.S. forces which were organized into River Assault Squadrons resembled, to a remarkable degree, the makeup of the RAG forces. The U. S. forces were, of course, better, because they were of the most modern design. The one great and decisive difference, however, was the amount of armor that the U.S. craft carried. That armor afforded great protection from the VC's recoilless rifles, which they had in large numbers.

The third major element of the Vietnamese navy was its Coastal Patrol Forces. Originally they were part of the paramilitary forces but had been integrated into the regular Vietnamese navy just prior to my arrival. The force was organized into 25 coastal groups. They were deployed in 20 rather primitive coastal bases strategically located along the South Vietnam coastal littoral from a location very close to the demilitarized zone separating the North from the South to Phu Quoc Island in the Gulf of Siam to the south. Many of these tiny bases were literally government outposts located in VC infested territory. These bases looked very much like the old wild west forts. Generally triangular in shape, they were enclosed by high stockade fences, which in turn were equipped with blockhouses, sally ports and lockable gates. The VC on the outside, unlike the Indians, were equipped with automatic weapons, AK 47s, mortars, bandoleer charges, and antipersonnel mines—certainly a much more dangerous and formidable enemy than the Indian-fighters faced in the old West.

Each coastal patrol group was equipped with eight to twelve motor junks, which operated in counter-infiltration missions, on patrol operations in the lagoons and river mouths, in fishing control operations, and in important psychological warfare operations.

It should be noted that the utilization of armed junks in naval war operations was strange indeed to the U.S. Naval advisors who typically came from powerful U.S. fleet units. The junks, when properly employed, were extremely useful in missions to which they were applied. Constructed of Sao wood, a kind of Vietnamese mahogany, they were armed with either a 30 or 50 caliber machine gun mounted on the bow and a 40mm mortar on the stern. Of equal importance, to the Vietnamese, at least, they were also fitted with prominent eyes fitted to both bows to ensure that the junks didn't make the calamitous mistake of running into evil sea spirits.

The remainder of the navy was comprised of its fragile and inefficient logistics support facilities. Its principal repair yard was located in Saigon, as were its principal supply and medical facilities. Training facilities were more dispersed. Prior to my arrival, they had already established Class A and B schools in Nha Trang and had an ongoing naval academy there as well, which offered a two-year course for officer candidates. They were also busily constructing a recruit-training center at Cam Rhan Bay.

To assist this expanding but weak navy, about 500 U.S. Navy officers and petty officers were assigned to the U.S. Naval Advisory Group, Vietnam and were under the direct command of the senior Naval Advisor. In the pages which follow I will describe their effort in some detail and then will follow with an account of the advisors interaction with their Vietnamese counterparts, drawing some conclusions as to their effectiveness and over all success in aiding the Vietnamese to develop a combat effective and efficient navy.

Typically, our officer advisors, either lieutenants junior grade or lieutenants, reported on board from the U.S. Navy's operating forces. Almost none of them had had any previous experience in the type of naval warfare in which the Vietnamese navy was engaged. What they essentially brought to the effort was a great deal of sea-based training which they received as officers in the fleet, plus almost universal enthusiasm and dedication to the tasks assigned to them.

The petty officers also largely came from the fleet. Generally either second or first class, they were typically in the deck ratings boatswain mates, gunner's mates, and so on. To respond to the need to advise in the development of logistics support initiatives several were in machinist and other artificers ratings.

Except for some concentrations in my command staff in the shipyard, in the supply base and at the various school commands, most of them were organized into small detachments typically made up of two officers and two petty officers. In several cases, however, such as on board fleet units, a single U.S. officer advisor was detailed on board.

They universally arrived in Vietnam with a determination and enthusiasm that was both remarkable and heartening. The Navy did its best to prepare them for the rigorous and dangerous duty which lay ahead. Almost universally they went through a 13-week grueling counterinsurgency course and 8 to 13 weeks of language training. Of course, their enthusiasm was understandably tempered by considerable apprehension, mostly of the unknown. They came to participate in a type of warfare that was largely foreign to U.S. naval experience. Almost none of them had ever been to Vietnam and none of them had ever been an advisor and in all probability they would never be advisors again.

Each of the forward detachments lived, ate, and fought alongside their Vietnamese counterparts. There were some conflicts between them, but they were rare indeed. When one became evident, both Commodore Chon and I took immediate steps to sort it out. By and large they got along famously.

It was a dangerous business. I insisted that the advisors train by doing. They had firm orders to accompany their units on all combat operations, including patrolling, ambushes, interdiction and assaults. That they generally performed wonderfully well was a tribute to those young Americans.

Combat was never very far from those in the operating forces. In spite of incredible efforts and genuine heroism, some of our units were defeated. I visited Lieutenant Bill Fitzgerald and his Coastal Patrol Group 16 during one of my regular trips to the various commands. We had a very rewarding visit and conference and I left them with a warm feeling of satisfaction with the efforts they were making. On the very night that I departed, a VC battalion attacked Coastal

Group 16's base. Using heavy mortars, the VC breached our mine-fields and punched through our stockade fences with satchel charges. Lieutenant Fitzgerald led his detachment into the advisors' fighting bunker. They continued to fire until the base was almost entirely overrun. While Lieutenant Fitzgerald gave them cover, Lieutenant (JG) Williams and the two advisor petty officers fought their way out of their bunker and managed to escape. Bill Fitzgerald, however, was shot and killed as he attempted to withdraw. Williams, although severely wounded, was rescued by Vietnamese villagers and survived.

This was typical of the heroism repeatedly displayed by our advisors. They almost universally believed in what they were doing and took enormous pride in their performance and in the performance of the Vietnamese units to which they were assigned.

The advisors attached to the riverine forces were equally dedicated and incredibly brave. Unlike the coastal patrol groups, the RAGs operated out of fairly well developed bases. These elite groups had a wonderful esprit. They were good, they were admired and they took great pride in their reputations. The advisors attached to the RAGs developed the same fierce pride in their outfits as did the Vietnamese. Each of them would argue with absolute conviction and certainty that their RAG commander was the very best officer in the Vietnamese navy. Invariably the advisors rode into battle alongside their counterparts on board one of the commandaments or on board one of the heavily armored monitors. I personally went into battle with a combined RAG outfit, but more about that later.

The Vietnamese took great pride and satisfaction that the U.S. forces operating in the Mekong Delta developed craft whose designs were heavily based on those operated by the Vietnamese and that they employed tactics that closely paralleled the tactics developed by the Vietnamese as well.

The performance of the RAGs in combat was a source of tremendous pride to the entire Navy. These battle tested outfits were frequently the subject of glowing reports from both U.S. Army and Vietnamese army commands. The RAG sailors rightfully took great pride in their performance.

Not only were the RAG operations dangerous but they generally extended over several days. This, of course, meant that our advisors had to learn to exist on these crowded boats and to learn to survive in a completely Vietnamese environment, including eating the rather exotic Vietnamese food. The latter took some getting used to, as American tastes do not exactly coincide with Vietnamese tastes, which I too soon learned. Surprisingly, here too, the advisors learned to adapt. It was not long before the advisors learned to enjoy Vietnamese rice laced with a native staple, Nhuc Mom sauce topped off with fiery hot red peppers. Nhuc Mom sauce, by the way, is essentially the liquid released by fish purposely rotted in the tropical sun. The smell that emanated from it was revolting.

The stuff had such an awful stench that, almost universally, U.S. pilots in country would fly almost anything including high explosives, napalm, and any other dangerous cargo, but they flatly refused to fly a bottle of Nhuc Mom, because if a bottle broke on board the only way to get rid of the stench was to burn the plane. I ran into this narrow mindedness and uncooperative spirit because the champagne of Nhuc Mom was made on Phu Quoc Island in the Gulf of Siam. I had a coastal group on the island and every time I visited there my Vietnam friends would beseech me to bring back some of that blue ribbon Nhuc Mom. I always did my best to smuggle at least a few bottles on my helicopter. When I was later assigned a Vietnamese army helicopter the problem of transporting that nectar became much easier.

The performance during the Tet Offensive of the two RAGs based at Vinh Long in the Mekong Delta is illustrative of their professionalism and their fighting spirit. Vinh Long, one of the major cities in the strategic Delta area, was a prime target of heavy enemy main force attacks very early in the offensive. Vietnamese army and U.S. Army units were initially driven out of their defensive positions but the RAG base, although surrounded, except on its river flank, held fast against repeated assaults. Those not engaged in defending their base manned their boats and, instead of giving ground, they maneuvered on the enemy's flanks, delivering along with Fleet Command LSSLs and LSLIS, a devastating fire against enemy formations and positions.

Anyone who claimed that the Vietnamese fighting man lacked courage just hadn't seen them in action. The Vinh Long RAGs held, they decimated the enemy formations and permitted the launching of counter attacks, which drove the enemy out of the city. There is an interesting footnote to this magnificent but by no means unique performance.

In order to stem the enemy advance, it was necessary for the RAGs to open fire on their own dependent housing which the enemy had occupied. Our advisors who were on hand reported that when the dreaded order to commence fire came there was only a moment's hesitation before the RAGs turned their fire on their own homes. The Vinh Long RAGs were officially credited with saving the city and their personnel received 72 personal decorations for their heroic performance.

The advisors assigned to Fleet Command were in a particularly unique position. Fleet Command consisted of all the navy's ocean-going and mine countermeasures assets. It numbered 41 patrol, 19 logistic lift and 17 mine craft. The Fleet Command shipboard advisor rode his ship as the only American on board. With patrols extending up to 45 days, this was often quite a problem for these young American officers. His problem was not only ensuring that his advisory effort was effective but it was also one of just existing on board. All of the fleet units were very small indeed. Contrary to popular belief, the weather in the seas surrounding Vietnam can be very rough. During the six months of the northeast monsoon, heavy seas, high winds, and generally inhospitable weather prevailed along most of the coast of Vietnam that fronted the South China Sea. When the monsoon shifted to the southwest the seas and weather in the Gulf of Siam became equally unpleasant and uncomfortable. Thus the advisors in the Fleet Command ships, as well as their Vietnamese hosts, endured much discomfort during a great portion of their underway time. Add to this the inevitable language problem, the often exotic and unappetizing Vietnamese food, and the loneliness of being without American companionship for long periods of time and you get some idea of the problems that these young American officers faced.

In spite of these difficulties, the great majority of them enjoyed their assignments. They almost all developed a pride in their ships along with a warm camaraderie with their counterparts, the skipper, as well as with the rest of the ship's company.

Obviously, those advisors who developed a feeling of belonging to and a responsibility for the ship to which they were assigned, not only derived great satisfaction from their tour, but also became the most effective advisors. The advisor who considered his ship's victory his own and his ship's failures his own took a great step forward towards developing the type of rapport that was so essential to an effective advisory effort.

Like sailors everywhere, the Vietnamese sailor was no slouch in working the angles. I was determined to rid the Vietnamese ships of rats. The problem was that the Vietnamese looked at rats as we look at squirrels. They didn't have the stigma that we assign to our rats. If the senior naval advisor held that no self-respecting navy tolerated rats on board, that was good enough for the Vietnamese. In a drive to rid the ships of rats we had camels built to hold the ships away from the piers and rat guards fabricated to rig to the mooring lines. In addition we enlisted the ingenuity of the skippers. Several offered special liberties to any man who proved the success of his anti-rat crusade by delivering the deceased's tail to the executive officer. He was rewarded with a special liberty. These programs appeared to be working well until it was discovered that many of the tails being offered up as proof were taken from rats caught at home.

We advisors were not in country long before we developed a great admiration and respect for the courage of the Vietnamese sailor. Witness the behavior of Petty Officer Coam. Like many Vietnamese sailors, Hai Si Coam had demonstrated his contempt for the enemy by having the words "SAT CONG" or "Kill Viet Cong" tattooed in large letters on his chest. He did his very best to live up to his slogan. Unfortunately, Hai Si Coam's luck ran out and he was captured by the Viet Cong. His captors soon discovered his slogan. Instead of killing him, however they tortured him by literally flaying the offending skin from his chest. They then released Coam, hoping that his pain and disfigurement would serve as an example to others. The VC's torture and indignities had just the opposite effect. Hai Si Coam bided his time until his terrible wounds had healed and, as soon as he could stand it, he sought out a tattoo artist and had his chest re-tattooed with an even larger "SAT CONG" than before.

I was present at a coastal group when word was received that contact had been made with the enemy. I wish that those who so maligned the courage of our Vietnamese allies could have seen the rush to the boats, and the disappointment of those who had to be left behind.

My favorite recollection of the wonderful courage and fighting spirit of the Vietnamese sailors centers around Coastal Group 11, one of our coastal groups located in I Corps and as close to the North Vietnamese border as any military unit in Vietnam. I was at my headquarters on a Sunday morning when I received an operational priority message from our advisors that they had made contact with a platoon of VC. They doggedly hung on for five hours and when they failed to make headway they asked for some help from the U.S. Marines who occupied I Corps. The battle eventually included two Marine battalions. It turned out that Coastal Group 11 had flushed a fully equipped North Vietnamese main force battalion. The 35 members of Group 11 stayed and fought the enemy to a standstill for almost five hours before relief arrived. Both of our enlisted advisors were severely wounded in the action.

The morale and discipline of our advisors during the year I was in command was uniformly outstanding. I only held one Captain's Mast during the entire year and that was on a second class boatswain mate attached to the heroic Coastal Group 11. He got very drunk and caused all sorts of problems. I fined him and broke him to third class. He was in the action that I just recounted with Coastal Group 11 and was seriously wounded. We had him evacuated to Japan. After he healed he insisted upon being returned to his unit. I promptly restored his 2nd class rate and ensured that he was properly decorated for his heroism.

How was it possible, the question was often asked, for the U.S. naval personnel to advise the Vietnamese effectively when their backgrounds, experience, customs, values and philosophy were so vastly different from our own? Actually, while the form of Vietnamese naval forces were quite different, the principles upon which naval effectiveness is developed are almost identical. Each advisor brought with him a wealth of experience and knowledge in naval organization, naval administration, naval training, equipment and ship maintenance and leadership. That background and previous experience was directly applicable to the Vietnamese naval unit to which the advisor was attached. How well he brought those and other attributes to bear was, of course, an excellent measure of his proficiency and performance as an advisor.

My association with Commodore Chon was both cordial and productive. He well knew my background and that I was number one on the major ship command list and that I was particularly chosen for my assignment. I assured him very early on that I was sent to him to help as best I could and that I would do everything in my power to assist him in improving the readiness and fighting efficiency of his navy.

Our advisory group developed 138 programs and initiatives designed to improve the navy. These efforts focused on materiel, logistics support, training, operational organization and performance, discipline, readiness, and most important of all, programs designed to get the Vietnamese navy ready to assume the roles and missions that were then being carried out by U.S. naval forces.

Our results were nothing short of dramatic. In the coastal groups, their performance increased markedly. From slightly under 21,000, junk searches increased to 48,000 a month, while the number of personnel checked increased from 81,000 per month to 156,000, which rivaled the performance of the U.S. Navy Market Time Forces engaged in the same mission. During the same period the number of small unit ground operations i.e. ambushes, sweeps, and search and destroy operations showed a similar dramatic increase.

The RAGs were already terrific but a series of initiatives were undertaken to improve their readiness and fighting capability even more. Fleet effectiveness also improved across the board. From an average of 15 gunfire support missions fired per month during the year prior to my arrival, we were able to increase the number to over 50 per month during April, May and June of 1968.

One of the prime families of initiatives which we developed was focused on the improvement of the logistic support facilities and personnel. I emphasized that without adequate and efficient ship repair, supply, personnel training and support, and medical support it would not be possible to grow the operating forces with any hope of reaching an acceptable level of combat effectiveness. An entire family of initiatives was undertaken to accomplish this vital task. The navy could not grow by 300 percent without first establishing a viable logistic support organization. It was my view that the navy's past weak performance was because neither the Vietnamese nor the Americans who were advising them understood this basic military truth.

Because of its dramatic improvement, the prestige of the navy soared. Towards the end of my year in country, the navy was receiving over 5,000 applicants per month. Since it could only enlist a few hundred per month the navy was only taking the very cream of the crop. An added bonus from my perspective was that over half of the recruits that they were taking had a good working knowledge of English.

The single aim of all these dramatic improvements was to permit the Vietnamese navy to assume more and more roles and missions that were then being carried out by U.S. naval forces. If the U.S was ever going to be able to withdraw this had to happen not only in the navy but in the other armed forces of the Republic of Vietnam as well. Oddly, many U.S. personnel resisted this idea. I didn't call it that then but what I was talking about was the Vietnamization of the war, which came into political popularity not long after my return to the fleet.

I developed a five year plan that would, when carried out, relieve all U.S. naval forces of the roles and missions currently being undertaken, with the exception of carrier strike and support operations. I was convinced that it would take that long because of the time required to develop adequate officer experience and effectiveness. A seasoned lieutenant commander cannot be produced in a year or two nor can you develop the crucial logistics support base in a short time. I well realized that in the delicate situation that existed in Vietnam it would most assuredly require time, but we could get started, and we did.

Its increasing effectiveness permitted the Vietnamese to assume exclusive responsibility for 10 U.S. Market Time or coastal blockade stations, and with the integration of better blockade assets this progress was set to accelerate. The increased performance and effectiveness of their mine forces were equally dramatic. During the previous year and a half the Vietnamese navy's contribution to mine counter operations on the Long Tau/Dong Nhai Rivers which form the shipping channel from Saigon to the sea averaged 24 miles per day. In June of 1968 this figure had increased to 196 miles per day.

Their performance had reached such a high level of professionalism that they were able to assume full responsibility from U.S. naval forces for mine countermeasures against command detonated mines in the Saigon shipping channel. This was a particularly significant attainment, as it represented the first full assumption by any of the armed forces of South Vietnam of a mission previously carried out by U.S. forces. The Vietnamese performance in this newly acquired role was flawless.

Their logistics lift ships made similar important improvements In the previous year alone their logistics ships increased their tonnage carried by 116 percent and the personnel carried by 60 percent. The Vietnamese were proud and delighted with their growing effectiveness and I was mighty proud and delighted right along with them.

In February of 1968, an event of transcending importance was approaching. Tet is a national holiday, which roughly corresponds to our combined Christmas and New Years. It was normally a joyous time for the Vietnamese but also a vulnerable time. We had early intelligence of a possible VC offensive that was timed to coincide with Tet. Saigon was filling with Vietnamese civilians coming to the big city to celebrate. On the eve before Tet there was a palpable tension in the air. At 2300 I ordered my headquarters detachment to general quarters in parallel with the Vietnamese navy headquarters personnel going to their battle stations.

At 0300 all hell broke loose. We were under attack! A VC sapper company had been ordered to overrun us as a similar outfit was assigned to attack our U.S. Embassy. The enemy killed our sentries and blew holes in our perimeter wall but never gained a foothold inside our compound. The Vietnamese counter-attacked and captured many of the assault team. The entire action lasted no more than 30 minutes.

I went down to the prisoner interrogations. We had about 20 POWs under heavy guard. They were so small that it was difficult to credit them as a major threat. They all looked more forlorn than defiant. If I didn't know that they would have cheerfully blown my head off if they had the chance, I would have been inclined to put my arm around them and tell them not to despair.

I think that you will agree that the information that we obtained through our interrogation is interesting and will to some measure define the type of warfare that we were waging in Vietnam.

> Q. How did you come to Saigon?
> A. We came in civilian buses that were bringing the civilian to celebrate Tet.
> Q. What did you do when you got to Saigon?
> A. We went to the movies.
> Q. After the movies what did you do?
> A. We went to a restaurant to have dinner.
> Q. What did you do after you left the restaurant?
> A. We went to our assigned safe houses and dug up our uniforms and weapons.
> Q. How did you get from the safe houses to our headquarters?
> A. We came by taxi.

When morning came, the Vietnamese navy was given a sector of Saigon to secure. Commodore Chon organized an offensive force consisting of personnel from the two RAGs stationed in Saigon plus personnel from our headquarters unit. Commodore Chon led the attack in our sector and our sailors fought wonderfully well. Here again we captured an assortment of VC. We had them collected in a fairly large group and they were chattering among themselves. I asked the interrogators what they were talking about. Apparently they were pissed off because they had to smoke those crummy Vietnamese cigarettes and their officers smoked U.S. brands.

Parenthetically, I was beginning to think that my counterpart had some of the MacArthur in him. He always insisted on leading his troops. He was supremely confident in his safety because he wore a magically powerful amulet, which his father had spent two years in the rainforest to perfect. It was designed to ensure that all bullets coming his way were safely deflected. He believed with all his might in that protection. I, of course tried to stay right with him but I felt obliged to point out that I had no such magic to protect me.

And what was the overall result of this enemy attack? The prime strategic objective was that through a broad based countrywide attack the enemy anticipated a mass defection of the Vietnamese civilian population and a mass mutiny of the armed forces of the Republic of Vietnam. Neither hoped-for result materialized. I know of no significant, if any, civilian defections and I don't know of a single armed forces unit mutiny or their otherwise going over to the VC.

Because of their very poor command and control facilities, their tactical objectives, of necessity, had to be reduced to detailed writing. After only a few days we had captured so many VC that we were able to recover the overwhelming majority of their written lists of tactical objectives. Except for their attack on Hue, they failed to gain any of these objectives. In Hue they did gain partial control of the city but were soon driven out by U.S. Marine and Vietnamese army forces. In the few days they were there they committed incredibly brutal atrocities against the civilian population. It was plain indiscriminate and wanton killing. Many civilians were murdered in cold blood. The VC also systematically destroyed many important historical buildings and sites in that ancient city.

And finally we come to the score keeping. The body count of the VC and North Vietnamese was enormous while our killed was minimal. For every twenty enemy killed we lost one of ours. We captured huge numbers of weapons and ammunition of all kinds. But one of the most telling statistics was the enormous movement of Vietnamese civilians toward our forces. They literally voted with their feet. The overwhelming sentiment among the South Vietnamese civilians was one of fear and dread of the VC and their North Vietnamese sponsors.

From Tet forward the VC were finished as a fighting force. From then on the North Vietnamese main force battalions assumed responsibility for the great majority of their war operations. That's not the way the U.S. media reported the battle. The U.S. media was always, reflexively at least, on the enemy's side. After the enemy launched their disastrous offensive the U.S. media almost universally reported them as the victor. Never mind the facts. To us who were there doing our duty for our country it was downright infuriating and discouraging. Although Walter Cronkite is held up as an American icon, he was the first major media representative who attacked our policies in Vietnam and, after the Tet offensive, he became our nemesis. I personally despise him for his perfidy. He became the nucleus of the growing anti-war effort in the U.S. If Uncle Walter was against it, it must be wrong. But more about the U.S. media's role in Vietnam later.

My relationship with Commodore Chon became not only professionally strong but also personally warm and congenial. He appreciated enormously all that I was doing to help his navy and I took growing satisfaction in his navy's progress. We spent a great deal of time together and he listened with both respect and interest to what I had to offer. On my side, my respect and admiration for him continued to grow. If I thought it was important for us to do something, after presenting my recommendations he invariably thought that it was important to do so as well and he did his best to make it happen. He became a great advocate of the 138 programs and initiatives, which the advisor group developed for the Navy.

I knew that the Vietnamese had a reputation for dishonesty which the media did its very best to foster and I was therefor very sensitive to any intelligence which indicated any official corruption in the navy. During the year that I was in country, there was only one creditable intelligence report that alleged dishonesty on the part of Commodore Chon. My intelligence sources informed me that he was taking money from loggers who were cutting timber in the Mekong Delta in exchange for Vietnamese navy escort of their wood barges on the Long Tau River.

After much soul searching I decided to talk with him about it. When I raised the issue he promptly owned up to it and was embarrassed that he had disappointed me. He indicated that he would immediately abandon the practice and I am firmly convinced that he did. With nine children to raise on a meager Vietnamese commodore's salary it was not surprising that he had to seek some sort of outside income.

In the course of our association he paid me a great personal compliment. His father was the head of the Buddhist sect in his native hamlet which was located deep in the rainforest. Every year the major celebration in the hamlet centered around the ancient custom of welcoming the village genie. It was truly the biggest event of the entire year, even surpassing the celebration of Tet. Commodore Chon invited me to accompany him to his hamlet for the big celebration. I was to be the only occidental there. I considered it a great honor and looked forward to going with him.

His father, who must have been in his upper 70s, greeted us. He spoke no English, but he did his best to make me feel welcome. He might have been a character in a movie. His face was weathered and he was a bit stooped but his eyes were alive and dancing and he took obvious pride in us being on hand. He asked me to feel his face on both sides of his mouth. I felt something like imbedded sticks. Through Commodore Chon he explained to me that they were golden needles that he had inserted to keep evil spirits away from him.

The hamlet looked like a scene out of a Cecil B. DeMille movie. Except for the elder Chon's house, which to them was grand indeed, but was by our standards quite modest, all the other structures were small cottages fitted with thatched roofs. There were no paved streets and no electric streetlights.

The celebration began with a procession led by torch bearers and several men beating on drums and crashing cymbals. They were followed by several large platforms heaped high with fruits of all kinds, large mounds of glutinous rice and game carried on the shoulders of strong young men. The senior Mr. Chon led the hamlet's citizens which formed up behind the procession and we accompanied him. We were en route to the temple for the big celebration. As we approached the elaborate little temple, several thousand fire crackers, which had been strung from the overhanging roof's eaves, were set off. What a magnificent racket! The Vietnamese were delighted.

We entered the temple and participated in an elaborate Buddhist service. Taking my cue from Commodore Chon I went forward with him and, in the true Buddhist tradition, I lit joss sticks and I carefully bowed to Buddha with my lit joss sticks between my hands.

Following the ceremony we watched exquisitely costumed Vietnamese women perform wonderfully choreographed dances, not unlike those native dances performed in Thailand. In that exotic setting it somehow had an unreal feeling.

After these beautiful dances we moved to another part of the temple where tables had been set for the grand banquet, and grand it was. The tables were overloaded with all kind of foods. The Vietnamese are enormously hospitable and invariably insisted on helping their guests to the various dishes. When Commodore Chon helped me to one meat dish, which tasted like venison, he asked me whether I liked it. I told him that I did, whereupon he informed me that it was dog meat. I immediately thought of my little dachshund Kartuffels at home and quickly lost interest in that dish.

The Vietnamese have some rather peculiar tastes in food. I have already described the joys of Nhuc Mom sauce, but there were many other exotic delicacies, which they thoroughly enjoyed. Basically the Vietnamese, like the Chinese, think that we are a little strange only eating the outside of the carcass. They eat that, of course, but everything else as well.

One delicacy which I never got the hang of was their *piece de resistance* hors d'oeuvre. They are 15-day-old chick embryo eggs which they put in boiling water just long enough to get the chill off them. They then clip off one end and drink it down, chick embryo and all. I tried it a few times and every time I got it only half way down and then couldn't make up my mind to continue to swallow it or bring it back up. What price diplomacy!

On one operation we were carrying out a fairly major sweep. Towards late afternoon we arrived at a district chief's house and he invited us to spend the night. He laid on a dinner in our honor. One of the many dishes that he served was chicken and banana leaves. Here again, being a fine Vietnamese host, he insisted on helping me. He rooted around in the dish with his chopsticks until he found what he considered the *piece de resistance*, the whole chicken head, which he proceeded to plop on my plate. I looked down at that chicken head and it stared back at me, eyes and all. On that one occasion I had to run up the white flag.

Commodore Chon was not only the commander of the navy but he was also commander of the Popular Forces who operated in the Mekong Delta. The Vietnamese Popular Forces were a cross between paramilitary troops and a national guard. They were tough little fellows who specialized in jungle warfare, especially in the Rung Sat (Forest of Assassins). For centuries this almost impregnable jungle served as base and refuge for pirates and other lowlife. It also was a place in which the VC sought refuge.

Commodore Chon, on occasion, took great satisfaction in accompanying Popular Force sweeps in this inhospitable place. I was never all that enthusiastic about going along, but my policy was to go where he went and along I went. The Rung Sat was awfully difficult terrain in which to move. In our first operation I came face to face with a personal problem. The area is completely tropical with a jungle canopy overhead. The place was populated with all kinds of monkeys, snakes and other assorted beasts. The place was laced with deep ravines which the Vietnamese solved by putting single plank bridges across. They have great balance and thought nothing of bouncing their way across those plank bridges with nothing to hold on to. Not me. My balance, especially in those steel-shanked combat boots, was tenuous at best. I had a hell of a time crossing them. If I ever fell into one of those awful ravines I would never be heard from again. What made it even worse, I knew that if I wasn't hit I had to recross those damn bridges on the way out. Here again, Commodore Chon came up with an answer. He assigned one of the troops to be my aide. The young Vietnamese preceded me across while I put my hand on his shoulder. That gave me the help I needed and I learned to cross with complete confidence.

When we stopped to have our lunch the PFs had little difficulty in coming up with food that they enjoyed. In addition to the ubiquitous rice and Nhuc Mom sauce, and tropical fruits, they invariably captured a snake which they threaded onto a stick and grilled over a fire. They thought that they were delicious but I was always less enthusiastic. We didn't make contact with the VC very often but when we did those tough little guys fought like hell. They hated the enemy and took great delight in killing them when they could.

All of the Vietnamese who I came in contact with loved Vietnamese beer. When I visited one of my detachments, they always had a briefing for me and then served refreshments, which was invariably beer served over ice. I don't like beer but I would be so damn thirsty that I would drink it anyway. I well knew that the water for that ice came from a drainage ditch, so my strategy was to drink down the beer as soon as they gave it to me and before the ice had a chance to melt too much.

I spent a great deal of time visiting my detachments. A visit from me was not exactly what our advisors dreamed about. I insisted on high standards, properly worn uniforms and meticulous attention to all military courtesies. They were U.S. Navy personnel and they were going to look and behave as representatives of the greatest Navy in the world. I wanted not only for the Vietnamese to look up to them but I wanted the Vietnamese to emulate them and to a large measure they tried to do just that. I demanded total dedication to their duties and their units and would accept nothing less. On the other hand I fought like hell for them. The proof of the pudding was their response, which was almost universally outstanding. Many tried to ship over. I rarely allowed it because I wanted them out of there while their luck held and I firmly believed that their careers lay in the destroyers, cruisers and other ships of the fleet from which they came.

I flew a great deal in Vietnamese army helicopters. They made one available to me without question. They were invariably Huey gun ships just like the ones the U.S. forces had. Their maintenance however did not live up to the same standards required in the U.S. forces. Their sides were always wide open and they seldom had safety belts. I often developed white knuckles trying not to fall out. Since our detachments were often located in VC controlled territory I generally sat on my flack jacket because I didn't want a VC bullet to penetrate my butt.

I had some near misses, some that I still think about. One that brings chills to me even now happened on a visit to Coastal Group 16. The helo pad was outside the stockade fence and was separated from it by about 100 yards. I landed about ten in the morning and on the way to the stockade the Vietnamese CO who met me pointed out two land mines that they had discovered in the path during a mine sweep just before my arrival. They were about 13 inches in diameter and encased in a blue plastic case with a pressure sensitive detonator rigged to the top. Whew!

One universal policy strictly enforced by General Westmoreland himself was the R & R program for all hands. It mattered not whether you were a private or a Navy captain, approximately half way through your tour you were guaranteed one week of R & R anywhere that you chose to go within reason. Many went to Thailand and others went to Hong Kong. I chose Hawaii. Since I had legitimate business there I was able to stretch my R & R to ten days and Mary Lee and the children flew out from Washington for a glorious family reunion.

Stan Hemino, a classmate and good friend of mine at the Harvard Business School, was delighted to make all the arrangements. He and his wife met me at the airport with a car for our use for the whole time that we were there. He arranged reservations for us, a beautiful hotel on Maui. He had us to some parties and arranged a beautiful New Years Eve celebration at Michelle's, the best restaurant in Hawaii.

Our very dear friends, Nev and Fran Shaffer, were on duty in CincPacFleet's staff and they too looked after us. We had an absolutely great time together and it was a wonderful break for all of us. When we said goodbye, we had only six more months to go which didn't seem quite so bad.

After Tet, we settled into a busy routine. We were moving the navy steadily along and we took great satisfaction in the start of the Vietnamization of the naval war as we made steady progress in relieving U.S. naval forces of an increasing number of roles and missions. At first the U.S. naval officers were extremely skeptical, but as the Vietnamese continued to perform well, they became more cooperative in ceding more and more duties to them.

One major discouraging change occurred during this period. As previously pointed out, the U.S. media never really supported us. They were always searching for the anomaly, the snafu and they always gleefully reported everything that was negative about our effort. The Mai Lai massacre was a case in point.

There was no doubt that a small unit of U.S. army forces led by Lieutenant Calley got out of control and killed some innocent Vietnamese villagers, although the village which they attacked was known to support the VC, who had recently killed some of the men in their outfit. There is no doubt that those killings should not have taken place. The VC, on the other hand, by policy routinely murdered villagers who were sympathetic to the South Vietnamese government. The press rarely if ever reported those atrocities, but it seems that they never got enough of the Mai Lai massacre. It came to symbolize our effort there. Mai Lai was inexcusable, but for every Mai Lai there were literally thousand of acts of human compassion on the part of our wonderful troops. Our officers and men were selfless and incredibly generous with both their time and what materials they had available to help the Vietnamese in the countryside. In addition, U.S. charities such as Catholic Relief were wonderful in supplying all sorts of assistance to the Vietnamese. Immediately after Tet, for instance, I was able to load up many Navy craft with mountains of supplies from the Catholic Charities, which we delivered to the people in the Delta who were hurting. I was and still am enormously proud of the humanity that was everywhere manifested.

The media, however, turned outright hostile to our effort and U.S. forces in general. The great British war correspondent, William Elegant, stated after the war that the U.S. media reflexively supported the enemy. You could read in any edition of *Time* magazine that the enemy was in the right and we were in the wrong. If the very fragile South Vietnamese government cooperated with us they were attacked as our lackeys. If they tried to hew to an independent position they were equally viciously attacked as being ingrates. They couldn't win. The drum beat of negative and inaccurate reporting eventually had a major catastrophic effect. It literally undermined the U.S. public's support for our war effort, not while I was there, but later, to the enormous discredit to the U.S. media.

I guess I have participated in more war operations than almost all living Americans. This long and varied experience in combat and in national crises situations around the world taught me a great deal about the motivation of the U.S. fighting man. In order for a man to go half way around the world and serve in a hostile, dangerous and inhospitable environment such as Vietnam in which he daily places his life in jeopardy he must feel that he is doing something of vital importance for his country. He must feel that his sacrifices and efforts are appreciated at home and that he is respected and admired for the enormous sacrifices that he is making for his country. He must feel special, as he did in World War II. Regardless of the politics of the situation, the U.S. fighting man is owed at least that.

William Manchester, a distinguished biographer and military historian, spoke to that point most eloquently:

> Esteem was personal too. You assumed that if you came through this ordeal, you would age with dignity, respected as well as adored by your children and memorialized in the pantheon of Americans who sacrificed their youth in combat so that others could live free.
>
> All these things and the certitude that victory in the war would assure their continuance into perpetuity—all this led you into battle, and sustained you as you fought, and comforted you if you fell, and, if it came to that, justified your death to all who loved you as you had loved them.

When the U. S. public's support for the war and the men who had answered their country's call to fight its battles was tragically withdrawn, and the soldier could read in the U.S. media, on any given day, that he was the enemy, his morale and feeling of self esteem was dealt a terrible blow, and that is exactly what happened in Vietnam.

Time magazine is a good case in point. Years later, after the war, at my urging, a dear friend of mine, Louis Banks, who had held the top editorial positions in the various Time Inc. publications and was then on the *Time* board won approval of his board to revisit the *Time*'s coverage of the Vietnam War. Its findings were hardly surprising to me. The review found that its coverage was fatally unbalanced in favor of the enemy. One very important *Time* stringer turned out to be an active North Vietnam major.

An article in *The Wall Street Journal* written by Mackubin Thomas Owens speaks eloquently to the distortions of the true facts by the U.S. media in attempts to cast those of us who fought there as victims. According to Owens, the genesis of the stereotype of the Vietnam War veteran as a victim was the antiwar left of the 1960s and 1970s:

> Initially vilifying the American soldier as a war criminal, the left eventually bestowed victimhood on him. He was victimized

first by his country, which sent him off to fight an unjust war. He was then victimized by a military that dehumanized him, turning him into a killer.

According to the conventional story line, those who served were largely young, poor and from ethnic minorities. Many if not all committed or observed atrocities. The horrors of war led many to turn to drugs and crime. Vietnamese veterans are disproportional represented among the homeless and the incarcerated.

But as Will Rogers once said, "It's not the things we don't know that get us into trouble. It's the things we know that just ain't so."

Let's look at some of the statistics. Thirty percent of those who died came from the lowest income group, but 26 percent were from the highest. As for the war's disproportionate burden on minorities, 86 percent of those who died were white and 12.5 percent were black, in an age group in which blacks comprise 13.1 percent of the population. Two-thirds of those who served in Vietnam were volunteers, accounting for 65 percent of all combat deaths. Other media-hyped contentions are equally baloney. The left's insistence that posttraumatic stress disorder and Agent Orange continue to victimize Vietnam veterans is just so much more hogwash. The number 3.3 million that is used to describe the magnitude of the posttraumatic stress disorder just isn't true, since only about 15 percent of this number actually were assigned to combat units. The Center for Disease Control made an exhaustive study of this and found that only 15 percent of Vietnam War veterans experienced symptoms of combat-related PTSD at some time during and after their tour in Vietnam, but only 2.2 percent exhibited symptoms at the time of the study.

The additional claim that more Vietnam veterans have committed suicide than died in the war is pure nonsense. The suicide rate for Vietnam veterans is no higher than for non veterans. This is also true of drug abuse, homelessness and incarceration rates.

... the press has been complicit in perpetuating the negative stereotype of the Vietnam veteran. B.C. Burkett's 1998 book

Stolen Valor explains how. Mr. Burkett used the Freedom of Information Act to check the actual records of the "image makers" used by reporters to flesh out their stories of homelessness, Agent Orange, suicide, drug abuse, criminality or alcoholism. What he found was astonishing. More often than not the showcase "veteran" who cried on camera about his dead buddies, about committing or witnessing atrocities, or about some heroic action in combat that led him to his current dead end in life, was an impostor. Many had never been to Vietnam, or even in the armed forces.

Don't be fooled by those fat slobs with beards in combat fatigues, which they bought at their friendly Army Navy Store. By just looking at them I can easily pick out the phonies.

Mr. Owens goes on to say that Vietnam veterans are not victims. A comprehensive survey commissioned in 1980 by the Veterans Administration reported that 91 percent of those who had seen action in Vietnam were "glad they had served their country." A healthy 80 percent disagreed with the statement that "the U.S. took advantage of me." Nearly two out of three said that they would go to Vietnam again—even knowing how the war would end.

Most of us who served there did so for the most part with honor and restraint and we veterans have fared at least as well as any other veterans of U.S. wars. I hold the U.S. media heavily responsible for the devastating destruction of the fighting spirit of our young soldiers, Marines and sailors in Vietnam. I loathe and detest the media for their nefarious behavior.

And years later, former Colonel Bui Tin who served on the staff of the North Vietnamese Army and received the unconditional surrender of South Vietnam on April 30, 1975 confirmed the American Tet military victory:

> Our losses were staggering and a complete surprise. General Giap later told me that Tet had been a military defeat, though we had gained the planned political advantage when Johnson agreed to negotiate and did not run for reelection. The second and third waves in May and September were, in retrospect, mistakes. Our forces in the South were nearly wiped out by the

fighting in 1968. It took us until 1971 to reestablish our presence, but we had to use North Vietnamese troops as local guerrillas. If the American forces had not begun to withdraw under Nixon in 1969, they could have punished us severely. We suffered badly in 1969 and 1970 as it was.

On strategy he said:

If Johnson had granted Westmoreland's request to enter Laos and block the Ho Chi Minh Trail, Hanoi could not have won the war.... It was the only way to bring sufficient military power to bear on the fighting in the South. Building and maintaining the trail was a huge effort involving tens of thousands of soldiers, repair teams, medical stations and communications units.... Our operations were never compromised by attacks on the trail. At times, B-52 strikes would cause real damage, but we put so much in at the top of the trail that enough men and weapons to prolong the war always came out at the bottom.... If the bombing had been concentrated at one time, it would have hurt our efforts. But the bombing was expanded in slow stages under Johnson and it didn't worry us. We had plenty of time to prepare alternate routes and facilities. We always had stockpiles of rice ready to feed the people for months if a harvest was damaged. The Soviets bought rice from Thailand for us.

Support for the war from our rear was completely secure, while the American rear was vulnerable. Every day our leadership would listen to world news over the radio at 9 p.m. to follow the growth of the antiwar movement. Visits to Hanoi by Jane Fonda, former Attorney General Ramsey Clark and ministers gave us confidence that we should hold on in the face of battlefield reverses. We were elated when Jane Fonda, wearing a red Vietnamese dress, said at a news conference that she was ashamed of American actions in the war and would struggle along with us.... Those people represented the conscience of America... part of its war-making capability, and we turned that power in our favor.

Colonel Bui Tin went on to serve as the editor of the *Peoples'*

Daily, the official newspaper of the Socialist Republic of Vietnam. Disillusioned with the reality of Vietnamese Communism, Bui Tin immigrated to France and now lives in Paris.

In late April 1968, I received my orders as prospective commanding officer of the heavy guided missile cruiser *Albany,* which was approaching the end of a long and major modernization in the Boston Naval Shipyard. I was delighted, and my focus began to shift to my prospective capital ship command.

On the seventh of May, however, I came very close to missing my major command opportunity—as well as the rest of my life. At about 0200 that morning I was knocked out of bunk by a huge explosion. When I picked myself up off the floor and found that I was unhurt I ran to the main house to find that the front half had been blown off. Through the smoke I saw our sentry lying in a heap. My immediate thought was that he was dead. I went to him and, to my relief, I found him badly stunned, but alive. He had been blown about thirty feet in the air. His flak jacket had saved him. We had taken a direct hit from a 7.2″ Soviet rocket which had come in over the back of our quarters, where I had been sleeping, and hit the front of the house. No one was seriously wounded but it was a miracle that we weren't. I had a strong feeling that it was time for me to go home, as my luck was apparently running out.

I received my orders detaching me from my command and, on the 2nd of July 1968, the Vietnamese navy had a formal review in my honor. Admiral Chon who had recently been promoted, graciously presented me with the highest Vietnamese decoration, The National Order of Vietnam, as well as The Cross of Gallantry for the several combat missions that we engaged in together.

On the 5th of July I boarded a charter flight to the United States and to a reunion with my family. All in all it had been an exciting and, to my mind, a worthwhile year. I was and still am proud to have served my country there and I would do it all over again if the circumstances dictated.

Looking back at that year in Vietnam I have formed some definite conclusions.

The performance, attitude and military judgment of the civilian hierarchy in the Defense Department headed by Robert McNamara were almost criminal. They repeatedly disregarded their military commanders' advice and did their best to belittle and humiliate them. Early on, in 1965, when the South Vietnamese forces were facing defeat by a heavily Russian and Chinese supported Viet Cong and North Vietnamese and Johnson decided to send combat forces to Vietnam, I saw, as I mentioned in an earlier chapter, a JCS paper that said that a force level in the vicinity of 750,000 troops would be necessary to bring us a quick victory. Since that meant that Johnson would have to call up the reserves and thereby endanger his enormously expensive Great Society programs, McNamara with the assistance of Allen Enthovan reprogrammed their systems analysis programs. They generated the strategy that would be followed to the detriment of the military effort for the remainder of our operations there. The reprogrammed computer solution was the Graduated Response Strategy. This approach, in substance, held that if the enemy had ten troops and you put eleven troops against him you would eventually win. If he raised his troop level to 15 then you put 16 against him. Under this terrible strategy McNamara was able to demonstrate that a force level of 250,000 troops was sufficient to do the job. This, of course, flew in the face of historical military experience, which said that if the enemy has ten troops you put overwhelming force against him—100 troops—and then you could contemplate quick victory.

The Graduated Response Strategy suited Johnson just fine because it meant not having to call up the reserves and it enabled Johnson to keep his expensive Great Society programs intact. The almost unbelievable disdain in which McNamara and his whiz kids held our military leadership made them very comfortable in demanding that they fight the war with one-third of the forces that the military said they needed. McNamara would bring success to this diminished effort by substituting his marvelous military judgment for that of his military commanders, which he disdained with continuing unsuccessful results.

McNamara had a great advantage over the military leadership at that time because he and his underlings understood the new science of computer based systems analysis and the military at that time did not. They were not able to challenge the fallacious programming that went into his scientific solution. In spite of all of this, the military was able to adapt and it fought wonderfully well in spite of being under-manned and over-controlled by militarily ignorant men.

In spite of the almost traitorous U.S. media and a bungling Department of Defense hierarchy, the U.S. was winning the war in Vietnam. That the U.S. population, through the successful efforts of the media and the radical left withdrew its support for the war and the young Americans who were doing their duty there was and still is a national disgrace.

This loss of U.S. support for the troops had an enormous effect on troop morale. The wonderful morale, which I experienced there, disintegrated in the face of this collapsing national support. It was little wonder that there were serious lapses of discipline after 1969. Regardless of whether the national policy in Vietnam was correct or not, the wonderful young Americans who went there at their country's behest deserved better. I am ashamed of the U.S. in its failure to support its committed young men and women. It shall remain an indelible black mark on our national behavior and history. Cutting and running is contrary to our national character, especially when we were doing just fine, despite the incessant civilian meddling and civilian blunders.

I have spoken of the incredible morale of the U.S. service personnel in country during my tour there. I rate the morale there superior to the troop morale in World War II and in Korea. There were three reasons for this. One—if you arrived in Vietnam on the 4th of July as I did, and if you were not hit prior to that date, you had to be on a plane home on the 5th of July the following year. No exceptions! Two—half way through your tour, whether you were a private or a captain, you were taken out of the line and given an R & R at a destination of your choice, guaranteed, no exceptions. And three—if you were hit and you made it to an aid station alive you had a 99 percent chance of making it. Medical evacuation using special helicopters and wonderful medical support all the way along the line increased your chances of survival enormously.

Another vitally important conclusion is that the absolutely uncontrolled media who almost always had an antiwar bias so inaccurately reported the war that it played a pivotal role in our political failure of will. When U.S. troops are committed to battle, the media cannot be allowed to subvert the military effort and military morale. If we learned one thing in our Vietnam experience it is that the media must be under tight military control in a war theater. That lesson was not only learned but it was put into practice in the Gulf War with great effectiveness.

And finally, we must never again commit our young men and women to combat without a powerful resolution to win. No more can we modulate our effort for political reasons. To do otherwise, like we did in Vietnam, is nothing short of criminal.

Chapter 19

The *Albany*, 1968–1970

L EAVING VIETNAM WAS somewhat of a bitter-sweet experience. I had grown very fond of my Vietnamese comrades and
especially Admiral Chon. I had developed a healthy respect
for them and I was enormously proud of their progress in developing
an effective fighting navy. While I had my plans well in place for the
continued Vietnamization of the naval war, I was leaving before we
were able to ensure the continued assumption of U.S. Navy roles and
missions. We just had a long way to go, but I took great satisfaction
knowing that we were at least well on our way. I recognized that we
had at least four more years to go before I felt that the Vietnamese
navy had the proper balance to be on its own, except for carrier aircraft support.

In 1968 I was absolutely confident that the United States would
stay the course and I did my best to reassure Admiral Chon of our national determination to stay with them for as long as it was necessary
to repel the Communists. I was proven to be wrong, of course, and it
still hurts when I think about how we lost our national will.

Admiral Chon, along with the senior members of his staff and
my relief captain, Paul Arbo, came to the airport to see me off. My
World Airways charter flight took off for the United States and carried me towards a completely new set of challenges and adventures.
It's a very long flight across the Pacific. We took the great circle route
that carried us to Japan and then over the North Pacific. Our destination was the Alameda Naval Air Station outside of San Francisco.

I must say that my homecoming carried none of the negative aspects reported by so many who returned from the war. There was no
sign of any hostility towards me, but in 1968 the U.S. resolve in Vietnam was still strong and those who were determined to undermine
that national resolve had not yet succeeded. I wore my uniform in

the airport in San Francisco and at my destination at Dulles Airport outside of Washington and felt very comfortable.

Mary Lee, Randy and Valerie were on hand at the airport to greet me, and a happy homecoming it was. I had been with them in Hawaii six months earlier, so it was not as bad a separation as it might have been. Mary Lee looked both beautiful and radiant and both children looked just great to me.

I had been given a full month's leave before I had to report to Boston to commence getting the *Albany* ready for commissioning and I looked forward to unwinding and enjoying my family, and getting a much needed rest after a very hectic and hazardous year.

Our home in Arrowood looked particularly beautiful as we drove up to the front door. I was home safe and sound and was damn glad to be there. As always after a very long separation, there were the usual family adjustment that had to be made. Mary Lee had done a great job of being both mother and dad in my absence and it took a little time to get used to my reappearance on the family scene.

I hadn't been home for more than two weeks when I received a call from the commander of the Boston Naval Shipyard. He informed me that they needed a qualified trial captain for the first underway sea trials for the *Albany* after her long inactivity during her two-year modernization. He got right to the point. He wanted me to come to Boston to fill that requirement. I pointed out that I had just returned from Vietnam and was getting a much needed rest and reunion with my family. He assured me that it would be for one day only. We discussed my legal responsibilities as trial captain and he assured me that the ship would continue to be his responsibility and not mine. Fair enough, but if I was on the bridge when disaster struck it would have been less than a great effect on my service reputation, legal responsibility or not. I told him that I would let him know as soon as I made a decision.

When I talked to Mary Lee about it she quickly concluded that I really wanted to do it and she encouraged me to go. She was right, of course. I really could hardly wait to see my new ship. So off to Boston I went. I arrived in late afternoon and I well remember my first real look at *Albany*. I walked down the pier to which she was moored and was truly awed by her huge size. Looking up at the massive superstructure, I stood there with enormous misgivings. How in the devil was I going to handle her from that distant bridge thirteen stories off the water? Her length exceeded the length of two football fields. She lay alongside in all of her awesome splendor and I was filled with a mixture of both great pride and not inconsiderable dread. It was a feeling I had each time I first walked alongside a new ship to which I had orders to command. *Davis* looked huge after the *Lester* and *Luce* looked huge after the *Davis* but the *Albany* was in a class by herself. This was going to be something else. I was thrilled with the idea of being her commanding officer but I was also a bit scared.

As I looked up at her and thought about getting her underway I wondered who was going to make up her trial crew. There was a small cadre of the *Albany* ship's company in the yard but not nearly enough to even think about getting her underway. The great majority of the ship's company was at the Newport training center under the direction of our prospective executive officer, Bob Brady. They would not report to the yard until just prior to her commissioning date. I soon learned that the trial crew was to be made up of a pick-up team taken from other ships in the yard and heavily supplemented with yard personnel from the various shops.

The next day I came on board and went directly to the bridge, as the various departments readied the ship for getting underway. A docking pilot came on board and we finally backed clear with the aid of three tugs. As soon as we were pointed fair I took the con, and from that moment everything started to go down hill. We almost immediately lost one of our two gyros. As we started to move out of the harbor the second gyro went down and we shifted to steering by magnetic compass. Then the surface search radar ceased to work and we shifted to a small Raytheon Pathfinder radar which was on board as a distant backup that could be used for navigation.

The weather had been clear, with excellent visibility, but as the ship approached the Boston sea buoy the wind suddenly shifted and we were enveloped in a dense fog. We shifted to dead reckoning as we started a very elaborate program of engineering trials. We used the Pathfinder to try to pick up contacts which might cause us problems. Here we were just off Boston harbor in a ship drawing 35 feet of water without a very real idea where we were because the heavy maneuvering required by the trial schedule raised havoc with our attempts to dead reckon the ship's position. We were truly lost. We picked up what we thought was a buoy on the Pathfinder and turned toward it. The idea was to close enough to read its number and thus establish our position. At a dead slow speed we approached. At 200 yards the lockouts on the forecastle could see nothing; at 150 nothing, at 100 nothing and finally at about 75 yards we could make out our "buoy." It was a small fishing vessel who apparently sighted us coming out of the fog at her, as we sighted her, and she was getting the hell out of there. I didn't blame her at all, as the huge monster bore down on her.

But there we were still lost, and I was conjuring up images of us grounding and becoming a permanent landmark off Boston Harbor. Luckily, as late afternoon approached, the wind shifted back to the west and the fog cleared as quickly as it had set in. At about the same time the yard engineers got one of the gyros back on line and we proceeded into Boston Harbor with no further difficulties.

I returned to Washington that same night and stayed at home until it was time for me to report as prospective commanding officer. On the 10th of August I reported for duty to the commander of the shipyard. He had arranged office space on a floating barge moored very close to *Albany*. While not particularly fancy, the accommodation would prove to be satisfactory for me and my staff.

My first priority was to have a careful look at *Albany*, and what I saw was alarming indeed. The ship was filthy. Apparently, to save money, there were no funds put into the modernization budget to cover ship-keeping. As a result there was debris everywhere. Some trunks that went down seven decks were more than half filled with all manner of yard dirt and trash. It was, in short, a damn mess.

I was in no mood for this obvious dereliction. Without delay, I put my observations and position into an operational immediate dispatch to the Chief of Naval Operations and that did it. In nothing flat the money spigots opened and the recriminations began. The yard commander was relieved and the Bureau of Ships attitude changed overnight. What I demanded I got, but it was almost too late. The money wasn't the problem anymore, it was the need for manpower. I scrounged men from everywhere that I could think of, including the Boston Naval Brig. We assigned small group projects, such as ladder refurbishment. There were literally hundreds of them needing retreading and painting and the prisoners did a great job. They liked having something meaningful to do and they made a fine contribution. Other similar, defined projects were developed and pursued.

At the yard's weekly commanding officers conference I wasn't voted Mr. Congeniality, but I was effective in motivating the various shops in the yard to focus on the *Albany*. As our commissioning date in November approached I started to feel slightly more confident that we were going to make it.

I very much needed a place to live during this precommissioning period and the Boston Navy League came to my rescue. Its president in Boston, Asa Phillips, called on me on board the barge soon after I reported and asked what he and his organization could do for me. When I told him of my housing needs he got right on it and the next day he picked me up at the barge and we drove together to Marblehead, Massachusetts. We went to a brand new rental development in a beautiful part of Marblehead overlooking Marblehead Harbor. The management was expecting me and showed me plans of the various units. I noted that as the units got closer to the water the prices rose appreciably. The one they took me to see was literally hanging over the water. It was a two-story townhouse, fully furnished down to the dishes, pots, pans and silverware. It was truly beautiful, but I dreaded finding out the price.

The manager asked me if it would be suitable and I rather tentatively replied that it would be just great, but I doubted that my budget would cover the cost. He asked if $150 dollars a month would be agreeable? It was a downright gift to me and I spent several happy months living there. The manager of Glovers Landing, as it was called, had been in the Navy and he quickly befriended me. He frequently came over to my apartment in the evening and we would sit on my deck overlooking the water and exchange sea stories. He had an amateur Massachusetts lobstering license which permitted him to deploy up to ten pots. When he found out that I liked lobsters he had his wife deliver a large cooking pot and I would frequently find live lobsters in my refrigerator when I returned from the ship.

I settled into the routine of inspections, monitoring, cajoling and encouraging progress. I know that I made enemies in the yard and on the type commander's staff, but I was working a minor miracle and everyone knew it.

There were bright spots. Buships (the Bureau of Ships) established a very generous budget to refurbish and decorate my in-port cabin. The yard hired an excellent Boston interior design firm to plan and execute the project and the results were spectacular. I loved it. In addition, the Navy assigned four Filipino stewards to my cabin. Since I did not live on board prior to commissioning I arranged through friends to have them accepted by the head chef at the Boston Ritz for training for a period of four months. They were directly under the supervision of the celebrated chef. He was glad to have them, since he did not have to pay them, and I was delighted to have them train in one of the best kitchens in Boston. In outfitting my cabin I had charbroilers, serving carts and all manner of food preparation and serving equipment procured. As a result, when we finally went into commission I had developed one of the finest messes in the fleet.

Perhaps this could be thought of, in hindsight, as extravagant, but consider this: I was taking command of the largest and most powerful cruiser in the world. The ship's company numbered about 1300 enlisted, 72 Marines and 86 officers. I carried eight missile systems, four Talos and four Tartar, as well as extensive antisubmarine armament. Talos missiles carried nuclear weapons, as did the antisubmarine torpedoes. I bore complete and unassignable responsibility for the safety and wellbeing of both a ship, worth about a billion dollars, and her ship's company, whose welfare and safety were beyond worth. My total compensation, including my rental and food allowance, came to just about $25,000 a year. The Navy well recognized that that modest salary in no way adequately compensated me or any other commanding officer in a similar ship, and that is why the Navy did everything that it could to come forward with non-monetary compensation. That non-monetary compensation included my splendid cabin, my assigned stewards, marine orderlies and marine drivers, personal writers, a beautiful gig, a private sedan and the use of the on-board helicopter.

As to the Filipino stewards in the fleet, they permitted the officers to live like gentlemen. They were a valuable addition to the ship and to the staff officers and it was a win-win situation for both the Navy and the Filipinos. At that time we had a treaty with the Republic of the Philippines whereby we would enlist 2500 Filipinos per year into the steward's branch. The program was so popular that we had about 25,000 applications a year to chose from, so we literally got the cream of the crop. Those young men would routinely serve for twenty years in the Navy and then would retire into the Fleet Reserve, return to the Philippines and live out their lives as the richest men in their barrios. Admiral Zumwalt, a highly political animal, had the treaty abrogated on the basis of racial discrimination and placed life at sea for the naval officer on a slippery slope indeed. Although this all occurred after I left the *Albany,* I understand that life in the wardrooms of the fleet shifted from gentility to an upscale mess deck with temporary mess cooks serving in the wardroom food service facilities. What a great shame!

Our commissioning date was set for the 9th of November and all of our efforts focused on getting *Albany* as ready as possible for that momentous occasion. The balance crew under Bob Brady not only spent their time in a total environment of training but they also produced the enormous paperwork required of a ship in commission, including the ship's organization book, watch quarter and station bills, battle bills and a host of other bills, covering every possible ship's evolution. It was a monumental task and they accomplished it with enormous professionalism.

I might digress a bit here to chronicle the correspondence that I had with Admiral Burke during this period. This was 1968, just after my return from Vietnam. I wrote Admiral Burke about my experiences in and observations of the war. I told him in some detail of my successes with shifting roles and missions from the U.S. Navy forces to the Vietnamese navy and stressed the point that if the U.S. was ever going to be able to withdraw from Vietnam with honor the war would have to be Vietnamized. I outlined my plan, which was succeeding so well in naval roles and missions, and held that, properly organized and developed, the same thing could be accomplished on the ground. I stressed that this could not be done overnight. In the Navy's case, my careful planning indicated that it would take about five years total, but I was certain enough in the quality of the Vietnamese naval personnel as fighting men that I was absolutely confident that it could be done. Admiral Burke was enormously interested in my positions and, as a senior advisor to Richard Nixon, then running for the presidency, he gave my letters to Nixon, who also, according to Admiral Burke, showed considerable interest and enthusiasm for the concept. I was enormously proud that as soon as Nixon was elected he announced that the national war policy was to Vietnamize the war. The problem was that he could not accept the five-year timetable and for political reasons he reduced the period to two years, with disastrous results.

I had hoped that Admiral Burke would be able to come to my commissioning and perhaps be the principle speaker, but he declined. In his stead, I invited Erasmus Corning who was the mayor of Albany New York and had been for the past twenty-five years. He turned out to be a great choice.

As is typical of the weather in November in Boston, the 9th of November dawned gray and cold. Happily, it didn't snow, but it was far from perfect commissioning weather. The very large number of attendees were protected from the elements by a hugh tent that had been set up alongside the ship. It was a fine commissioning. The speeches were mercifully short but eloquent. The commandant of the First Naval District, Rear Admiral Benson, presented me with a Legion of Merit with a V for valor for my service in Vietnam and read the orders placing *Albany* in commission. I read my orders, made some brief and probably forgettable remarks and ordered the executive officer to set the watch. The ship came alive. The crew quickly came on board to the tune of "Anchors Aweigh," and manned the rail. The missiles were run out on the launcher rails and the launchers were trained and elevated, much to the delight of the spectators. The marine honor guard came to present arms and the national ensign was broken on the stern and the jack broken on the jackstaff on the bow. The ship's commissioning pennant, the symbol of a U.S. man-of-war in full commission, was broken on a pig stick at the peak. It was an enormously proud moment for me. Here I was in command of the Navy's and the world's most powerful surface ship—something I had dreamed about all my professional life.

And now we were a ship of the Navy in full commission. We

looked great on that gray November afternoon but we still had a hell of a lot of work to do before we would be truly ready to join the fleet. The weather continued to deteriorate and it became an important factor in our continuing efforts to make progress in our long fitting-out schedule and in our equipment and hull maintenance. The yard also had a long way to go in its SHIPALT and ORDALT programs, so yard workers continued to work all over the ship. The fitting-out process was a particularly long and arduous job, mostly because we were so damn big.

Mary Lee and the children left our Washington home and came to live in our beloved Newport where, thanks to our old and delightful realtor, Peter King, we were able to rent the Auchincloss home on Barkley Square. It was an absolute gem. Sited on four acres of land overlooking the sea, it was a perfect house for us, and all hands loved it. Randy and Valerie entered the Newport school system and flourished. Randy became quite a football star as an outstanding place and field goal kicker and we were both very proud of him and delighted for him. He didn't miss a point after touchdown all season.

As December began, I became terribly ill with pneumonia and was turned in to the Naval Hospital at Newport. I was one sick puppy. I eventually recovered enough to be discharged and I rejoined the ship a few days before Christmas. The day after I returned, the exec asked me if I felt well enough to attend a Christmas party on the mess decks which the ship was organizing for our enlisted families. I told him that I thought I was. At the appropriate time, the chief master at arms escorted me to the mess deck where I greeted everyone and stayed for a little while to enjoy the wonderful party in progress. I was so weak that I was barely able to make it back to my cabin. It took over a month for me to feel truly well again.

And I was champing at the bit. We were just not making the progress that we wanted in organizing ourselves or in physically getting the ship ready for operations. I hit on the idea of getting the ship out of the yard and taking her to the warm waters and clement weather of the Caribbean. Eventually I was able to convince the type commander that it was a good idea, and so for the first time we got *Albany* underway in early February and headed for Roosevelt Roads, the site of the Atlantic Fleet missile range. We didn't intend to fire any missiles; we just wanted to move into warm weather and be by ourselves for a while, where we could work on the ship and work on making the ship's company into an operating team.

We stopped in New York for a much deserved liberty and, incidentally, to take on feed water for our boilers, since our evaporators were not operating efficiently. The cruise was a great idea. We worked the ship's company hard but all hands enjoyed the effort. Our progress was remarkable and the ship started to look beautiful. Being moored alongside in Roosevelt Roads was the perfect place for what we wanted to do. When we left Roosevelt Roads the ship looked terrific. It literally sparkled, and all hands were mighty proud of her. In addition, we had a good handle on what additional work needed to be done in the yard.

From the time we returned in March until our scheduled departure time in early July we focused on remedying the long list of material deficiencies that still existed in the ship, completing our fittings out and loading the mountain of stores that a ship of *Albany*'s size must carry.

Officers continued to report on board. One, our senior surgeon, was a delightful young doctor. During his call on me he told me a little of his background, including the fact that he was a graduate of Suffield Academy located in Suffield, Connecticut. Since Mary Lee and I were wondering what to do about Randy's final year in high school, I immediately became interested, because of his obvious enthusiasm for the school. Mary Lee and I decided to look into the possibility and the whole family promptly drove down to visit Suffield Academy. We were all enormously impressed. Randy was particularly enthusiastic. The headmaster said that they would be delighted to have Randy but the school's policy was only to accept students for a minimum of two years. This suited Randy, as it did Mary Lee and me. It was a wonderful choice. Randy loved the place. He loved his teachers and he thrived both academically and on the athletic fields. He was well suited to the school and the school truly liked him. He often stated that the two years that he spent at Suffield were the two best years of his academic experience.

As our departure date approached, all facets of the ship's life accelerated. With money readily available, we were able to put enormous shipyard focus on the ship and we made great progress in reducing the number of discrepancies in our material condition that still remained. As the physical condition improved so did our organizational efforts prosper under our outstanding executive officer. Bob Brady did an excellent job of completing the written organization of the ship and in carrying out an intense training program for all hands.

Finally, our departure date arrived on the 1st of July, 1969. Since we did not carry a flag officer, I decided to invite some of my civilian friends to sail with me from Boston to New York. Included among my passengers was the economics professor whom I had while attending the Harvard Business School, my good friend Larry Fouraker. I also included young Randy among my invited passengers. It was a very foggy passage which required my presence on the bridge most of the night. I did have a splendid dinner in my mess for my guests. During the course of our conversation at dinner, I took the occasion to inform my friends that I was thinking about retiring from the Navy after my capital ship command. I told them that, politically and socially, the Navy was moving in a direction that was making me uncomfortable and that I was starting the long process of coming to grips both personally and professionally with that reality.

The weather cleared as we made landfall off of Sandy Hook and we entered New York Harbor in bright sunshine. Taking the ship under the Veranzano Bridge was always a thrill, since the top hamper on the mast just cleared the center span by a very few feet. To successfully clear, it was absolutely necessary to hit the center span of the bridge exactly. A few yards one way or the other could prove disastrous. Although I was right on, there was an optical illusion which made it appear that the ship would not clear, but clear it did.

The ship looked absolutely beautiful. Its paintwork was perfect, the enormous amount of topside brightwork had been polished to a brilliant gold and it shone in the sun. The ship had a huge quantity of topside white canvas which also reflected the sun. Our crew was in the uniform of the day, drawn up in careful ranks at quarters for entering port and our wonderful band was at its station playing its usual repertoire of stirring marches. We were quite a sight indeed! We were surrounded by all manner of craft as we moved through the harbor. Several of the numerous ferries that move cars and people across the harbor from Staten Island and elsewhere diverted from their course in order that their passengers might admire us. We received countless whistle salutes. It was the kind of experience that made it all worth while. I wouldn't have swapped being commanding officer of that ship that day for anything in the world.

We moored at a pier at 54th Street, and Mary Lee was there to greet me. After I said goodbye to our embarked passengers I called on the commandant of the Third Naval District. At noon several of my Harvard classmates had a luncheon in my honor at the New York Athletic Club. Gerry Donovan, my old friend from Harvard was the president of the Bulova Watch Company and he presented me with an elegant Acutron Bulova watch. I invited all of them to visit the ship and most of them did. And I had a wonderful dinner on board for many of them that evening. The next day, the Fourth of July, Mary Lee, Randy and I went up to Yankee Stadium to see a double header. At least Randy stayed for the second game. We left to drive to Chapaqua to have a picnic lunch with the Peers, another Harvard classmate.

On the 5th of July I said goodbye to Mary Lee and Randy and we got underway for the Atlantic Fleet Missile Range at Roosevelt Roads, Puerto Rico. Since we had a great deal of shaking down to do I was in no hurry to get to Roosevelt Roads. We availed ourselves of the transit time to continue the long dreary process of organizing and training our ship's company. Two weeks later we entered Roosevelt Roads.

After settling in at our berth, I looked forward to a little relaxation after the vigorous at-sea period that we had just completed. One of my stewards brought me a current copy of the *New York Times* and I was both surprised and delighted to find a picture of my pal Larry Fouraker on the front page, accompanying a news story reporting that he had been named dean of the faculty at the Harvard Business School. His appointment, although I didn't know it at the time, was to change my life dramatically.

We were scheduled to fire six Talos and 10 Tartar missiles in the first real test of our new and revolutionary digital fire control systems, our new Naval Tactical Data System, and our super sophisticated three-dimensional SPS 48 air search radar.

While many features of our technologically advanced system functioned quite well, I would have to characterize the Talos shoots as failures. The missiles, it turned out, had not been properly tested at the missile depot and they contained a number of material glitches that made successful shots impossible.

I'll never forget the very first one that we fired. Talos, by the way was a huge missile. It measured 18 inches in diameter and with its booster it was well over 30 feet long. It was a programmed beam rider with active radar terminal guidance. Its effective range was about 100 miles. On the first day of our scheduled firing we acquired the high speed drone that was to be our target at about 120 miles. I gave the order to fire when the target closed, to make the intercept within our effective range. The missile unfortunately was not captured by the capture beam, so instead of flying towards the target it did a complete loop over the ship, at a not very comfortable altitude. It scared the hell out of all of us topside and we were relieved when missile control destroyed it.

I had raised hell about the lack of any offensive power capability on our very best cruiser. I repeatedly pointed out that in effect the *Albany* was nothing more or less than the weapons department of the carrier. If the carrier got taken out, the *Albany* might as well go fishing. That, by the way, suited the aviators just fine. They had no use for the idea that the missile was going to displace piloted aircraft in many of its cherished roles and missions and so they were comfortable trying to starve the Navy's missile program to death, except where it supported the carrier. To be responsive to this argument and to keep me quiet at a late stage in our modernization the Navy authorized the installation of the short-range, 50-mile, Nuclear Armed System. It was a geographic system, meaning that, to be effective, the firing ship had to be able to fix its position within 50 yards. To do that, the Navy authorized the first installation of the the the new Navy GPS system in *Albany*. The idea of the GPS now is not very exciting but in 1968 it was a gee whiz concept. It was a slow process because the Navy only had a few GPS satellites, which meant that we needed more than one pass to fix our position. It was, however, at least a start. We fired only one surface shot using a conventional warhead and happily made a direct hit.

After spending about three weeks at Roosevelt Roads, we set course for Boston and our final post yard availability. We spent the next two months in Boston reworking many of our systems and fixing numerous engineering, weapons, fire control and electronics discrepancies which we uncovered on our cruise in the Caribbean.

And finally we were able to say goodbye to the Boston Naval Shipyard and report to the Atlantic Fleet for duty. I was overjoyed to set our course for Mayport, Florida which was assigned as our home port. Having had a wonderful experience there in the *Luce*, I looked forward to being based there again. Unfortunately, since Valerie was finishing her senior year at Holton Arms School in Washington and since *Albany* would not be spending much time in Mayport, Mary Lee elected to remain in Washington. While I realized that it was a sound decision, I missed having her with me in Mayport, as did the many Jacksonville friends which we had made during the *Luce* tour there.

Many of our old friends had learned that I was returning in the *Albany* and they gave me a warm welcome. Rear Admiral Ike Kidd, Commander Destroyer *Flotilla Four* broke his flag in *Albany*, but elected to keep his staff on board the destroyer *Tender Yellowstone*.

Ship keeping in Mayport was a commanding officer's dream. The weather was almost always clement and never really cold. It made everything so much easier on the ship than it was for those who had to fight the long dreary and cold northern winters.

Everyone including the Second Fleet commander was anxious to prove the Talos system again. A series of 14 Talos shots were authorized and planned. This time the 14 missiles to be fired were specially selected and painstakingly readied for fleet use. We took them on board and headed back to the Atlantic Fleet missile range. This time we had enormous success. We fired eight Talos and had seven direct hits and one near miss. We were in business!

These missiles were not cheap. During World War II when we fired a nine gun salvo from the *Massachusetts* it was common to hear members of the crew say, "There go nine Buick cars," because in those days a Buick cost about $1,100 dollars, exactly the same as a 16-inch shell. In *Luce,* when I said "fire" on the Terrier battery, it cost $63,000 per missile. In *Albany,* when I said "fire" on the Talos battery, that missile cost $363,000. In 1969 that was one heck of a lot of money.

After returning from Roosevelt Roads in early February, I was ordered to proceed to Yorktown Virginia to take on missiles and other ordnance to replace all that we had expended. Proceeding from Mayport to Yorktown in early February we ran into a hellacious storm off of Cape Hateras. Fleet doctrine required that the ship be slowed so that it would not be pounded by the seas. We continued to slow until our speed was so reduced that we had difficulty maintaining a course. I then had to make the decision to turn the ship around and take the seas on the stern. That was easier said than done because the seas were about 50 foot and turning that huge ship through that trough was hazardous at best. Using both engines and full rudder we started the long evolution to turn. The ship rolled violently as we reached the trough but she kept turning successfully until we had the seas on our stern. We rode that way until the storm abated. Other than some broken crockery we made it with no mishap.

When we moored in Yorktown I decided to drive to Washington to have a visit with Mary Lee. When I arrived at our home, our next door neighbor came out to tell me that Mary Lee had been taken to the Bethesda Naval Hospital in an ambulance. Earlier that day she had fallen out of our car while trying to collect the mail from our mail box and the car had rolled over her foot, breaking some bones. The hospital had set her foot and had given her some Darvon for the pain. It turned out that she was enormously sensitive to the Darvon and went into shock, thus the emergency trip back to the hospital. She damn near expired. That was not exactly what I planned to find but I was glad I had come so that I could give Mary Lee moral support and some tender love and care.

After taking on missiles and ammunition, we headed back down the York River. We had a pilot on board, but I had the con. We had a fair current of about six knots. As we approached a railroad bridge, I mistakenly slowed too much as we neared the open span of the bridge and, to my horror, the current started to swing the stern to starboard just as my bow was pointed fair into the bridge opening. The stern was going to hit the bridge abutment unless I took immediate evasive action. I ordered "right standard rudder" and as the bow started to starboard the stern swung to port and we eased through the opening without disaster striking. Damn, it was a close thing though, and I still get a little shaky thinking about what might have happened.

And now we faced shakedown training at the fleet training center at Guantanamo Bay, Cuba. I hadn't been in Gtmo since shaking down the *Lester* in 1957. It had changed enormously. I found a heavily armed base situated on a hostile island. The Marines had prepared and manned strong defensive positions along the entire base perimeter. Strangely enough, each day hundreds of Cuban nationals crossed into the base to work their numerous jobs there. Castro apparently allowed this because it was advantageous to him. The workers were paid in dollars, something that was in critically short supply in Cuba. The workers were allowed to keep their greenbacks just long enough to cross the border back into Cuba where there was a mandatory exchange of every one of them into Cuban pesos. God help the poor Cuban who tried to keep a few bucks for himself.

What hadn't changed at Gtmo was the incredibly rigorous training which fleet units were obliged to undergo. It was tough and it was purposely painful. The underway training teams conducted a battle problem every day and carefully graded every aspect of the ship's performance. On the first day we received a damage control grade of −156. Up until then I didn't know it was possible to get a grade below zero. We had six weeks to turn the ship into a well organized and trained fighting machine and we collectively set out to do just that. It was slow going but our progress in all departments was steady and encouraging.

At the end of our forth week our progress was judged to be such that the fleet training group commander authorized us to shove off for a long weekend in Jamaica. Since Jamaica lies just an overnight cruise south of Gtmo, it was a convenient place to go for a break.

I hadn't been in Jamaica since visiting there in the *Lester* in 1957 and I remembered it as a delightful, out-east kind of British possession with all of its colonial airs. I remembered the police in their beautiful red coats and white pith helmets. I remembered that the streets were immaculate, that everything worked and that there was a wonderful gentility about the place. I remembered going to the governor's mansion to sign his guest book and then being invited back for tea, but most important I remember the warm hospitality shown our bluejackets. There was a venerable old hotel in Kingston named the Myrtle Bank. It was at this venue that the people of Kingston threw a wonderful party complete with local girls. What a warm and thoughtful thing to do! I always carried warm feelings for Jamaica and Jamaicans from that 1957 visit.

Regretfully the place had changed dramatically for the worse. The British had relinquished sovereignty over the island and the radical socialists had taken political power. Sagan, a black rabble rouser had gotten control of the country and immediately set out to ruin the place. He destroyed the local economy, which was largely based on tourism and the export of bauxite. The infrastructure started a long decline. We found the streets filthy, the buildings shabby, and the natives surly. The gangs had taken over the streets. Nothing seemed to be right.

On our leaving, the Jamaican committed a purposeful act of downright meanness which I shall never forget. In our prearrival logistics request to the port authorities in Kingston, which they acknowledged, was a request for a bar pilot to assist us in our departure. The channel into Kingston Harbor is long and tortuous with about 30 changes of course and a buoy and lighting system unlike that which we were used to.

The exec had the ship ready to get underway at 1500 and we waited for the bar pilot, who was scheduled to arrive just prior to 1530. At 1530 he was not in sight. When 1600 arrived and still no bar pilot we sent a dispatch to the port captain requesting that he be expedited. We received no reply. As hazardous as the channel was in daylight it would be infinitely worse in darkness, because the navigational light system was appreciably different than what we were used to. It had already started to get dark. We had to get underway that evening in order to be ready for operations at Gtmo early the next morning. Knowing that I was taking a hell of a chance I got the ship underway without a pilot at 1730. The evening was moving from dusk to darkness. Drawing 35 feet we were okay only as long as we stayed in the channel. Straying outside just a few feet and we were in grave danger of grounding. Our navigation team performed magnificently, using visual bearings on the navigational aids, radar, fathometer soundings, lookouts and careful navigational plotting in both combat and on the bridge. I conned the *Albany* through that awful channel. When we finally safely reached the sea buoy we gave a great collective sigh of relief. I shall never forgive those damn Jamaicans.

We faced our final exam at Gtmo after six weeks of grueling work but work that brought our ship to a marvelous state of readiness. The final exam consisted of an operational readiness inspection which involved the entire ship in a battle problem which included a great deal of simulated battle damage. The ship engaged both submarine and air attacks and was carefully graded in all of its offensive, defensive and damage control performance. The battle damage imposed by the observers was particularly severe, making all sorts of adjustment and modifications in controlling our various systems very difficult. The ORI lasted for five hours. In the hottest actions in the great battles of the Pacific War we never encountered such grueling combat situations. *Albany* was ready, however and she performed magnificently.

During the many weeks that we were at Gtmo I had time to think about my future. There was no doubt that I was doing very well indeed in the Navy but the Navy was changing and not to my liking. I had always believed in discipline, high standards and excellence in everything that we did, from shining brightwork to wearing our uniforms correctly and with pride and to maintaining the highest standards of material condition and combat readiness—with no compromise for race relations, social engineering or any of the liberal tendencies that were rapidly influencing the way we went to sea.

Through the year I became convinced that only through such effort and standards could we compete successfully in the U.S. manpower market. *Lester, Davis, Luce,* and now *Albany* were all splendid examples of what could be attained if we pursued excellence with every fiber of our being. It was all up to the commanding officer. His job was not to run a popularity contest. His job was to set the standards for the ship and then to have the courage to hold all hands to them. His goal was not love but respect. I know that my ship's companies never loved me, but they had a healthy respect for me and, since we were always considered the very best ship, they had enormous pride in their ship and in themselves. And, incidentally, we always had re-enlistment rates that were at or very near the top of our force.

But my philosophy of command was coming under increasing pressure as the Navy moved into the Zumwalt era. No longer was the captain's word law. We were being increasingly undermined by politically correct attitudes and procedures that were being forced on us at an ever increasing tempo by Zumwalt and his minions. If, for instance, a seaman apprentice felt aggrieved he could write directly to an ombudsman in the Bureau of Naval Personnel and the commanding officer would have to respond officially to the complaint. This put the commanding officer of a man-of-war in an impossible situation and I wasn't buying it.

Although I was well ahead in the competition among my peers I found myself very much at odds with the changing Navy policy and although I was successfully commanding the most powerful surface ship in the world, what should have been a source of joy and fulfillment was rapidly turning into a source of unhappiness for me. I made up my mind that I had to leave the service. This was a tough and wrenching decision. It's tough to quit while you are ahead and a decision like this was not unambiguous, but I made up my mind and I was determined that I would not change it.

Remembering my warm relationship with Larry Fouraker, now the dean of the faculty at the Harvard Business School and my later growing friendship with him when *Albany* was in Boston, I wrote him a letter reminding him that I had discussed the possibility of my retiring after my capital ship command and asking him to keep an eye open for a position in the civilian economy. Being in his distinguished position would almost certainly bring appointments to major corporate boards and I thought that he would be in a good spot to help me find a suitable job.

In due course, I had a letter from him in which he told me that there was a very large company in New York on whose board he served that knew all about me and was anxious to talk with me about the possibility of joining them as vice president for personnel at a possible salary that was about three times what I was receiving in the Navy. In the last paragraph of his letter he wrote that if I could run the Business School as I was running the *Albany* he would very much like me to join him at the Business School as a dean and member of the faculty. Bingo!! Just what I wanted; coming off a high prestige position as commanding officer of a capital ship I aspired to a position of prestige. Going to Harvard as a dean and member of the faculty at the Business School was just what I wanted and needed, subject, of course, to Mary Lee's concurrence. When I put the idea to her, as usual she was completely supportive. The down side was that my salary in academia would not approach the salaries possible in industry. Nonetheless, I was more than a little intrigued. I wrote to Larry Fouraker telling him of my great interest in his proposal and asked him if it was possible to wait until I extricated myself from the Navy. He wrote immediately to tell me he would hold my job as long as necessary.

As our shakedown approached the end I was informed by my detailer in Bupers that my relief was being ordered. He was to be Captain Bob Penniston, someone I did not know. He had been serving as commanding officer of *New Jersey*, which was being decommissioned. I informed my detailer that I had decided to leave the Navy and asked for a billet in Washington where transitioning to civilian life would be as easy as possible. He didn't believe I was serious but did order me to the Chief of Naval Operations in the Pentagon.

We returned to Mayport and I started to prepare the ship for a change of command and to start preparations to return to Mary Lee and Washington. My change of command went very well, but it was a sad day for me. In my farewell remarks I informed everyone there that I was leaving my beloved cruiser destroyer force, this time never to return. My dear friend Admiral Nev Schafer was in attendance but he failed to pick up my remark. When Captain Penniston said, "I relieve you, Sir," that effectively brought my naval career to an end. It now became a case of extricating myself.

I eventually reported to OpNav and again informed my detailer that I intended to retire. There was general disbelief in the Navy. On the authority of the Chief of Naval Personnel, my detailer informed me that I was being ordered to the "Charm School" conducted at the Naval War College for new admiral selectees. They wanted me to see first hand what was probably in store for me if I would change my mind. I at first declined, then I agreed to go if they would put me on per diem and permit Mary Lee to accompany me to Newport. They agreed and off to Newport we went. It was an interesting experience to be with all the flag officer selectees. M.I.T. participated in much of the course and, while I enjoyed it, my focus while in Newport was the Business School. I used some of the time to negotiate with them and by the time we left Newport I had accepted a firm offer from them. My entire energies now were directed to getting our home sold, moving to Boston and entering civilian life.

Chapter 20

A Dean at the Harvard Business School

As a long chapter in my life came to a close, I looked back at the 30 years that I spent in the Navy with a feeling of both pride and satisfaction. The wars, the combatant ship commands, the exciting shore tours, the educational experiences and the wonderful encouragement and love of Mary Lee, made it a long chapter in my life, which I shall always cherish. But now was the time to change course and to look to the future. I resolved never to look back and never to think about what might have been, but to direct my focus, my energies, and my enthusiasm to the future and to make the most of the wonderful opportunity that Harvard had afforded me.

Of course it was a wrench for the whole family. We were leaving the warm womb of the Navy where we were comfortable and where we were loved. We were heading for a new life in New England where we understood that the people would be less than welcoming and friendly. At least that was our impression.

For the first several months after joining the Business School faculty, I lived in Cotting House. The school made a beautiful suite available to me and I was most comfortable. We decided that Mary Lee would stay in our home in Washington until Valerie graduated in May from the Holton Arms School.

In preparation for Mary Lee joining me, I found a temporary rental in Winchester, which would make an ideal base for our search for our permanent residence. Since my Boston friends almost universally recommended that we narrow our search to the Weston-Wellesley area, it enabled us to bring some early focus to our search.

We soon found a suitable home in Weston. While not ideal, it was close enough and would lend itself to the modifications that we felt were necessary. We purchased it and immediately made plans to modify it to better suit our needs. Through friends, we found a wonderful old craftsman to undertake the rather extensive construction work, which involved expanding the master bedroom and adding dressing rooms and a bath for me, and adding hardwood floors and a covered lanai off the back of the house. These additions made it a truly beautiful house that was perfect to our needs. And we loved it even more when we had designed and executed a lovely landscape plan, which included beautiful gardens consisting mostly of azaleas and rhododendrons, a lovely raised vegetable garden, a white picket fence and a great irrigation system.

To complete our happiness, we found a miniature Dachshund who became our best friend. Mary Lee chose the name Aristotle. It was perfect for him. What an absolute delight he was! He was beautiful, smart as a whip and completely loving. He soon became an important and full-fledged member of our family.

Coming off the bridge of a heavy guided missile cruiser, Harvard was quite a cultural shock for me. On the other hand, I am sure that I was quite a cultural shock for Harvard.

The organization of the administration of the school was changed to accommodate me. I was appointed administrative dean and member of the faculty and was given responsibility for all non-teaching functions except for finance and fund raising. My responsibilities covered buildings and grounds, food service, security, planning, personnel, new construction, and membership on almost all university committees as representative of the Business School.

As I would have done on taking command of a ship in the fleet, I immediately inspected every single space in our physical facilities. I literally looked at hundreds of rooms, all aspects of our extensive engineering plant, our storage areas, our classrooms, and so on. I also took a close look at the school's central administration. What I found was not reassuring.

At the first faculty meeting that I attended, Larry Fouracker, the dean of the faculty, welcomed me to the school and introduced me to the faculty. I responded by saying what an honor it was to join the faculty of this distinguished school. I observed that in my view its world-renowned academic reputation should not be mutually exclusive from the administrative and material condition of the school. I told the faculty of my exhaustive physical survey of the buildings and my examination of the school's administration. I told them that I found both areas severely lacking and certainly not up to the standards of its academic programs. I further told the faculty that I intended to bring these areas up to the same distinguished standards presently enjoyed by its academics. And that is exactly what I worked hard to do during my ten years at the school.

Years later, long after I left the school, the then dean of the faculty, John McArthur, invited me for a visit so that I could see the incredible progress that had been made in rebuilding the school's facilities. During my visit I reminded the dean what I had said at the first faculty meeting that I attended, that academic excellence was not mutually exclusive from facility and administrative excellence. John McArthur replied, "Allan, I have quoted you a hundred times."

I soon learned that politics in the Navy was childs' play compared to politics in academia. I also learned that those academic giants that made up the world-renowned faculty were as much or even more sensitive to rank and privilege than officers in the Navy. In the Navy we were at least more honest. We wore our rank on our sleeve and made no secret of our signal number. I found academics much more hypocritical on that score. Most of them were exquisitely aware of their relative rank and their prerogatives.

I also quickly noted that the very organization of the academic aspects of the school almost guaranteed intensive competition and hard feelings. When I was on the faculty, the academic disciplines were divided into eight subject areas: marketing, human behavior, business policy, finance, control, business and government, business history and real estate. Under a firm policy of the dean of the faculty, the school was restricted to making only three tenured appointments a year. Thus the competition among the eight areas for those appointments was intense and often unpleasant. Five of the areas were guaranteed to be disappointed each year. I watched this process with great interest. Since I was not involved I could be impartial and above the fray.

The other big problem was tenure itself. Once gaining tenure, an academic cannot be fired except for flagrant acts of moral turpitude. To add to the problem, soon after joining the faculty, federal law changed to extend the age for normal retirement from 65 to 70. This had an immediate deleterious effect. First of all, the truly able professors did not want to wait until 70 to retire, as they had many outside interests and opportunities. They left to pursue those interests. The less able stayed on. It was a reverse enrichment process. Secondly, the old Navy expression "retired on active duty" to describe those officers who had run out of gas, equally applied to the Business School in spades. Many tenured professors were of little further use to the school but they could not be involuntarily retired. The school was literally stuck with them. They were assigned to "course development" a euphemism for "the shelf."

There was another major force in play here as well. Unlike almost all other universities, Harvard was almost completely decentralized. The university consisted of nine independent faculties or schools. There was absolutely no subvention. Each school had to stand or fall on its own. The expression "every tub on its own bottom" was the underlying principle of management. Someone described Harvard as a collection of nine independent faculties having a common interest in the heating system. Each school was taxed at two percent of its gross income to support the university administration. And finally each school derived income only from the endowment that it raised itself. Harvard College, which had been building endowment since 1635, owned the overwhelmingly largest share of the Harvard endowment.

To give some cohesion to the operation of the university, several inter-university standing committees were in force, the senior being the Council of Deans. I was a member of the Council of Administrative Deans and many other university committees. These committees met, some on a regular basis and others on an ad hoc basis. They literally formed the glue that held the university together. I made some fine friends throughout the university through those committees.

The Business School had a beautiful campus when I arrived, but, like its physical structure, it had been neglected. I took great delight in improving it. During my tenure I installed three parks and planted thousands of specimens of plants and trees. I expended great efforts and treasure to try to protect the campus's magnificent elms from the Dutch elm disease and installed a replacement program for the ones that we gradually lost. Through contacts at the Arnold Arboretum, I was able to get first whack at their surplus specimens, which meant that I got some beautiful plants and trees at no cost except for transportation and planting.

Several years into my tenure, Larry Fouraker informed me that the city of Boston had chosen me to be the annual recipient of its "Golden Trowel Award" which the city gave each year to an individual whom the city considered made the greatest contribution to the beauty of Boston. I was, of course, delighted and proud to win the award that Mayor Kevin White presented to me in his office.

Another great area of interest was in the school's food service. When I first joined the faculty, the MBA students were required to purchase a meal contract. There was a great deal of student resentment of this policy and not without merit. After a careful analysis I concluded that there would be negligible impact on the school's financial position if we changed the policy, especially if we made our restaurants places in which our community enjoyed dining.

I set about improving all aspects of the food service. I was determined to offer our community excellent food at a fair price. To this end I hired an Austrian by the name of Kurt Kramer to head up the food service activities and hired other fine professionals, including an outstanding pastry chef. We expanded considerably and refurbished the Faculty Club using funds obtained from the Kresge Foundation. We built a wonderful outdoor café, complete with tables, awnings, a hot dog cart and a popcorn machine. We built a splendid food and snack bar facility and a beautiful pub.

We had great fun and enormous success and we actually made money. Our reputation grew throughout Boston and it became a genuine treat to be invited to lunch or dinner at the Faculty Club. *Boston Magazine*, in one issue, cited our Faculty Club as one of the best places to eat in Boston.

I made some great personal friends at the school. Howie Whitmore, the financial dean was also my compatriot. Joe O'Donnell, an administrator in the MBA Program, and others formed a wonderful group of close friends. We had great times together, including going to Fenway Park on numerous occasions to see the Red Sox play. Joe had close friends in high places in the Red Sox organization, which resulted in terrific tickets to important games, such as several to the great World Series against the Cincinnati Reds in '76. Many years later in 2002, my friend Joe O'Donnell, who had made a great deal of money in the movie food concession business, came within an ace of being the successful bidder for the purchase of the Red Sox.

In writing of my experiences at Harvard, I would be remiss indeed if I didn't address the problem of affirmative action. The EEOC had been established in the years just prior to my joining the school. When I arrived, the EEOC had a blowtorch on Harvard's feet. They reasoned, I guess, that if they could make Harvard bend, the other schools would follow. At my first faculty meeting, the faculty voted overwhelmingly to establish a separate entrance track for black students. As a result, the school admitted a very large number of blacks. We didn't change the academic standards, so many of the students just could not keep up academically. Many of them became frustrated, then angry and finally belligerent. It just was not working. Two years later, the faculty voted to return to a single-track entry system and to make a genuine effort to find qualified blacks. Our black population declined by over 65 percent but the blacks that we took in were intellectually on par with the other students and all the frustration and militancy disappeared.

We also had similar problems appointing blacks to the faculty. There were some very qualified blacks in the business teaching area but every business school in the country was trying to recruit the same qualified black teachers. Thus the school never was able to attract as many blacks to our faculty as we would have wished.

Mary Lee and I relished our life in Weston. We were dead wrong in our impression that we would find New Englanders unfriendly. We lived next to Pete and Marge Fellows and soon became close friends. The Fellows had a great old house on Lake Sunapee in New Hampshire. We were soon frequent houseguests there during the summer months. They unsparingly extended their warm hospitality to us and ensured that we met their many friends that lived in the Sunapee area. Eventually we would settle there for our summers as well.

Others in Weston were similarly welcoming and hospitable. Friends proposed us for membership in the prestigious Weston Golf Club where Mary Lee, in particular, enjoyed the golf course enormously. Several of our new friends owned ski lodges in New Hampshire and Vermont and we started to be invited for ski weekends. There is nothing duller to be in ski country for a few days at a time if you do not know how to ski. We decided to give it a real try. We enrolled in a weeklong ski school at Mittersill, New Hampshire and by the end of the week we were actually skiing, not well but skiing nevertheless. We both found that we loved it. While we never became experts like many of our friends, we became very passable intermediate skiers and enjoyed skiing at that level. We pursued our new sport at every opportunity, not only in New Hampshire and Vermont, but also in Canada and out west in Vail, Sun Valley and Jackson Hole.

I became greatly interested in Republican politics and eventually became the chairman of the town Republican committee. We were mainly interested in trying to defeat the congressional representative from the Massachusetts 12th Congressional District, Robert Drinan.

Probably because of my position at Harvard, I was asked to chair a town committee ostensibly to look at the needs of the school system but actually as a way to show citizen support for ever increasing spending on public education in Weston. At the time, 75 percent of every dollar paid in ad valorem taxes went to support the schools.

My committee and I embarked on an intensive examination of the entire system and what we found essentially was a school system out of control. Every hair-brained idea that the school administration dreamed up was funded. I concluded that it was scandalous. While certainly not universally so, many of the teachers were on the liberal left and seemed to revel in being members of the counter culture. The system seemed to lose sight of the fact that over 90 percent of the graduates of the system went off to college. One anecdote seems to underline this observation. As was my practice, I made numerous visits to all the schools in the system. One evening I visited the high school and the school's principal was my host. We toured the resource center better known to us as the school library. Off the resource center was a very large room that contained nothing but long racks of tapes. I asked the principal what was on the tapes? He replied that most of them contained many copies of the required reading. He added that they were unable to get the "kids" to do the required reading so they made the tapes available to them so that they could listen to them and would not be required to read their assignments. I pointed out to him that 92 percent of the students went on to college and if the school system didn't teach them to read effectively, write effectively and reason effectively they were producing intellectual cripples. That didn't seem to make any impression on the principal.

Thus the entire initiative didn't work out at all like the superintendent of the schools envisioned. After an exhaustive examination of the school system, a very lengthy bound final report, I concluded that the system was out of control. At an overflow meeting in the town hall I reported our findings to the Weston citizens. I told them that if the Harvard Business School were run like the Weston School System it would probably go bankrupt. As a result of our study three schools buildings were closed and many of the fiscal abuses were stopped. As a result, the tax rate in Weston stayed level for four years. I was not exactly voted "man of the year" by the school administrators and teachers but most of the rest of the Weston citizens thought that I was great. The superintendent, by the way, resigned.

In 1978, my dad suffered a stroke that incapacitated him. He signed an enduring power of attorney giving me complete control over both his finances and his business which I was to inherit on his death. It was a small company indeed. The Luzerne County News Company was the wholesale distributor of all magazines and paperback books in an exclusive area in northeastern Pennsylvania.

Fortunately, being a full member of the Business School Faculty, I was given 1/5 time to pursue private initiatives. I took every week to fly to Wilkes Barre to visit my dad and to look in on his company. In April of 1979 my dad died. I continued to go to Wilkes Barre weekly to check on the company.

Mary Lee and I had to decide whether to try to sell the company, which at the time had a negative net worth, or to move to Wilkes Barre and try to do something with it. We decided that, although we hated to leave the Business School and Weston, it was in our best long-term interest to try to build the company. That of course meant resigning from Harvard for our move to Pennsylvania. I informed Larry Fouraker of my decision to resign. The school didn't want me to leave and offered me three one-year contracts at my full salary to stay on as a consultant. I accepted with both enthusiasm and pride.

To make it even better they were able to pass all of my remunerations into my retirement account.

We hated to leave our wonderful life and our good friends in Weston but we were convinced that it was in our best interest to do so. We sold our lovely home on the first day it went on the market for the full asking price and moved to Wilkes Barre to a beautiful rental home in Dallas, Pennsylvania. I was about to commence my third career, this time in business.

Chapter 21

My Later Years

W HOEVER COINED THE expression "you can't go home again" really had it right. Returning to Wilkes Barre after an absence of 40 years was difficult to do. My boyhood friends had either moved away or had established very close interpersonal relationship with those who chose to stay in Wyoming Valley. While everyone was cordial, we really didn't make any close friends.

We lived in Four Views for a little over a year and were obliged to move because the owner decided to make it his home. We found an adequate condominium at the Newbury Estates in Dallas. Mary Lee did a great job in decorating it and we were very comfortable there.

We knew from the get go that we were never going to settle permanently in Wilkes Barre, so we devoted considerable time to thinking about where we would like to end up. We both loved Bermuda and during a visit at the Coral Beach Club there we did some house hunting and found a place with which we both fell in love. It was named Spanish Grange and belonged to the great British playwright, Sir Terence Ratigan. We made an offer, which was accepted, pending our ability to arrange proper financing.

We went back to Bermuda over the Christmas holidays to look into financing and other matters incident to buying property in Bermuda. After looking at the situation there carefully we decided to back off for a number of reasons, mostly political.

If we were going to find a place in the sun for the winter that pretty much left Florida. I didn't much like Florida based on our two tours in Mayport, but we decided to have a look at it anyway. We spent a couple of weeks touring the state. Our visit took us to Naples where our dear friends the Banks had bought a condo and they invited us to be their houseguests. As we drove up Gulf Shore Boulevard looking for their condo I turned to Mary Lee and said, "I think we found our place." Naples was elegantly beautiful and located on the southwest coast, ensuring that we would have delightfully warm winters.

Once we saw Port Royal we knew that that was where we wanted to live. The problem was that any house that we could afford there we didn't like and those that we liked we couldn't afford. Thus we decided to buy some property and build our own house. One undeveloped property was spectacular and, while it was much too expensive, we bought it anyway.

We then went through the process of finding an architect. I used a method that I developed at Harvard to interview architects for commissions at the Business School and Mary Lee and I chose Dick Morris. We decided that we wanted to build an authentic Japanese style home. Dick Morris had never done one; however, Mary Lee did a fine job of researching Japanese architecture in the Philadelphia Library and I wrote a 25-page program outlining precisely what we wanted in our new home. He came up with a plan that we both loved. We held our breath that we could get financing because we were right at the limit of what we could hope to obtain. At the time mortgage rates were a historic high 15 percent but we accepted the bank's offer. Dick Morris did a great job of developing the drawings and specs and we chose a builder on a competitive bid basis. We were off and running in Naples.

In order that we might monitor the construction of our new home we found a small, furnished condo on Gulf Shore Boulevard, which we happily rented. And so we had started the process of organizing the rest of our lives.

I had, of course, become familiar with the Luzern County News Company during my weekly visits, which extended over a 14-month period. Therefore, when I finally reported for full-time duty, I had already determined that the scale of the company was entirely too small, its plant was antiquated and the basic system for order control and financial control was hopefully out of date.

I set about trying to remedy these and other inherent weaknesses. We made contact with the Hazelton News Company and were able to make a deal for its purchase. The Hazelton territory was contiguous to ours and its integration into our area was logical and easily accomplished. A few years later we were able to acquire the Potstown Agency. It was a stretch but we were able to integrate this territory as well and to service all the new accounts from our Wilkes Barre plant. Together with other bits of territory that we were able to acquire we increased our business from about 300 hundred accounts to over 600. At the same time we pursued a major marketing effort to expand our business in all of our accounts.

But the more I looked at the industry, the more I concluded that—with the advent of the computer—the business as presently constituted could not survive very long. Large chains now had the option of dealing with one or two large wholesalers, cutting out the small companies such as mine. They were also in a position to demand larger discounts from the wholesaler putting even the largest distributors at great risk. I therefore concluded that my best bet was to sell the company at the earliest possible date.

I found a wholesaler who was anxious to have the company and was able to make a deal which I felt was fair to both sides. Thus in July of 1986 I sold the company. My decision was prescient indeed, as the industry changed dramatically. All the small companies like mine were driven out of business and the remaining large companies who landed the big chain accounts were squeezed by them to the point that none of them was able to make a profit.

We had already decided on our winter home and now we had to decide where to spend our summers. The decision was really very easy since we had spent so much time in the Lake Sunapee area and knew so many people that a move to New Hampshire was a no brainer. We went to visit our friends, the Fellows, for the purpose of looking for an adequate home and we found a new development in New London that suited us perfectly. We purchased a lot and signed a contract to build. Since we purchased before our unit was built we were able to expand and modify it to better suit our needs.

We now had two homes, each in a delightful venue and we set about furnishing them. Our home in Naples being of Japanese design demanded furnishings and decorating in a Japanese or at least a Far Eastern motif. We slowly assembled some beautiful materials.

We eventually added significantly to our home. Dick Morris designed an addition to the main house off the master bedroom, which was to serve as a study and dressing room for Mary Lee and a beautiful and authentic seventeenth century Japanese teahouse that he situated over our Japanese water garden. It contained two luxurious guest suites, which included a large bedroom, a private bath and a morning kitchen. The house included a veranda, which surrounded it and stretched out towards the water garden to accommodate outdoor furniture. We had a landscape architect completely relandscape the property to the rear of the house. The next year we converted an unneeded bedroom and bath in the main house to a study for me.

Our home in New London was really of typical New England design. On a wonderful trip to the Far East however, we visited Bangkok. While there, we found a lovely antique shop and discovered that the young owners also had a furniture manufacturing company. While still in Bangkok we contracted to purchase some furniture and expanded our order when we got home. We also purchased numerous very attractive Thai antiques and accessories. Thus our New London home looked very New England on the outside but was strictly Thai on the inside.

During our early days in Wilkes Barre we were invited to be the guests of our friends, the Peers, in Chapaqua, New York. Other Harvard friends, the Peppers, were also guests. During our visit, George Peer suggested that since we were such good friends we ought to be in business together. Ed Pepper and I agreed and George volunteered to start searching for a suitable opportunity. In due course George did find a tiny company which we could buy and came up with a plan that envisioned five partners. I nominated Pete Fellows, my neighbor and good friend in Weston and now in New London and Ed Pepper nominated Steve Howe, a Boston lawyer. The name of the company was Labsphere and it was in the electro-optics business. The CEO and chief scientist was a man by the name of Phil Lape. The company had seven employees and was housed in an A frame ski chalet in North Sutton, a small town adjacent to New London. Soon after we purchased control I sought an appointment with Phil Lape and asked him to explain the underlying physics upon which our technology was based, at the Naval Academy physics level. It was at that level I understood the science of Labsphere. Phil Lape, by the way, was not only a brilliant scientist but he also turned out to be a superb CEO.

Labsphere grew like a weed. We constructed our first building, which contained 43,000 square feet. We made an addition to bring it to 73,000 square feet and finally expanded to over 150,000 square feet. We went from seven employees to over 170 and we became quite profitable. George Peer decided to withdraw and we found a friend to purchase his equity. Upon his departure I was elected chairman of the board. Through the years we added new owners, as Phil Lape who suffered a heart attack, decided to convert some of his equity into cash. At the end we had ten partners, all of them friends.

The situation became such that we decided that we had to sell. Some of the owners were plagued by physical problems and Phil Lape decided that he had enough. We sold to a public company Xrite for an excellent price and closed a very satisfying chapter in our lives.

Mary Lee and I traveled extensively, going on some fabulous cruises as well as tours of our own. We started with a grand tour of Europe, either visiting friends or staying in elegant hotels in England, Scotland, Denmark, Sweden, Holland, Switzerland and Italy. Our next major trip took us on a four-week tour of the Orient. We spent considerable time in Hong Kong, China, Singapore, Thailand and Japan.

We returned to the Western Pacific on board the Royal Viking *Sea*, which took us on a cruise to New Zealand and Australia. We left the ship in Sydney to enjoy a two-week exploration of the outback including a visit to Alice Springs and Ayres Rock where we encountered first hand the almost completely primitive aborigines. A trip to Northeast Australia permitted visits to the rainforest and a wonderful day out on the Great Barrier Reef.

We joined our Harvard AMP friends in England and Scotland as well as in Puerto Rico, Bermuda and Canada. We also joined them at several delightful venues in the United States including Pebble Beach, Santa Fe, Houston and Boston.

We joined close friends for a cruise to Alaska. We concluded that when they invented the word "awesome" they had Alaska in mind. We cruised the inner passage, visiting many interesting Alaskan cities as well as Glacier National Park and Tracy Fiord.

We were really into world travel when we took a cruise in the Baltic with a visit to Saint Petersburg as the main attraction. Before we embarked we had read an article in *Town and Country* magazine about the art of Saint Petersburg that said, "think of the art in the Louvre and then multiply it by 20." From our experience there, *Town and Country* had it right.

We also enjoyed a fabulous river cruise in Europe. We embarked in a brand new deluxe river cruise ship near Frankfurt on Main and cruised down the Main to the Main Danube Canal, through the canal and down the Danube terminating in Vienna. We left the ship and stayed an extra several days in the Imperial Hotel. Marie Antoinette couldn't have enjoyed a more elegant suite. It was little wonder to us that the Imperial Hotel was judged the very best in the world at that time. While in Vienna we, with great good fortune and excellent planning, were privileged to see the weekly performance, which was held on Sunday, of the Spanish Riding School. The word "spectacular" comes to mind when describing it.

I had always wished to visit the beaches at Normandy where the D-Day invasion was launched. Our dear friend Air Chief Marshal Sir John Barraclough volunteered to arrange our visit there. With his help we saw all of the important places that have become synonymous with that great military operation. It was an emotional visit for both of us. Visiting that beautiful military cemetery at St. Lo, which sits on a bluff overlooking Omaha Beach, was awesome. We were both moved to tears. We combined that visit with one to Mont Saint Michelle and a leisurely visit to many of the lovely French chateaux built along the Loire. We ended our trip in Paris where we met some good friends.

Probably the most incredible trip was a round the world cruise on the fantastic liner *Crystal Symphony*. We covered 40,000 miles and visited 38 countries. We had a penthouse suite and enjoyed both the comfort and luxury of that fabulous ship, including our own butler. We sailed west out of Los Angeles, stopping in Hawaii, and other Pacific islands including Guam, Okinawa, Palau, Truk and Taiwan. All through the Pacific part of the cruise we had on board a retired Marine colonel, who had been the Marine Corps historian, to tell us of the battles that were fought in the waters through which we were cruising. Since I had been in several of those battles, it was truly a voyage filled with nostalgia.

We also visited both North and South Vietnam. I went on a tour to Hanoi and was impressed with the beauty of the place. While we could not go inside, we visited the infamous Hanoi Hilton. Visiting Saigon was another nostalgic experience, having spent such an intense year of war there. We flew to Cambodia to visit the famous ruins of Angkor Wat. Then on to Singapore, Ceylon, Burma, India, including the Taj Mahal, then across the Arabian Sea to the Persian Gulf with a fabulous visit to Dubai in the United Arab Republic. Dubai was one of the greatest surprises of our long and event-filled cruise. Dubai looked like a place where the streets were paved with gold. The gold souke alone was worth the visit. At least a thousand jewelry stores were crowed into this incredible area. The unbelievable hotel Burj Al Arab was nothing short of spectacular. Built on an artificial island, the hotel was the most elaborate and luxurious we had ever seen. It looked like a giant sail. The rooms went for $1250 dollars minimum. Our dinner there was something out of *The Arabian Nights*.

From Dubai, we sailed south along the east coast of Africa visiting such counties as Oman and islands such as the Seychelles, the Comoros and Madagascar. When we reached Kenya we went on a game drive in the Masa Mara, another fabulous experience. Lots of African animals and a wonderful experience in one of those African game camps added to a memorable trip. Then on to South Africa, a visit with the Zulus from Durban and an incredible visit in Cape Town which included the mandatory visit to the Cape of Good Hope. Then we cruised up the West Coast of Africa visiting Namibia, Ghana, Bon Bon Island in Principe, The Gambia, Senegal and Morocco, which included a visit to Marrakech.

We visited Madeira, where we went on a basket ride down a steep hill, which was thrilling, but scared Mary Lee to death. After visiting the Canary Islands we stopped in Malaga where we were able to visit the Alhambra. Then we were off to Bilbao, the site of the famed Guggenheim Museum.

Our last port of call was Bordeaux. Neither of us had been there before and we found it to be an absolutely beautiful city. We visited the famed wine country of which Bordeaux is the center. Our tour took us to the elegant little wine city of St. Emillion and to an operating vineyard and winery.

The cruise ended in Southampton, were we disembarked and drove to London for a visit of a few days, after which we flew home on British Air. We both agreed that the experience was truly one of the great highlights of our lives.

As I write this chapter in July of 2002, Mary Lee and I are looking forward to spending two weeks in Provence as we celebrate our 54th anniversary. And in July 2003 we are included in the passenger list for the maiden voyage of the new *Crystal Serenity*.

As we were both approaching our 80th birthdays we decided that, although we loved our home in Port Royal, it was time to make a move to make our life less complex. We sold our home on the first day it reached the market and moved to a beautiful new condo on Gulf Shore Boulevard.

And I come to the end of this long journey through my life. To say that it was satisfying, exciting, fulfilling and delightful would be an understatement. Having Mary Lee with me most of the way made the whole life experience something that I treasure. I wouldn't change a thing if I had it to do over again.

Epilogue

Looking Back

A S I ENTER my eighties, I have time to think about the incredible life and experiences that I have enjoyed through these many years. From these many, varied and exciting experiences I have distilled some philosophies, observations and conclusions which I hope the reader finds both pertinent and worthy.

Much has been written about our generation. Tom Brokaw flattered all of us when he dubbed us "The Greatest Generation." Long before Tom Brokaw wrote about us I had thought about the very same thing. What made our generation so special? I have concluded that two cataclysmic events largely shaped what we were and are and why we are unique.

The first was the Great Depression. It had an enormous impact on all of us. While it was a tough period it had a major influence on the development of our underlying values and our collective character. It taught us the importance of fiscal responsibility, of working hard and not assuming that somehow the government had a responsibility to look after us. Of course, through necessity, as a group we were frugal. That conditioning became part of our very character and influenced greatly how we behaved for the rest of our lives. I still go around our house to turn out the lights and feel guilty about making overly long long-distance telephone calls.

The second cataclysmic event was the Great War in which nearly all of us participated in an active way. While it was a very trying and tragic period, it left an indelible mark on most of us. We learned the importance of sacrifice. We were unabashedly patriotic. We took pride in the incredible teamwork in which America fought the war to a successful conclusion. We felt an intense responsibility to fight. The worst thing that could befall us was to be classified 4-F, not physically fit for military service. We became hardened to the rigors and dangers of combat and willingly accepted casualties in the hundreds of thousands. While a single fatality was a tragedy, we didn't hear the word "quagmire" as we did when we lost a few hundred in Iraq. We came out of that incredible World War II struggle with a feeling of pride and a determination to succeed in our great country. That aggregate determination combined with the incredibly successful G.I. Bill has helped us as a group and our country to become astonishingly wealthy, unbelievably powerful, and wonderfully compassionate.

***

Along the way, in the fleet, at Harvard and in industry I developed several principles and philosophies that in the aggregate proved to be enormously effective and contributed to my personal success and, I hope, in some small way the success of the United States.

Early on, I concluded that the pursuit of excellence would be the hallmark of my success. I distilled a personal philosophy that held: "The pursuit of excellence is man's noblest endeavor and its attainment is man's noblest achievement."

That philosophy became my guiding light through these many years. But how to translate that philosophical concept into concrete performance? I have thought and written extensively in an effort to answer that question. The first specific task is to establish standards of excellence. Extremely high standards, whether they are established in a man-of-war, at a distinguished university or in a company, are the basis for success. Those standards must be comprehensive, covering every aspect of the organization's endeavors. In a man-of-war it encompasses the highest standard of personal conduct, performance and appearance, of comprehensive ship-keeping standards, of the highest possible standards of administration, and of course, the highest standard of operational excellence. Everyone in the ship must understand these required standards and must be convinced that they will not be modulated by events, or by a weakened resolve on the part of the commanding officer.

Man is not by nature a completely consistent animal. His attitudes and his pursuit of his responsibilities are influenced by his mood, by his inertia, by his desire for approval, or by circumstances.

The trick is to strive for consistency. Inconsistency in the pursuit of standards is poison to ship's morale and to its drive towards excellence. It introduces uncertainties and eventually impacts on both morale and performance.

The commander does no one a favor to overlook a departure from his established standards for whatever reason. Demanding in a uniform and consistent way the highest standards of performance is axiomatic to success. It makes little difference whether you are a commanding officer of a billion-dollar ship or head coach of a football team. In the case of the latter, the Lombardies and the Parcells of this world understand this truth very well. They were and are tough. They demand and expect outstanding performance and will not accept less. They are not loved nor should they be. What is of far greater importance for a successful leader, they are respected.

The outstanding ship is uniformly outstanding. I have often heard the observation when discussing a man-of-war, "She's not very pretty but she's an operator." Baloney! I can stand on the pier at the fleet landing and by observing the ship's boats that come alongside tell which of the ships are great operators. Excellence cannot be a hit and miss thing. It must be universal in a successful man-of-war. Such a ship is outstanding in everything that she does, and this same basic truth applies to a school or a company. At a school, its academic performance must be supported and enhanced by its administrative and facility excellence. In a business, the product or service must be outstanding, but also the plant and equipment must reflect excellence. The catalogues, correspondence, customer relations, all must also reflect these same high standards of excellence.

But just saying and believing all this doesn't in itself assure excellence. Starting with highest standards of excellence, the commanding officer must be able to manage, inspire and, yes, even drive his personnel towards that excellence. Normally a commanding officer has a relatively small span of direct control i.e., his executive office and his heads of departments. This, in a cruiser, represents no more than six officers. Each of those six has what I choose to call a maximum standpipe of capability. That is, he is capable of just so much performance and no more. Human beings' motivations are arranged along a normal distribution curve. At one end of the curve are those who will only perform if they are forced to do so by external pressure. On the other end of the normal distribution curve are the self-starters. They perform at their peak capability because they are self-motivated to do so. They need no outside stimulus. Most individuals are arranged along a normal distribution curve. Depending where they are on the curve, they require a combination of outside motivation and their own inherent desire to perform.

It is the commander's responsibility to observe those within his span of control and determine what combination of external demand and internal motivation is necessary for each to perform at their maximum standpipe of capability. If left to their own devices, except for those few way over on the right of the normal distribution curve, they will not perform at their maximum capability. The trick is to get each officer in the commander's span of control to perform at his maximum capability. The danger is to demand more than an individual's maximum capability. Such miscalculation can seriously demotivate and even demoralize the person who is being overdriven.

The result of the intelligent, forceful, uniform and consistent application of both the standards and the human motivation results in a truly outstanding ship or, for that matter, any other organization. A ship may have an outstanding engineering department or an outstanding supply department. That is the result of having an outstanding engineering officer or an outstanding supply officer. It has little to do with the capability of the commanding officer. When a ship is uniformly outstanding, then that ship has an outstanding commanding officer.

If what I have observed was easy to accomplish all ships would be outstanding. That is decidedly not the case. In an eight-ship destroyer squadron, usually one ship and possibly two ships are truly outstanding. Since each ship is more or less dealt the same officer and enlisted manning, the difference is that the successful captain understands either implicitly what I have observed or he understands it intuitively.

In regard to ability, I found in the Navy that there was a stratification of talent. There was a thin veneer of the conceptualizers, the innovators and those who had the wisdom and ability to challenge the assumptions. Then there was a much larger strata of what I called "store keepers." They were dedicated and willing and they performed very well in accordance with established requirements. They were essential to the efficiency of the endeavor. And finally there was a strata of incompetence. Although most in this strata really tried, they were not capable of performing at an acceptable level of competency. I thought that this stratification was unique to the Navy but in later years I found the same stratification at both the Harvard Business School and in industry. The depth of the various strata varied but they all existed.

***

Many negative things have been said and written about young Americans today. They are accused of being lackadaisical, unpatriotic and undisciplined. They are often characterized as having no moral rudder. They are accused of rejecting the notion of right and wrong in favor of relativism. I have commanded thousands of young Americans in the Navy. I have interacted with them on a daily basis at Harvard and I have observed their attitudes and their performance in industry. Based on these comprehensive and diverse observations, I have concluded that young Americans are just as good, if not better, than we were at their age. They have their shortcomings but the rap that is put on them is seriously misplaced. Their failures, in most cases, are directly related to a dismal lack of leadership by a generation that should be setting and insisting on high standards of excellence. Properly led, these young Americans perform magnificently. Witness the exemplary behavior, the wonderful courage and the superb performance of our young men and women in Iraq and Afghanistan. They are and should be a source of great national pride.

Properly led, they will work their hearts out to make their ship the very best. I can personally attest to this. I am enormously proud of them and proud to have them assume the responsibility that they must and will assume in these very troubled times.

***

There has been much written about the problem of homosexuality in the fleet. Recently, Harvard University voted to retain its ban on having a Naval Reserve Officer Corps on its campus. Its reason was the Navy's position on homosexuality onboard our ships. To sanction homosexuality in the fleet is absolutely impossible. Let's examine the problem on a typical destroyer. Our enlisted personnel, even in ships with the most advanced habitability standards, live in compartments containing about 40 men. The only nod to privacy is a curtain which can be drawn on bunks that are stacked three high. The showers are open, as are the commodes. These steel boxes routinely get underway for months at a time. In my experience, the deployments were routinely for nine months. Thus, during those long deployments, the ship becomes the crew's home. There is no going ashore after the day's work is done. Insert two homosexuals into that enlisted compartment and the situation becomes sociologically explosive. It is akin to putting two male heterosexuals into a compartment of 40 women at a time when the hormones are literally gushing through their bodies. It is an impossible situation and an invitation to disaster.

The homosexual is intellectually as able as any heterosexual and will receive promotions in accordance with his capabilities. Now a homosexual who is also a petty officer is in a position to exert exquisite sexual pressure on the nonrated personnel with predictable disastrous results.

A companion problem is women in combatant ships. In discussing this problem with a distinguished admiral he said "Allan, what difference does it make whether a woman or a man presses the missile firing key?" The answer is, "Of course it makes no difference." That's not the problem. I am absolutely confident that I could train an intelligent young female officer to be a splendid officer of the deck. I am confident that a fine female officer could well handle the pressures of being a top watch stander in a combatant ship. The problem is that sexuality cannot be repealed. Again, in those long fleet deployments, forced to interact for months on end with each other in an incredibly cramped environment, the irresistible sexual drive among these young men and women is bound to have enormous effect on the good order and discipline of the ship. Pregnancy among our enlisted women is enormously serious but it is a carefully suppressed crisis in our fleet operating forces.

***

I cannot conclude this survey without addressing once again the incredible deleterious effect that the left wing media has and will continue to have not only on the morale of our fighting men and women but also on the deterioration of the resolve of the American public. During the major military operations in Iraq the liberal media again looked for the anomaly, the snafu, the tactical set-back to report almost with glee. "Quagmire" found its way into coverage when our forces paused to hunker down in a blinding sandstorm and to allow its logistics to catch up. Much to the surprise and, I truly believe, the disappointment of the hostile media, we gained a great and decisive military victory. Since the end of major military operations, every setback, whether it was the looting of a museum or a successful terrorist attack on our troops, is headlined. Thus far about 300 Americans have been killed in Iraq, about two-thirds of that number from enemy action. That is 300 tragedies, but those casualties are astonishingly small. There is almost no coverage about the continuing success of our efforts there even though every on-site observer has returned to the U.S. with glowing reports of our successes. This astonishing anti-military and anti-U.S. bias is reinforced on many of the U.S. campuses by tenured professors who were the hippies and violent war protestors of the 60's and 70's. The left wing politicians are also loud and persistent in their denunciation of our military efforts. The situation is frightfully similar to the drumbeat mounted by the same communities during the Vietnam War. We don't have a Senator Church who led the charge for the withdrawal of U.S. financial and legislative support for our Vietnamese allies but there are many others vying to take the leadership in an effort to cut and run once again. This time in Iraq.

***

I have often reflected on my long years in the Navy. Was the enormous effort worth it? The personal dangers inherent in battle and just going to sea, the long separation from family, the less than commodious habitability standards and the comparatively poor pay for the enormous responsibilities that routinely had to be shouldered were certainly important negatives.

I remember well being in command of one of our combatants during a gale in the North Atlantic. Exhausted after rolling and pitching for days on end, being on the bridge without respite, cold and wet with little or no sleep, experiencing frustrating communications difficulties and the chief engineer reporting significant engineering casualties; I'd sometimes ask myself, "What the hell are you doing here?"

But when the weather clears and the ship is squared away with her paintwork perfect and her brightwork gleaming in the sun and she is steaming into a foreign port with her ship's company arrayed in perfect ranks at quarters for entering port and the ship's band is playing "The Stars and Stripes Forever" and you look up at our magnificent national ensign flying from the peak and you are in command of the mightiest guided missile cruiser in the world and thousands of people are lining the banks watching you steam up the channel and you know you and your ship are tangible and powerful representatives of your great country, I wouldn't swap that thrill of command for any job in the world! It's an honor and a feeling of pride that only a few men are privileged to experience.

One day, some years ago I was beefing about the Navy to Kenmore McManes, a dear friend and distinguished admiral. He put his arm around my shoulders and said,

"Allan, the Navy isn't what it used to be and never has been."

I am certain that he was right, and by extrapolation the same thing might be said about the United States. In retrospect, in spite of its detractors both foreign and domestic I am confident of its continuing enormous success. I shall be an enthusiastic observer when it is my turn to join the Great Destroyer Squadron in the Sky.

CAPTAIN ALLAN SLAFF grew up in northeastern Pennsylvania. He graduated from the U.S. Naval Academy in 1944, and served on board the fast battleship *Massachusetts,* which participated in many of the great battles of the Pacific War as a unit of the famed Fast Carrier Task Force. After the war, he served in many of the combatant ships of the Atlantic Fleet, including the light cruiser *Houston,* the destroyer *Holder* and the destroyer *Hazelwood.* He commanded the destroyer escort *Lester,* the fleet destroyer *Davis,* the guided missile destroyer leader *Luce* and the heavy guided missile cruiser *Albany.*

He served a tour on the staff of Commander Cruiser Division Twelve, as aide and flag secretary to Commander Destroyer Force, U.S. Atlantic Fleet and as personal aide to the famed Admiral Arleigh Burke when he was Chief of Naval Operations. He also served in the immediate office of Secretary of the Navy Paul Nitze.

Captain Slaff was the first naval officer ordered to the Korean War, where he headed up the Navy's black chamber activities for the first eighteen months of the conflict. He also served in Vietnam in 1967 and 1968 in command of all naval advisors during some of the heaviest fighting there, including the Tet Offensive.

He holds 22 personal decorations, unit commendations and campaign medals, including the Legion of Merit with a V for valor, a Bronze Star, the Vietnamese National Order of Vietnam, which was the highest decoration for service in Vietnam, and the Vietnamese Cross of Gallantry.

He is a graduate of the U.S. Naval Postgraduate School, the U.S. Naval War College and the Advanced Management Program at the Harvard Business School.

He served for ten years as a dean and member of the faculty of the Harvard Business School and as a consultant to the school for an additional three years. He has also been chairman of two small but highly successful corporations.

Captain Slaff has authored numerous magazine articles about the Navy and the sea. He has served on more than a score of corporate, educational, civic, social and club boards of directors or trustees.

He currently makes his home with his wife Mary Lee in New London, New Hampshire in the summer and in Naples, Florida in the winter.